MW01520029

After Genocide

Critical Human Rights

Scott Straus & Tyrell Haberkorn, Series Editors;
Steve J. Stern, Editor Emeritus

Books in the series Critical Human Rights emphasize research that opens
new ways to think about and understand human rights. The series values
in particular empirically grounded and intellectually open research that
eschews simplified accounts of human rights events and processes.

After Genocide

*Memory and Reconciliation
in Rwanda*

Nicole Fox

The University of Wisconsin Press

The University of Wisconsin Press
728 State Street, Suite 443
Madison, Wisconsin 53706
uwpress.wisc.edu

Gray's Inn House, 127 Clerkenwell Road
London EC1R 5DB, United Kingdom
eurospanbookstore.com

Printed in the United States of America
This book may be available in a digital edition.

Library of Congress Cataloging-in-Publication Data

Names: Fox, Nicole, author.
Title: After genocide : memory and reconciliation in Rwanda / Nicole Fox.
Other titles: Critical human rights.
Description: Madison, Wisconsin : University of Wisconsin Press, [2021] |
    Series: Critical human rights | Includes bibliographical references and index.
Identifiers: LCCN 2020047424 | ISBN 9780299332204 (hardcover)
Subjects: LCSH: Genocide—Rwanda. | Memorialization—Rwanda. |
    Memorials—Rwanda. | Memory—Sociological aspects. | Reconciliation. |
    Rwanda—History—Civil War, 1994—Atrocities.
Classification: LCC DT450.44 .F69 2021 | DDC 967.57104/31—dc23
LC record available at https://lccn.loc.gov/2020047424

For Avi Jacob, Mira Jane, and my beloved Robin
and the resilient survivors of mass atrocity in Rwanda and beyond

Bezichronot yeshnam chaim (In remembrance there is life)

Contents

Acknowledgments

The saying "it takes a village" may apply to completing a book as much as it does to raising a child. My work on this book was made possible by a vast village. First and foremost, I would like to thank the Rwandan survivors who are featured in this book and all those who helped me along the way during my time in Rwanda. Participants welcomed me into their homes; introduced me to their families; and invited me to church, family dinners, weddings, funerals, outings, and commemorations. They all suffered a great deal in the aftermath of the genocide, and their courage in speaking about their experiences and dedicating themselves to the memory of their loved ones inspired me throughout. Those who survived the genocide witnessed the worst atrocities of which humankind is capable. However, participants often responded to these acts of violence and brutality with true heroism by rescuing others at the risk of their own lives, ensuring the survival of orphaned babies by breastfeeding them, adopting orphans after the genocide, organizing resources for vulnerable populations, and caring for younger siblings. The list of their displays of humanity goes on and on, and I will forever be humbled by these individuals' acts of courage.

While I was in Rwanda, the most incredible family hosted me, inviting me not only into their home but also into their family. They taught me Kinyarwanda in the evenings, lent me the family car, hosted my sister and mother, and included me in birthday and holiday celebrations. My Rwandan family unreservedly supported my research and cared for me when I was sick, sad, and exhausted. During one of my trips, I gifted this family a cow. In Rwandan culture this means that our families will be united in heaven for eternity. In many ways, this was a selfish gift, as I cannot imagine a greater bequest to bestow on my own family than to unite them forever with such a remarkable group of human beings.

In addition to my Rwandan family, amazing friends in both the US and Rwanda were a source of constant encouragement. I would like to thank Father Leonard for our adventures in both countries and for always finding the time to talk with me and for becoming family. I would also like to thank Father Elisee, who showed me the finest of Rwandan cuisine and debriefed with me more than once during the mourning months. My invaluable and knowledgeable research assistants have earned my deepest appreciation. Hollie Nyseth Brehm's expertise, encouragement, and generosity were extraordinary. Additionally, I had a cohort of colleagues who showed me unwavering support: Merry Berry, Casey Clevenger, Ashley Mears, Brianna Remster, Alexa Sardina, Emily Sigalow, Christina Simko, Chris Smith, and Katie Young. Thank you for your time and wisdom. Erin Hatton's unparalleled encouragement took many forms, from uplifting emails during my fieldwork abroad to thoughtful feedback on the manuscript drafts. She is everything that is right in academia and a true unicorn. My beloved friends Amanda and Stephanie Borellis, Lily Johnson, and Kim Richards cheered me on throughout the research and writing process. Their belief in this project, and in me, made all the difference. My dear friend Mary Lou Swiencicki was a source of inspiration, joy, and laughter during the dark days of writing and revising. Rest in peace, Mary, you are deeply missed and truly loved. My beloved soul sister, best friend, and cousin Robin died suddenly as this book moved into the final stages of production. She provided me with support while I conducted fieldwork and laughter when I came home, and she rooted for me during every stage of the writing process. This book would not have been possible without her unconditional love and support.

Wendy Cadge, Janet Jacobs, Sharyn Potter, and Ernest Uwazie served as mentors to me, modeling true academic excellence through their intelligence and expertise as well as their fierce dedication to social justice and research ethics. David Cunningham sparked my interest early on in graduate school by introducing me to scholarship and theories that served as the foundation for this project. He was a sounding board for initial findings, a thorough early reader, and a model of ethical and rigorous research, generous mentorship, and writing for social change. Furthermore, I am grateful to the National Science Foundation, the Andrew W. Mellon Foundation, Prevention Innovations Research Center, Society for the Scientific Study of Religion, TAG Institute for Jewish Values, and the Research Circle on Democracy and Cultural Pluralism for their substantial funding for this project.

Last, but certainly not least, I would like to thank my family, who have been steadfast in their support for me. My parents, Tom Fox and Jean Schuldberg, are the ones who first instilled in me a passion for justice and thirst for education.

My mom was the one who first taught me about the genocide in Rwanda as it unfolded in those horrific days in spring 1994. She and my dad have always believed in me, giving me courage to travel around the world and attend graduate school across the country. They also cared for my children (and me) in the final days of writing, making this book possible. My grandparents were an inspiration for how to create community and family in the aftermath of adversity. Thank you to my incredible siblings: Joey, Louise, and Joey, I love you. Finally, I would like to extend my deepest gratitude to my beautiful children, Avi Jacob and Mira Jane, who are brilliant and kind human beings and who fill my life with boundless joy and meaning.

Abbreviations

ACLED	Armed Conflict Location and Event Data Project
AERG	Association des Etudiants et Elèves Rescapés du Genocide (Association of Student Survivors of the Genocide)
AIDS	acquired immunodeficiency syndrome
CDR	Coalition pour la Défense de la République (Coalition for the Defense of the Republic)
CFC	Center for Commemoration
CGPE	Center for Genocide Prevention and Education
CHH	child-headed household
CMSR	Center for Memory, Survivors, and Reconciliation
CNLG	Commission Nationale de Lutte contre le Génocide (National Commission for the Fight Against Genocide)
DRC	Democratic Republic of the Congo
EPI	Everyday Peace Indicators
EU	European Union

FARG	Fonds d'Assistance aux Rescapes du Genocide (Genocide Survivors Support and Assistance Fund)
GPI	Global Peace Index
HDI	Human Development Index
HIV	human immunodeficiency virus
ICC	International Criminal Court
ICMP	International Commission for Missing Persons
ICTR	International Criminal Tribunal for Rwanda
ICTY	International Criminal Tribunal for the Former Yugoslavia
IDP	internally displaced persons
INGO	international nongovernmental organizations
MDR-Parmehutu	Mouvement démocratique republicain–Parmehutu (Republican Democratic Movement–Parmehutu)
MRND	Mouvement révolutionaire national pour le développement (National Revolutionary Movement for Development)
NGO	Nongovernmental Organization
PHR	Physicians for Human Rights
PIH	Partners in Health
PTSD	post-traumatic stress disorder
RPA	Rwandan Patriot Army
RPF	Rwandan Patriotic Front
RTLM	Radio Télévision Libre des Mille Collines

SES	socioeconomic status
SGBV	sexual and gender-based violence
TRC	Truth and Reconciliation Commission
TRP	Trauma Recovery Programme
UCDP GED	Uppsala Conflict Data Program's Georeferenced Event Dataset
UN	United Nations
UNAMIR	United Nations Assistance Mission for Rwanda
UNAR	Union Nationale Rwandaise (Rwandese National Union)
UNICEF	United Nations International Children Emergency Fund
USAID	United States Agency for International Development
WHO	World Health Organization

After Genocide

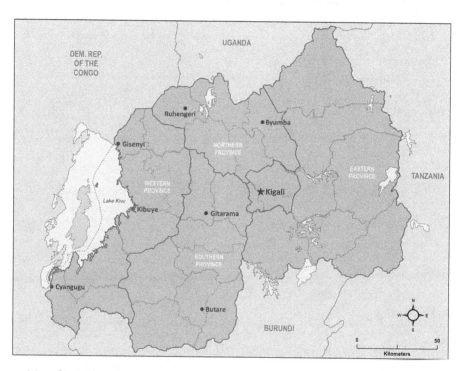

Map of Rwanda

Introduction

On a rare sunny morning in April 2012, Anitha walks out of her small home across the road from the church she attended with her family when she was a child. However, the church no longer holds services as it became a memorial site after April 1994, when the genocidal militia arrived at her village. Her mother and siblings were among the thousands who sought shelter in the church while she stayed behind in her grandmother's home. The militia threw grenades into the church and attacked people outside with machetes, ultimately killing the majority of the village. Today, the church is a space for people to commemorate and honor the victims killed there. The memorial features signs of the destruction that have been left for visitors to see: the blood of victims on the walls, pews piled high with their clothes, bricks broken from grenades, and skulls lining the shelves on the back wall. These material reminders of the atrocity invite visitors to learn firsthand about the genocidal violence that took place here. Anitha honors her family members buried at this memorial by sweeping the grounds with a broom made of twigs and planting flowers near the remains. Most mornings, Anitha arrives at the memorial early before walking to school to make sure it "looks beautiful"; this is particularly important in April, the mourning month. Anitha finds strength in this work, even though she still experiences flashbacks to the brutal violence that occurred almost twenty years ago.

Twenty-five miles from where Anitha tends the church memorial grounds, Mihigo arrives at a memorial outside the capital city. During the 1994 genocide against the Tutsi, Mihigo rescued several people, some of whom he had never met before, risking his life to feed and shelter them by hiding them in his home. The militia came after him, accusing him of betraying his kind, but he courageously stood up to them. One day, the militia men demanded he kill three young girls he was sheltering. When he refused, they hacked off his right leg with a machete. One of the young girls he rescued carried him to the hospital, with a ripped towel tied around his thigh to prevent him from bleeding to death. When the violence ended, Mihigo was applauded by the new government for his heroism. He now participates in a reconciliation program at a memorial where he regularly shares his story. He also works with former perpetrators to demonstrate the choices they had other than killing. While he still has nightmares about those weeks in April 1994, he is grateful to participate in reconciliation programs that might help his country move forward.

Less than ten miles from Mihigo, Honorine arrives at her job at a memorial in the capital city. Working as a memorial guide, in April she puts in particularly long hours to assist with all the visitors, including survivors, who come there. On April 12, 1994, when Honorine was three years old, her father was taken from their home in the middle of the night and killed. Along with her mother and older brother, Honorine managed to escape unharmed by crossing the border to Uganda. They returned in late 1994, and while her mother struggled with the trauma of witnessing her husband's murder, she worked hard to support Honorine in school. Honorine attended two years at the National University of Rwanda and secured her current job as a guide. Offering several tours a week to high school students, whom she teaches about divisionism and Rwanda's violent past, Honorine particularly values the opportunity to participate in vital education that is key to coexistence and recovery in Rwanda.

In April 1994, one of the most heinous atrocities of the twentieth century unraveled: the intimate and meticulous killing of almost one million Rwandans over approximately one hundred days. Rwandans were killed by their neighbors, religious leaders, and friends, who murdered using grenades, machetes, and guns. The 1994 genocide represented an utter failure on the part of the international community: the UN refused to provide adequate support; the media proliferated misguided reporting of "tribal warfare"; and powerful nations failed to intervene, in part because Rwanda lacked profitable natural resources for them to exploit.[1] In the twenty-plus years since those three brutal months, Rwandan citizens, international NGOs and donors, and the Rwandan government have together created more than five hundred memorials throughout the small African nation. Among these, seven memorials are national sites controlled and supported by the Rwandan government. These national sites aim to create a national collective memory of the genocidal violence, pay tribute to the victims, and facilitate unity across a previously divided nation; in practice, they also divide survivors.

Anitha, Mihigo, and Honorine, all survivors of the genocide, spend a significant part of their lives at memorials. Their stories of survival differ, as do their experiences at their respective memorial sites. Anitha works to clean the memorial—a space left intact since 1994 and the resting place of her beloved family and community. She lives in poverty, and the psychological trauma she endures daily is so severe that she was unable to care for her child.[2] She misses him and visits him at the convent where he now resides, grateful to the nuns who care for him. Anitha feels deep shame about being raped during the genocide, explaining she will never marry because of it. While she values the memorial, declaring that it brings her much needed peace, she also feels that Rwanda's remembrance processes have left her behind because she is poor and the victim of trauma and rape.

Mihigo, who participates in a reconciliation program at a site that was destroyed during the genocidal violence but later transformed into a beautiful memorial, believes he followed God's will and made the right choice for his country and himself when he rescued Tutsis in 1994. The Rwandan government awarded him livestock for his heroic acts, deeming him a national hero, and he expresses great pride in having since married and started a family. However, life has not been easy. In 1997 his neighbors killed his cows in retribution for his act of saving those they were trying to kill in 1994. Today, with his amputated leg and aging body, he is unable to farm in the same capacity he once did, and he lives in poverty. While the Rwandan government once awarded him for his heroism, he is ineligible for many of the government's survivor services because he is not considered part of the persecuted ethnic group. Mihigo regularly shares his testimony at commemorations, memorials, and jails. He is proud of his actions and values memorialization, but he wishes his life were easier.

Honorine curates a memorial education center where she gives tours to hundreds of visitors from around the world, carefully avoiding sharing potentially traumatizing details. As a genocide survivor, Honorine has benefited from government social support and education and strongly believes memorials are vital to reconciliation in Rwanda. Her older brother, now a financial advisor at a prominent bank in Kigali, the capital city, regularly gives testimony at large-scale commemorations during the mourning months, but Honorine does not. Honorine thinks of her father often and is devastated that she can no longer remember the sound of his voice.

Anitha, Mihigo, and Honorine all describe their time at their respective memorials as an investment in the future—not only for themselves but also for their country. However, because of their different relationships with these diverse memorial sites, their particular social status, and how they have weathered the aftermath of the traumatic events in Rwanda, they hold significantly different perspectives on the possibilities for reconciliation and the priorities for remembering the 1994 genocide against the Tutsi. These three individuals' stories, along with those of almost seventy others I interviewed, reveal how memory projects such as memorials and commemorations have powerful and deep significance in the aftermath of atrocity crimes. The narratives told and withheld at these sites empower communities, heal trauma, and validate pain and experience. When survivors question their own memories, because of the difficulty in believing that the brutality they survived was real, such narratives can productively mediate the cognitive dissonance associated with genocide, an event in which human beings act inhumanely. Memory narratives—those shared as well as those not shared—can also stratify, for they make claims about who is worth remembering and who is not. I am using "stratify" to refer to the process by which groups of people are divided into hierarchies, resulting in a lack of resources, opportunities, and empathy for those at the bottom of the social order. The "stratification of collective memory," a term I develop in chapter 4, refers to how memory projects in particular, in both process and outcome, can serve to reinforce previously existing hierarchies and their attending ethnic, gender, or socioeconomic cleavages. This stratification can lead to civic disengagement and nonparticipation as well as further violence, pain, and social isolation.

Given these simultaneous but contradictory processes of stratification and empowerment at memorial sites and commemorations, this book explores how memorial projects impact and function in the lives of those who survived the violence that these spaces aim to remember. The stories of Anitha, Mihigo, and Honorine make visible how memorialization processes are embedded in some survivors' lives and everyday routines, shaping their understandings of the past and the future. In many ways, this is a book about everyday memory and everyday reconciliation. Narratives about how memorials impact and function in survivors' lives shift the analytical focus from the memorial sites' material aspects to people's engagement with those sites. How do survivors understand the role memorials and memorial rituals play in shaping memories of the genocidal violence? How does their engagement with memorials shape local reconciliation, transitional justice, and civic engagement? And finally, what social processes in and around memorials create a collective memory that can both empower and stratify survivors from different social locations?

While this book explores these questions in the context of Rwanda, mass human rights abuses are occurring throughout the world, from South Sudan to Syria. Memorials are crucial today in all these contexts because the stories told about violence and its aftermath shape individual and communal-level experiences of justice, peace, and healing. The insights offered here are vital because, while studies have examined the different forms that reconciliation can take after human rights abuse—ranging from nonlethal coexistence to social harmony—they have failed to examine how such forms of memorialization affect everyday life for survivors of violence. How atrocity is remembered affects not only whose stories are told but also how those stories impact people's lives.

While the genocide that occurred in Rwanda was unique, the struggles of its survivors unfortunately are not. Marginalized, impoverished, and traumatized, survivors of atrocities all over the world must struggle to restore meaning to their lives and regain their livelihoods. Memorials are one mechanism that communities, governments, and NGOs employ to attempt to transition from mass violence to a functioning society. Even while at times silencing, occluding, serving state interests, and further stratifying communities, memorials can also provide a crucial source of hope and cathartic healing to survivors of genocide—something that few other institutions or social structures can replicate.

Many Rwandan genocide survivors, like survivors of other mass atrocities, envision national collective memorialization as a central mechanism in the enduring quest for accountability for human rights violations. Survivors commonly believe that such memory work can prevent future atrocities, particularly if it prioritizes reconciliation and social harmony through forgiveness, redress, and public acknowledgment of past wrongs. States also promote memorialization as violence prevention, making it impossible to disentangle nationalism and state-sanctioned collective memory from governmental memorial efforts. National memory is remembrance through the lens of present-day circumstances by those who are currently in power. The stories told on a national level most often support present-day political leaders and administrations; this is true in Rwanda and across the globe.[3] Citizens, as subjects of the state, interact with national narratives of past atrocities. Survivor communities, in particular, resist, debate, reproduce, and reconstruct national narratives of state violence at different moments in time and in different contexts. While political leaders, propaganda, curricula, or new state laws may impose national narratives upon survivors of violence, survivors have the agency to choose which elements of state memory to resist or reproduce. This dialectical meaning-making process is further impacted by the survivors' own social locations and experiences.

In Rwanda, this means that survivors and the government of Rwanda alike often definitively assert the role of remembering the 1994 genocide against the Tutsi as a means of preventing future violence. However, their motivations are starkly different: while survivors are deeply committed to this narrative because it gives some meaning to their loved ones' deaths, the government of Rwanda is motivated to correlate memorials to violence prevention in order to validate, consolidate, and maintain its own power. For survivors, the creation of memorials means that some good could come out of their loved ones' brutal murders and their own enduring grief: the transmission and dissemination of their knowledge of the genocide could lead to a future in which history does not repeat itself. For those who work at the memorials, the narrative of memory as violence prevention gives their work meaning. Caring for the sites where their family members are buried gives them not only proximity to their loved ones' remains but also the chance to contribute to a larger goal: a society without the kinds of mass killings that robbed them of their lineage and livelihood.

Yet, while national collective memorialization may bring hope and empowerment to some survivors, it can disappoint and exclude others. Collective memory in a stratified society is itself stratified. Those survivors most vulnerable in a postgenocide society—particularly poor women survivors of sexual violence—endure public silence around their stories, primarily because the government of Rwanda considers those stories as detrimental to national reconciliation. Thus, in a sense, those who endured some of the most traumatic forms of violence and loss are pressured to forgive (even when their forgiveness has not been sought) for the sake of a national healing project that would prefer to ignore and forget their experiences altogether.

By foregrounding the narratives of individuals, this book shows that survivors' stories are paramount to understanding how communities of survivors rebuild after mass human rights abuses.[4] In analyzing local dynamics of memory and everyday practices of reconciliation, this book challenges implicit conceptions of Rwanda's memorials as part of a uniform national project that has unfolded evenly across space and time. Attention to local cases highlights the diversity of individual experiences with memory projects and the local dynamics that interact with evolving national discourses in ways that reproduce and resist nationalist collective memory efforts. Furthermore, engagement with memory processes is stratified not only in terms of ethnicity and region but also, as we will see in the chapters that follow, in terms of class and gender. The way this stratification plays out in local settings offers insight into bottom-up reactions to top-down state narratives and initiatives.

While official government memorial initiatives in Rwanda bring necessary hope to some and offer practical services that help rebuild destroyed communities, survivors also have created forms of reconciliation that have received less attention. "Everyday reconciliations," which occur when a neighbor offers another neighbor a ride to a doctor's appointment, or an individual is allowed to attend a school that had previously been off limits to that person's ethnic group, play a key role in long-term peaceful coexistence. Because traditional studies of memorial culture have largely neglected these micro experiences, evaluating them provides a more inclusive, if more complicated, understanding of survival and rebuilding after mass human rights abuses. In interviews, survivors attributed much of these "everyday reconciliations" to memorial rituals—the process by which the nation acknowledges the damage mass violence has done to a region, a nation, a village, a family, a home, or even the ecosystem. These survivors framed memorials as a catalyst for the small acts of reconciliation that occur at ground level but cumulatively amount to significant social change.

A Brief Note on Constituencies and Naming

Here I provide a brief note on constituencies and naming, both of which are addressed in much more detail in the appendix. In this book, I define genocide survivors as those who feared for their own or their families' personal safety during the period of genocidal violence from April to early July 1994. This includes Tutsi, Hutu, and Twa who, during those horrific three months, faced danger because of the perception that they were either Tutsi or were associated with Tutsi, the direct target of the genocidal project. The memory and voices in this book are from that specific constituency: Tutsi genocide survivors and Hutu survivors who rescued Tutsi.[5]

In this book, I call the genocidal violence that occurred within Rwanda's borders in spring and summer 1994 "the 1994 genocide against the Tutsi." For those readers new to the scholarship on Rwanda, the government of Rwanda is the source of much divided and intense scholarly debate, and the title used to discuss the genocide is no exception. Again, I detail why I use this particular title for the genocide in the appendix but briefly summarize my reasoning here.

Beginning in 2007, the government of Rwanda asserted that the genocide should be called "the 1994 genocide against the Tutsi" in order to highlight that Tutsi were the targeted population. Previously the genocidal violence had been referred to as "the Rwandan genocide." Some, including highly regarded scholars from the West, felt that this new title left out Hutu and Twa survivors and gave the present-day government too much control in categorizing victimology. In early 2018 the UN General Assembly formally amended the title of the annual genocide observance (resolution 58/234) to declare April 7 the International Day of Reflection on the 1994 Rwandan Genocide Against the Tutsi. The change in the UN's nomenclature was perceived by those in favor of it as a move against the denialism of those seeking to forward a theory of "double genocide" between the Hutu and Tutsi. Others, including me, were hesitant to use the new title as it seemed inconsistent with the naming of past genocides and offered the current government a tool for consolidating power by positioning itself to both name and police the naming of the genocide. The proposed enforcement of the new nomenclature within Rwanda and in academic scholarship about Rwanda raised concerns for me about how this move would influence research, memorialization, and free expression.

Ultimately, what pushed me to use the name for which the government of Rwanda pressed was not an alignment with the current regime or its politics; rather, my usage was instead a response to what I heard consistently from people I interviewed. During field trips in 2019 for another project in Rwanda, I asked survivors I had interviewed for this book (both Hutu and Tutsi) how they thought I should refer to the genocide in my book. For the most part, they agreed that I should call it the official (government) title because Tutsi were the ones targeted, and the targeted Hutu were being singled out for their relations with Tutsi. Throughout this book, I will honor the view of these survivors of the violence by calling the mass violence that raged from April 1994 to early July 1994 "the 1994 genocide against the Tutsi."

Transitional Justice and Reconciliation

Forgiving is not forgetting; it's actually remembering—remembering and not using your right to hit back. It's a second chance for a new beginning. And the remembering part is particularly important. Especially if you don't want to repeat what happened.

Desmond Tutu

Scholars, activists, communal and political leaders, and victims of mass violence across the globe are fervently trying to understand how memory and forgiveness can contribute to violence prevention. One point of consensus is that societies experiencing ethnic cleansing, war, or mass human rights abuses must undergo crucial social, political, and economic transition processes to become healthy societies. These transition processes may include poverty reduction programs, educational reforms, judicial pursuits, changes in political leadership, and other measures that can help to democratize atrocity-torn countries. These diverse processes, composed of mechanisms that are often termed transitional justice, aim to heal communities whose social fabric has been torn apart. Transitional justice centers on truth-seeking and reconciliation as a means to prevent future violence and create "a second chance for a new beginning." After atrocity, a range of mechanisms can help address human rights violations and the transition toward justice, including amnesties, truth commissions, trials, lustration, and financial compensation. This book shows that memorialization efforts are a central transitional justice mechanism that should be combined with more traditional ones such as truth commissions, trials, or reparations to increase memorialization's power in facilitating reconciliation and justice.[6] No approach thus far has been lauded as a one-size-fits-all model; however, mechanisms can be combined or adjusted to fit specific post-atrocity circumstances, locales, or goals. These circumstances may take into account the length of time a country aims to spend on judicial remedies, the budget allotted to the pursuit of such remedies, or the types of crime being evaluated in the community or country. Combining approaches could assist in meeting multiple goals for communities and nations.

According to scholars, transitional justice mechanisms fall primarily into two categories—retributive and restorative.[7] Retributive justice focuses on proportional punishment for crimes, whereas restorative justice is based on the social importance of reconciliation and focuses on victims.[8] These two types of justice, while centered on different goals or social actors (victims vs. perpetrators), are deeply intertwined.[9] Restorative justice can occur before, during, or after retributive justice (i.e., parallel to court decisions or after trials). Because restorative justice can refer to a diverse and broad range of concepts and practices, scholars have struggled to come up with a single definition. One definition understands restorative justice as a continuum. Paul McCold suggests that fully restorative practices incorporate victim reparation, offender responsibility, and communal reconciliation, all with the inclusion of multiple stakeholders.[10] Restorative justice may involve punishment, but, unlike retributive justice, the outcome is not measured by how proportionate the punishment is to the crime.

Trials are one of the best-known forms of retributive transitional justice. In the aftermath of the genocides in Rwanda and Bosnia, the International Criminal Tribunal for the Former Yugoslavia (ICTY) and the International Criminal Tribunal for Rwanda (ICTR) became the first trials after the Cold War to convict perpetrators of genocide and crimes against humanity. These tribunals advanced legal jurisdiction, brought perpetrators to justice, and shaped public policy.[11] The most famous advancement in legal jurisdiction was achieved in the Akayesu trial, which culminated in a landmark decision. It was the first ever conviction for genocide, the first time that an international tribunal ruled that rape and other forms of sexual violence constituted genocide, and the first conviction of an individual for rape that had been ruled a crime against human-ity.[12] This verdict recognized that sexual and gender-based violence (SGBV) targeting the destruction of part or all of an ethnic group (e.g., rape, gendered torture, sexual slavery, or forced molestation) is indeed a form of genocide.

Even though it produced the landmark Akayesu decision, the ICTR casts light on the shortcomings of efforts by international courts to address sexually violent crimes. International law, by and large, has significant room to grow before it can effectively prosecute SGBV.[13] In part because of flawed investigative methodologies, the ICTR had less success in prosecuting additional cases of sexually violent crimes than did the ICTY.[14] International and domestic trials can be slow and expensive; during the ICTR's twenty-year tenure, the court rendered only fifty-three judgments and ninety-three indictments, and it completed trials of only seventy-two persons.[15] The total cost of the trials neared $1 billion, a cost of $10–15 million per accused.[16]

Truth commissions, which can also be costly and marginalize gendered dynamics of violence, fall on the restorative end of the transitional justice spectrum. Based on the assertion that truth is essential to achieve unity and peace after human rights violations, truth commissions frequently involve an official investigation that produces accessible public knowledge and details about perpetrators and past crimes. The contours of such programs have significantly varied across the more than two dozen Truth and Reconciliation Commissions (TRCs) enacted to date.[17] A key difference between truth commissions and trials is that the majority of truth commissions offer amnesty in exchange for testimony; this dimension can present challenges to victims and provide governments with a tool for power consolidation.[18]

For some victims who share their stories of violence and atrocity, truth-telling accelerates healing because they have placed their stories and those of their loved ones on record, ensuring that these memories will not be lost.[19] Truth programs can also lead to forgiveness because once victims know who has committed the crime against them or their loved ones, they can choose to forgive.[20] In the wake of South Africa's Truth and Reconciliation Commission (TRC), therapists reported that torture survivors perceived the public as more respectful and empathetic toward their experiences and needs, and this in turn led to reduced feelings of isolation and shame.[21]

However, not every victim involved in a truth commission experiences healing and empowerment, and amnesty can sometimes contribute to impunity.[22] Like memorials, truth commissions can marginalize certain victims by not providing them the appropriate space to share their stories. Additional trauma can occur when victims, especially survivors of sexual and gender-based violence, detail the violence they experienced.[23] Only after pressure from women's organizations did the South African Truth and Reconciliation Commission include an all-women hearing that allowed some women to feel safe enough to testify about SGBV.

National-level truth commissions, however, are only one mechanism associated with the reconciliation process, and their goals of social harmony are sometimes too broad and ambitious.[24] Localized reconciliation programs also work to find practical solutions to postconflict tensions.[25] In Rwanda, these efforts include free legal assistance for those accused of genocidal acts such as looting and property seizure, soccer teams organized to include children of both victims and perpetrators, church groups that discuss coping or church involvement in the 1994 genocide against the Tutsi, and orphan educational programs for those whose parents are in jail or deceased. Local programs like these elucidate for researchers and activists how people engage on a daily basis with the challenges, both social and physical, that arise after atrocity. Individuals rebuild their sense of self and their understanding of their place in the social world through routines of worship, community engagement, commemorating, and micro processes of reconciliation.

Several transitional justice research centers and initiatives are now considering the ways memorials fit within the bounds of transitional justice and how different transitional justice efforts connect with one another to address pressing contentions in post-atrocity communities.[26] Tribunals and truth commissions share with memorial projects a dependence on collecting documents and other materials to establish historical truths. To establish historical truths that provide the foundation for truth commissions, communities, researchers, and international actors must collect, manage, and analyze an overwhelming number of documentary materials.

While some scholars and practitioners have used memorials to rebuild communities or establish a record of past atrocities, memory projects are often not considered a key strategy in larger-scale transitional justice processes.[27] Using the case of Rwanda, I argue that memorials should be conceptualized as a form of restorative justice through their ability to provide information on past atrocities, facilitate localized reconciliation and educational programs, and give survivors a sense of hope for the future. Like other transitional justice mechanisms, memorials have strengths and weaknesses, both of which can provide valuable insights into memorialization, trials, and truth commissions. The struggles memorials have with representing histories marred by sexual and gender-based violence illuminate why those histories could be difficult to share in the context of a truth commission; these same struggles also suggest the need for communities to structure circumstances in which individuals can share their experiences.

Globally, transitional justice efforts are built upon the idea that societies and individuals are entitled to know the truth about mass human rights violations in the wake of armed conflict or repression. Transitional justice highlights the importance of proper mourning to achieve personal and communal healing.[28] International law also recognizes the right of victims and survivors to have access to knowledge concerning both the circumstances of serious human rights violations and the identities of those responsible.[29] Documenting and disseminating information on human rights abuses depends on civic engagement, including organizing and providing information. Truth-telling, civic participation, and mourning are also central facets of memorialization efforts. In the case of some memorials, scholars even go so far as to measure their success based on the reactions they provoke. Those reactions may take the form of civic debates, public dialogue, or responses by constituent groups of stakeholders—victims and their families, perpetrators, civic groups (schools, nongovernmental organizations, government organizations), and individuals (artists or even tourists).[30] Truth commissions depend on survivor testimony, in which social actors, including international ones, bear witness to the crimes victims survived, ensuring that victims' experiences become incorporated into the nation's (and world's) collective memory.

Collective Memory

The past is an overflow of the present. It is oriented from the present.[31]

George Herbert Mead

Like the driving ideology behind truth commissions, the construction of a collective memory aims to resist the collective forgetting of a past event and depends on an audience willing to bear witness to past traumas. Collective memory scholars have demonstrated the many ways in which the past is socially constructed and collective memories reflect the interests of present-day social actors.[32] One way that communities aim to create a cohesive narrative of a fragmented past of cultural trauma is through the construction of permanent memorials and rituals aimed at creating a collective memory that can be drawn upon for years to come. Building a collective memory through permanent physical memorials is a complex process. Commemorating a difficult and often controversial past involves negotiation with variously situated stakeholders, such as community organizers, victims of past abuses, policy makers, and political officials. Sociologists have evaluated several dimensions of this process, analyzing physical memorials themselves, the politics of who constructs memorials and why, changing concepts of memorials across time and space, and reactions by the public and other stakeholders to memorials.[33] This range of work emphasizes the physicality of memorials—the artists who create them, the physical landscape on which they stand, and the creative features that shape the relationships different groups of people have with memorial sites.

This work on the physicality of memorials helps us to understand the negotiations communities, artists, and political leaders make in developing a collective memory built upon a narrative rehearsed and repeated during commemorative rituals and in spaces such as monuments or memorials. In this literature, however, there has been little focus on the micro-level experiences of those who live around, work at, or interact with memorials on a regular basis. Most prior work on memorials has focused on elites who have shaped the physical forms of memorials or on the experiences, interpretations, and reactions of visitors and the general public to memorials.[34] This book takes place after the memorial setting has been constructed and as survivors are consistently engaged in creating meaning in its space.[35]

The focus of this book is on a subset of survivors: those who engage with memorial spaces on a regular, sometimes daily, basis. It is about what happens day to day in these spaces for the people the memorial is dedicated to remembering. The social actors in this book are the survivors who are guides, gardeners of the memorial, counselors at the memorials, memorial program participants, and neighbors. I inquire whether memorials matter to survivors on the micro level, and if so, how and why? How do these spaces facilitate healing, and how might they further pain or marginalization? I did not base the book on interviews with the general public, the architects, or visitors from faraway places; rather, I spent months talking to survivors, observing their daily lives and their meaning-making practices at memorial sites. Even with the explosion of social memory studies and the social science inquiries into collective memory and memorials, few have asked survivors about their own experiences with memorials.

Over the past twenty years, social memory studies have expanded in depth and breadth across the humanities, social sciences, and natural sciences. These diverse approaches share a commitment to engaging memory spaces and rituals as a heuristic for understanding history, identity, behavior, and social relations.[36] While the rediscovery of Maurice Halbwachs's 1925 book *On Collective Memory* sparked a resurgence in work that interrogates how the past affects the future, such questions were not new to philosophers or sociologists, even in Halbwachs's time.[37] In 1852, Marx stated, "The tradition of the dead generations weighs like a nightmare on the brain of the living."[38] Like Marx, Halbwachs saw the past as a force that affects the future through collective identities, social norms, and responses to present-day conflict. Halbwachs's major contribution to social memory studies is the foundational idea that groups have a collective memory, outside of individual memory, based on their social location and their access to power and resources. Past events are reconstructed through the lens of the present; the past thrives in the present when individuals from various social locations see it as relevant to the present moment and evoke it continuously.[39]

Approaches to understanding how the past shapes the present vary among disciplines. Two schools of thought, differing in both methodology and ontology, have emerged based on a distinction between "collected" and "collective" memory.[40] This difference most dramatically divides sociological and psychological studies, with the former adopting a more collectivist perspective and the latter an individualistic perspective.[41] "Collected memory" approaches, while acknowledging that "social frameworks shape what individuals will remember," ultimately believe "it is only individuals who do the remembering," not groups, spaces, or institutions.[42]

In the "collective memory" tradition, scholars assert that collectivities have memories that are "more than the aggregation of individual subjectivities . . . It is not just that we remember as members of groups but that we constitute those groups simultaneously in the act," demonstrating how power and institutions can stimulate and dictate memory.[43] For Halbwachs, "social frameworks" make it impossible to develop coherent memories outside of a social setting; in other words, all memory is collective.[44] While his analyses acknowledged and incorporated both collected and collective memory, Halbwachs argued that "group memberships provide the materials for memory and prod the individual into recalling particular events and into forgetting others," even if they are doing the remembering as individuals.[45] Groups can remember events in patterned and predictable ways; however, the lens of the present differs according to the social location of such groups.

Karl Mannheim's classic work on generations was among the first to apply this idea by demonstrating how individuals of a similar age were significantly influenced by major historical events that occurred during formative stages of their lives, shaping what scholars term "social memory."[46] Not all generational cohorts develop a shared memory, for "contemporaneity becomes sociologically significant only when it also involves participation in the same historical and social circumstances."[47] Mannheim's work sparked contemporary sociologists to consider how generation and age shape collective memory through factors such as which national events people name as most important to their lives.[48] From a generational perspective, much of what we remember emerges not from personal experience but from intergenerational, national, or institutional narratives. As Eviatar Zerubavel reminds us, we remember as "members of particular families, organizations, nations and other mnemonic communities."[49] Collected memories can become collective when groups remember in a way that makes them feel connected and united.

Communities, movements, and nations often remember their pasts in ways that create a sense of solidarity or exceptionality within the larger global community. Benedict Anderson famously described how such "imagined communities" make individuals feel allied with one another in nationalist projects. "Imagining a community" means sharing traditions, or "inventing" shared traditions, practicing communal rituals, or encouraging ideas of common descent.[50] War memorials often assert, through narrative or architectural design, that those who died did so for a morally justifiable cause, evoking national pride and honor.[51] To be remembered, such traditions and communities must be narrated; narration includes a process of gathering social memories together so that the past becomes identifiable, recognizable, and thus recallable.

One way that institutional powers have constructed collective memories is through the creation of physical memorials and monuments as well as commemorative events. Commemorations depend on participation, which is facilitated by "overcoming the separation from which otherwise unaffiliated individuals suffer. . . . Commemoration suggests that such separation is a sham."[52] Commemorations encourage group cohesion through shared rituals; their "master narrative is more than a story told and reflected on: it is a cult enacted."[53] In this understanding, for commemorative ceremonies to be effective, "participants must not simply be cognitively competent to execute performance: they must be habituated to those performances."[54] However, memory formation is often a contested process, structured by those who can access and secure institutional power.[55]

Institutions can struggle with developing a collective memory through memorials or commemorations when the past is contentious or shameful, or when a lack of national consensus about traumatic events produces emotions such as guilt and grief.[56] One way to address this problem is for institutions to situate the remembrance process within various stories, sites, and spaces.[57] Having multiple memorial sites or narratives within a single memorial allows for flexibility. Flexibility can also result from changes over time in memorial narratives, physical dimensions, or internal structures to more appropriately match present-day interpretations of a contentious past. Such flexibility maintains a strong national collective memory. For example, the American national narratives and commemorative projects associated with the Vietnam War have significantly transformed over various decades, with memorials evoking attitudes that have changed over time.[58]

In addition to salient temporal variation, memorials dedicated to the same event or atrocity can significantly vary depending on geographic location. Young's study of Holocaust memorials found that sites differed considerably from country to country. For example, Israeli memorials offered stories of heroism and national redemption while US memorials focused on the centrality of rescue workers and soldiers.[59]

Memorials tell stories about the nations that construct them, and these are often highly gendered accounts of mass trauma, social change, or war.[60] Narratives of war or atrocity often confine women's experiences of violence to traditionally feminine roles, such as mothers, nurses, or victims lacking protection from men.[61] In Jacobs's analysis of Holocaust memorials, she finds that women are either absent or strategically represented as grieving mothers or sexual victims of perpetrators—static roles in Jewish Holocaust memory. Jacobs's work draws attention to the genderblind lens that is often used when analyzing memorials and treats women's and men's experiences as identical, thus ignoring the ways that social roles and gendered norms shape collective memory.[62]

While memorials can enforce rigid societal norms and reflect social inequalities, they are also thought to be a vehicle for illuminating aspects of truth and reconciliation after atrocity.[63] This book takes this intersection of transitional justice and collective memory as its point of departure, expanding work on restorative justice and the importance of truth-telling to include less conventional sites. This study is invested in the interaction of the micro- and national-level narratives about violence. Taken together, these narratives demonstrate the dynamics of how decisions are made by guides, community members, professionals, survivors, and political leaders to create a collective memory through memorials and commemorations. By considering how decisions are made, we can better understand what processes matter in memory projects and how those processes can both empower and stratify communities. This matters more broadly for studies of contention and inequality because how a country remembers its past shapes its future. How survivors feel they fit into national collective memory affects their participation and perspectives as citizens in a nation that hopes for peaceful coexistence.[64]

The stories of survivors in this book document the lived experiences of people who physically survived horrific violence: rape; the murder of their children, spouses, and loved ones; torture; and dismemberment. By knowing what makes survivors' lives more hopeful, bearable, and stable, we can better assist efforts to build similar resilience in Rwanda and beyond with appropriate and adequate aid, resources, and research. In the chapters that follow, I discuss the ways that some survivors engage with memorials and commemorations, the stories shared at these spaces, and the challenges memory projects in Rwanda encounter in representing survivors, unifying communities, and facilitating reconciliation.

After Genocide

This book is based on nine years of field work, including multiple interviews with seventy-two survivors of the 1994 genocide against the Tutsi who live near, work at, or regularly engage with one of three national memorials that I selected for this project. I first visited Rwanda after conducting preliminary interviews with Rwandan refugees living in the US.[65] I was in Rwanda in 2009 with Global Youth Connect, a program that aims to advance human rights by connecting activists from around the globe to meet face-to-face, exchange ideas, and collaborate with Nongovernmental Organizations (NGOs), policy makers, and other stakeholders. After the program, I extended my trip to visit friends and memorial sites, exploring the landscape. From 2009 to 2018, I made seven trips to Rwanda, interviewing survivors from 2011 to 2012. I visited memorials throughout the country and attended commemorations and burials throughout the mourning months (further detailed in the appendix).

I interviewed those who had survived the most horrific of circumstances, and their stories still haunt me today.[66] In response to the most inhumane violence that any individual could imagine, many performed heroic, almost superhuman acts. Some risked their lives by saving others; breastfed babies they found in mass graves; lived in swamps for months; survived injury, rape, forced sexual slavery, and torture—the list goes on and on. Some went on to become leaders. Others, sometimes the only living survivors in a long family lineage, became heads of households composed of adopted family members. These survivors have persisted in ways that are unfathomable, and some are rightfully angry to the core of their being. A few have forgiven those who harmed their families and destroyed life as they knew it. Many clench their fists until their knuckles turn white at the thought that they still don't know who killed their loved ones. All tell stories steeped in the unwavering belief that remembering past violence is inextricability linked to the possibilities for justice in its aftermath. Their beliefs, stories, and experiences are detailed in the pages that follow.

Before delving into these stories, chapter 1, "The Context of Violence in Rwanda," provides a foundation for interpreting contemporary Rwandan memory culture. I outline the social construction of ethnic identities during the colonial period, independence, the civil war, and the genocidal violence that followed in April 1994. What follows is a description of the aftermath—a scene difficult to fathom for those who have not experienced war or atrocity. It is within this historical moment of destruction, fear, and trauma that memorials were erected by government leaders, survivors, and members of the international community.

Chapter 2, "Memory Landscapes after Human Rights Violations," moves beyond the historical context to explore the physical landscape of Rwanda's memory culture, describing the memory objects and symbols that occupy every facet of social life during the national mourning months. Banners stating "never again" marked with white crosses alert visitors to burial sites and commemorative spaces throughout the country. Commemorations occur annually during the national mourning period (April–July), drawing crowds of up to five thousand. I draw on ethnographic research and participant observations to describe the enormity of the devastation, trauma, and memorial culture in Rwanda. These spaces, which are attended year-round, not only serve as sites of redress and remembrance (discussed in chapter 3) but also, I argue, have significant physical and logistical functions, such as housing the evidence of genocidal violence and the many bodies found post-1994.

Inquiring beyond the pragmatic functions of memorials, chapter 3, "The Role of Memory Work in Violence Prevention," provides an analysis of how survivors made sense of the 1994 genocide against the Tutsi and the role of memorials in two main ways: identifying culpability through a narration of history, and honoring the innocent people who died. While survivors assert that remembrance rituals lead to violence prevention, a sentiment echoed by the government of Rwanda, this chapter argues that survivors both embrace and contest state narratives, making these narratives personal through individual ideological processes of meaning-making. This chapter will be of particular interest to readers attuned to narratives and the power of storytelling and meaning-making after trauma.

Chapter 4, "Trauma and the Stratification of Collective Memory," is the first of two chapters that dig into how decisions are made about what Rwanda's collective memory includes or leaves out. Chapters 4 and 5 will be of particular interest to memory scholars as the field is only beginning to address the creation of collective memories at the micro level. While the survivors I interviewed are deeply dedicated to memorials and commemorative events, as seen in chapter 3, a significant challenge in remembering the past is the increasing traumatization of survivors during commemorative events. Rwandans have a word for survivors' distinctive bodily response to memories of extreme trauma: "traumatizing." This chapter examines how different groups of survivors understand trauma and shape decisions about how commemorations are structured. I show that different constructions of trauma inform decisions about who is included in and excluded from public testimony. Although these and a series of other decisions are often made in an effort to keep people safe and move the nation forward, they ultimately serve to stratify Rwanda's collective memory. An unintended effect of such decisions is the marginalization of stories by some of the most disenfranchised survivors: rape survivors, those with mental health challenges, and the poor.

Chapter 5, "Gendered Violence and the Politics of Remembering and Forgetting," focuses on decision-making behind memorial tours that incorporate discussions of gender-based violence perpetrated during the genocide, when an estimated 350,000 rapes took place, along with countless other forms of sexual violence and torture. Rape was considered the rule rather than the exception, with many women publicly tortured before being left for dead. These experiences are fresh in survivors' minds, and many still experience physical and emotional scars. I foreground how memorial guides use memorials' physicality and orientation to discuss gender-based violence. Some guides find unique ways to bring the experience of women survivors into the larger narrative of past violence. Not all memorials, however, make this choice. I argue that these choices reveal how some memorials relegate stories of genocidal rape and gendered violence in favor of ones that offer more inspiration and justify practices of forgiveness and reconciliation.

In chapter 6, "Survivors' Lived Experiences of Reconciliation," I turn to how survivors experience reconciliation—a central goal of memory initiatives. This chapter addresses two aspects of reconciliation. The first is what I refer to as the "reconciliation formula": an idealized, but ultimately mythic, notion that reconciliation occurs when a perpetrator admits wrongdoing, asks the survivor for forgiveness, and is forgiven. Despite the dominance of this narrative among participants, not a single participant I interviewed reported experiencing the formula. While the formula provides inspiration for some, it also has ramifications for survivors who see their own hopes of reconciliation dashed when no one seeks their forgiveness. The reconciliation formula highlights how stories intended to heal can sometimes add to victims' struggles. The second aspect of reconciliation addressed in this chapter has to do with the everyday markers of reconciliation and progress, such as daily experiences between people of different ethnicities or with different degrees of access to education. These markers have both symbolic and practical significance in survivors' lives and offer hope that social harmony may be achievable. In the aftermath of mass atrocity, social change can be measured in the contradictions between imagined and experienced reconciliation. The unfulfilled hopes for reconciliation can serve the broader purpose of working at the local level toward achieving peaceful coexistence and protecting human rights.

In the conclusion, I highlight the lessons from my study: Memorials organize memories in ways that concretely affect the lives of survivors and their experiences of reconciliation. Memorials and commemorations order narratives of the past that are chaotic, disjointed, and traumatic. Ordering memories facilitates hope and offers survivors overarching narratives; however, elevating a unifying metanarrative to order memories disregards the stratified effect violence has on communities. I argue that stories about past violence and future hope—both those publicly shared and those silenced—impact the present-day possibilities for reconciliation and justice. Finally, I suggest that the lessons learned from Rwanda can be applied to present-day cases of violence and terrorism, informing transitional justice policy and positing directions for future research.

The appendix details my methodology and research design; it describes highlights of my fieldwork and moments that required ethical considerations. My aim in this section is to provide an honest and feminist reflection on data collection, secondary trauma, and my own positionality as they impacted my qualitative international research. In this section, I hope to stimulate and continue a dialogue about ethical feminist research on vulnerable populations.

1 | The Context of Violence in Rwanda

When I first spent time in Rwanda, and before I had visited any memorials, I found it nearly impossible to imagine the horrors that had occurred more than a decade earlier. The luscious green hills and meticulous landscaping I saw through the car window were incongruous with the atrocity I had read about. I, like most Western tourists visiting Rwanda, walked in admiration of the perfectly manicured Kigali streets, drove around the beautifully designed roundabouts marked by their distinct statues or fountains, shopped in the vast and colorful markets, and ate lunch at four-star hotels. Kenyan friends who visited me while I was in Rwanda also noted the tidy sidewalks, the clean capital city, and the efficient bus system. Some Rwandans, too, were proud to show off rooftop coffee shops, lavish hotels, ethnic restaurants, and sparkling pools. It was indeed impressive.

A survivor once said to me, "History is part of today—it is part of us and who we will be." The many memorials dotting the Rwandan landscape are an obvious reminder of the past's influence on the present-day built environment, but the past is also in the paved streets and the pride over present-day order, detail, and development. The past is likewise in the dirt roads, the ones that are not on display. When I was living in Rwanda, when traffic was particularly congested, I would drive home on the unpaved, uneven backroads. On this route I caught glimmers of women selling bananas that were in baskets on their heads and kids running around shirtless and barefoot. Fountains did not appear on these streets; in their place stood fences and walls marked with bright blue and yellow paint and a red Primus beer logo in the center—an effective way of advertising one of Rwanda's most ubiquitous beers. Small bright-yellow umbrellas stood in stark contrast to the deep red dirt holding them up, with young people nearby, wearing matching yellow vests, selling phone cards to passersby. When I first came to Kicukiro to stay with a few graduate school friends in 2009, it was much less developed than it was in 2011, when I embarked on fieldwork for this book, or when I returned in 2019. The roads were rocky and surrounded by open space, allowing goats and other animals to roam free. Houses were beautiful yet modest, unlike the mansions one can see in Nyarutarama today.

The order, detail, and development that now mark Kigali's city space especially command attention because of the contrast with the not-so-distant past. It was jarring to enjoy a lavish poolside brunch buffet at the very hotel where people sought refuge in 1994 and resorted to drinking pool water to survive dehydration. Indeed, comparatively, few cities in the world have experienced the exponential population, political, and socioeconomic change of Kigali since 1994.[1] The spatial dimensions of a city tell a story about power relations, social control, and political processes. As Ine Cottyn points out, "Urban areas are strategic political locations in post-conflict societies, gaining and retaining control over them is a critical concern of the post-conflict state . . . [and] urbanization is an important strategy of the government in rebuilding and reconstructing the country."[2] In Rwanda, such rebuilding has included both traditional urbanization and the creation of memorials.

Through Rwanda's Master Plan for 2020, Kigali has become a model city with a level of urban security few cities have come close to achieving.[3] What I witnessed in admiration as a foreigner in 2009 was undeniably the result of a deliberate plan. I saw a city worth investing in—a city of security, control, and promise. However, this transformation has materialized in large part due to a range of political consolidation strategies and an abundance of foreign aid, both of which have done little to improve the difficult lives of the urban and rural poor.[4] The women selling fruit on the side of the road have disappeared from the roundabouts because they are no longer allowed to be there—the city's low-paid street economy has been forced out of the public eye to protect the promise of Kigali as a development site for investment.[5] As is true of other postconflict societies, Rwanda's present-day development aspirations, memorialization projects, and respective inequalities are a product of history. Thus, I begin with background on Rwanda's distant past to lay a foundation for understanding the present-day proliferation of memory projects.

Rwanda is a landlocked country located in the Great Lakes region of Central Africa, surrounded by the Democratic Republic of the Congo (DRC), Burundi, Tanzania, and Uganda. Rwanda has long been one of the most densely populated African nations. Historically, the forests in Rwanda have served as a barrier against tsetse flies and malaria-carrying mosquitos. Known as the "land of a thousand hills," the country features countless stunning grassy knolls and mountains. Lake Kivu separates Rwanda from the DRC, and on the eastern side, marshes extend into Tanzania. Rwanda's seasons are marked not by fluctuating temperatures but by rainfall. Yearlong moderate temperatures and mild elevations have fostered productive farming and population growth. Agriculture flourishes, with intricate vegetable gardens lining the slopes of hillsides like staircases. Rwanda's densely populated landscape contributed to a highly social human culture but also led to the demise of large African animals, such as elephants and lions, outside the wildlife preservation areas of Akagera National Park.

Today, Rwandans often assert in public, and especially to tourists, that there are no longer ethnicities such as Hutu, Tutsi, or Twa because "we are all Rwandan."[6] Such claims mark a significant change from both the rather recent past (i.e., the years leading up to the 1994 genocide against the Tutsi) and the more distant past of colonial rule. The meanings of the names Hutu, Tutsi, and Twa have shifted over time, transforming with the changing political landscape of Rwanda. Many Rwandans and scholars of Rwanda alike argue that, prior to colonial rule, Hutu, Tutsi, and Twa represented social classes rather than ethnic or racial categories. Generally speaking, Hutu were agriculturalists (84 percent of the population), Tutsi were cattle-raisers (15 percent), and the Twa were potters (1 percent). However, during this time period it was possible for some Hutu to become Tutsi and vice versa. Thus each group's overall percentage of the population has fluctuated over time.[7] State power at this time rested with the king and chiefs installed by the Tutsi court. As Anuradha Chakravarty explains, the chiefs "acted as patrons, providing security guarantees for 'Tutsi' cattle-owning lineages in exchange for receiving cows and luxury items as a sign of submission. . . . For non-cattle-owning farming lineages, defined as 'Hutu,' the patron extended the loan of a cow for usufruct use to the farmer client who was expected to reciprocate with labor, gifts, and of course, loyalty."[8] Even with social, economic, and political inequality, Hutu, Tutsi, and Twa for the most part shared the same culture—speaking the same language, eating the same food, and intermarrying.[9]

While the categories of Hutu and Tutsi were fluid, this fluidity did not translate into equality or equity across the approximately eighteen clans, with agriculturalists generally having less economic prosperity than cattle-raisers.[10] J. J. Maquet describes this period in terms of a caste system that kept intact a (rather fragile) social harmony between the Hutu and Tutsi, while anthropologist Helen Codere argues that these categories were wrought with social tensions over economic inequality and the Tutsi's consolidation of political and military power.[11] Economic inequalities increased between 1865 and 1895, when the system of kingdoms, previously comprising both Hutu and Tutsi kings, shifted organization from lineages to chiefs and peasants, with the chiefs being mostly Tutsi and the peasants mostly Hutu.[12] While in power, King Rwabugiri diminished local control by implementing stratified economic institutions for all those in his kingdom, including *ubuhake* (cattle clientship that favored Tutsi) and *uburetwa* (a forced unpaid labor system from which Tutsi were exempt).[13]

King Rwabugiri executed expansive leadership, "massively expanding Rwanda's territory during his three-decade rule," until his death in 1985 while on an expedition on Lake Kivu.[14] During a period known as the "Scramble for Africa" in 1897, German colonizers offered support to the new king, fifteen-year-old Yuhi Musinga, who welcomed their backing and in return allowed Missionaries of Africa, known as the White Fathers, to establish bases throughout Rwanda.[15]

The Germans chose a path of indirect rule by centralizing political power, creating fixed borders, and, most importantly, beginning the transformation of political identities of Hutu and Tutsi into racialized ones through the reiteration of the "Hamitic" myth.[16] The "Hamitic hypothesis" racialized previous categories of Hutu and Tutsi by contending that Tutsi were taller, had thinner noses, and appeared more like Europeans, having supposedly originated from somewhere outside East Africa.[17] German colonizers, as well as Belgians years later who solidified this ideology, assumed that Tutsi were originally from Northern Africa, and, because organized politics and practices existed within the region, they believed that "the ruling group must have come from elsewhere."[18]

The White Fathers followed the lead of German colonizers by enforcing the belief that the Tutsi were a superior group and that Hutu were less "civilized." For instance, the White Fathers assumed that all chiefs were Tutsi and all subjects Hutu; they therefore ignored Hutu chiefs.[19] These artificial divisions had the effect of creating two distinct groups, establishing Hutu as the group indigenous to the area and Tutsi as having originated elsewhere. Colonialists gain power through division. The Germans' approach to ruling Rwanda was both to assert divisions between the colonizer and colonized and to impose categories of ethnic superiority and inferiority upon those they colonized.[20]

Germany lost its rule over East Africa to Belgium in 1916, ending the German presence in Rwanda. While German leaders had believed the Hamitic hypothesis, "Belgian power turned Hamitic racial supremacy from an ideology into an institutional fact by making it the basis of changes in political, social, and cultural relations."[21] The Belgians and White Fathers consolidated power by controlling the elite and crystalizing racial divisions.[22] To reinforce the racial hierarchy Germany had sketched out, Belgians deliberately furthered the careers of Tutsi by institutionalizing inequality in key areas such as education, labor, and the Catholic Church through taxation, employment, and social policies.[23] Under Belgian orders, the White Fathers removed all remaining Hutu chiefs from power and, by the late 1920s, Tutsi held virtually all ranks of political power. By the 1930s, the missionaries' efforts began to pay off when Tutsi started sending their children to Catholic schools and becoming heavily involved in Catholic churches.[24]

During this time, the modern eugenics movement was gaining traction across Europe, Australia, and the Americas, heavily influencing the practices of colonizers.[25] The Belgian colonizers imposed eugenic ideology in Rwanda through the use of mandatory identity cards and a census. These cards marked an individual as Hutu, Tutsi, or Twa, thereby eliminating any gray areas around ethnic identity and essentially asserting these categories as biological, fixed, and measurable. The identity stated on one's card delimited one's access to political, educational, and communal opportunities and resources. This colonial construction of race was further reinforced in Rwanda by being taught in the schools, churches, and communities.

However, by the early 1950s, the Hutu-Tutsi divide was only one of many social issues that had percolated into what had become the most Catholic nation in Africa. Opposing communism and secularism—and supporting democracy, modernization, and economic prosperity—largely defined the White Fathers' agenda.[26] Globally, the post–World War II era saw a range of nationalist social movements across Africa, all centering on decolonization and justice, ranging from Pan-Africanism in Ghana to anti-apartheid in South Africa. At this time, even East African Belgian colonialists started using the language of "partnership," discussing issues of autonomy and even African independence.[27] Belgians and the White Fathers were instrumental in significant early socioeconomic policy changes to eliminate *uburetwa* and then later *ubuhake*: patron-client exchange relationships that favored Tutsi (the patrons). The elimination of these, in turn, did little to actually redistribute land or eradicate inequalities.[28]

By the mid-1950s, Hutu-Tutsi tensions arose in the church and throughout public life. Under pressure from the UN and a vocal disenfranchised Hutu majority with Catholic support, reforms were implemented that allowed Hutu to occupy select leadership positions in public life. However, these reforms only escalated tensions as they had little effect on improving the everyday lives of poor Hutu.[29] In early 1957, Tutsi leaders issued a "Statement of Views" in which they emphasized self-governance with a focus on educational opportunity for all and denounced the inequality between colonizers (Europeans) and Rwandans (Africans). The "Statement of Views" lacked any mention of Hutu-Tutsi inequality, and months later a group of Hutu intellectuals responded with their own statement.[30]

The 1957 "Hutu Manifesto" also called for equal access to education, employment, and social resources regardless of ethnicity, but it elevated the inequality between Tutsi and Hutu rather than highlighting European oppression, as the "Statement of Views" had done. While the manifesto's demand was for power sharing regardless of ethnic background and liberation from both Tutsi and colonial powers, the document was steeped in racist ideology and terminology.[31] Compelled by a fear of losing power, Tutsi elites condemned the manifesto for both its racist ideology and its call for land redistribution and to claim that such a reallocation of resources could trigger violence and threaten the social order.[32] On November 1, 1959, a Hutu leader from the newly established (1957) Parmehutu political party, Dominique Mbonyumutwa, was killed by a group of Tutsi associated with the Union Nationale Rwandaise (UNAR, Rwandese National Union), a recently mobilized elite Tutsi political party.[33] After the murder of Mbonyumutwa, violence from rural Hutu aimed at Tutsi elite erupted throughout the country. At this time, there were still multiple political parties and moderates—Hutu, Tutsi, and Twa—who emphasized poverty as a concern to all ethnic groups, underscoring the issue of widespread rural grievances.

Violence and social revolution from 1959 to 1961 motivated some Tutsi to leave Rwanda for neighboring Uganda and Zaire (now the Democratic Republic of the Congo).[34] During this period, the framing of grievances shifted when patterns of violence, ethnic nationalism, and exclusionary rhetoric coalesced in ways that facilitated generalizations about entire ethnic groups.[35] During this time, the marginalization of political moderates of all ethnicities gave rise to a new phase in Rwandan history known as the Hutu Revolution. The Hutu Revolution successfully paved the way for independence from colonial rule in 1962. Grégoire Kayibanda, a Hutu from the south representing the Hutu political party Mouvement démocratique republicain–Parmehutu (Republican Democratic Movement–Parmehutu, or MDR-Parmehutu), served as Rwanda's first postcolonial president.[36]

Over the next several years, through violence, neocolonial support, and strict policies of inequality, power dynamics shifted. Hutu gained representation and domination in all social and economic institutions, including politics. The use of violence and massacres against Tutsi communities, as well as quotas that restricted Tutsi presence in schools and public life, constrained any chance of Tutsi regaining power and ensured Hutu authority. Some of the anti-Tutsi violence during this period included acts of reprisal after a series of raids between 1963 and 1967 led by Rwandans who were living in exile in Uganda. Susan Thomson notes that in areas where "ordinary people were hesitant to scapegoat their Tutsi neighbors, senior government officials returned to their hills of origin to incite attacks on Tutsi."[37]

In 1973 General Juvénal Habyarimana, a Hutu from the north and senior officer of the army, took power in a relatively peaceful coup on a platform of "peace, unity, and development."[38] President Habyarimana founded the political party Mouvement révolutionaire national pour le développement (MRND, National Revolutionary Movement for Development), which garnered vast international financial support in part due to his focus on education, development, and national security. Habyarimana's regime had significant assistance from churches, and as in previous historical periods, the churches promoted leaders who supported the president.[39] During the first decade of Habyarimana's regime, ethnic violence declined after the persistent ethnic-based killings during Kayibanda's regime, and the economy prospered.

In the second decade of Habyarimana's rule, he asserted that a single-party political arena was needed for Rwanda's security and development.[40] However, in the late 1980s, with the onset of significant economic turmoil, violence and tensions once again rose, but this time centered around region and class.[41] Coffee, which accounted for 75 percent of Rwanda's foreign income, swiftly dropped in price, and Rwanda became indebted to the World Bank.[42] Tensions increased in 1989 when Rwanda experienced a severe drought and food shortage that exacerbated the already substantial divide between rich and poor.[43] Habyarimana responded with additional quotas and policies that further disenfranchised Tutsi and privileged Hutu. While this disenfranchisement aimed to lift up Hutu, even conditions for the middle class deteriorated to such an extent that both Hutu and Tutsi expressed widespread uproar. Public clamor emphasized discontent over corruption, the AIDS epidemic, class disparity, and growing ethnic tensions.[44]

During this time, East African and European allies pressured Habyarimana to democratize Rwanda. With the decline of communism in Europe, Western donors no longer wanted to invest in single-party dictatorships, and Rwanda was no exception.[45] In 1990, under demands from France (Habyarimana's principal international investor and ally), President Habyarimana agreed to transition to multiparty elections and the creation of a commission to examine a range of possibilities for political reform. However, before these reforms had a chance to come to fruition, in October 1990 the Rwandan Patriot Army (RPA), an armed rebel movement composed of exiled Rwandans living in Uganda, attacked Rwanda, shifting priority from democratization to national security.[46]

The attack was the first of many by the Rwandan Patriotic Front (RPF), and it sparked a civil war that continued until the 1994 genocide against the Tutsi. The civil war was framed by the Habyarimana regime as being rooted solely in ethnic divides.[47]

In response to repeated RPF attacks, Habyarimana's administration led a public propaganda campaign linking the RPF rebels with Tutsi civilians living in Rwanda. Labeling Tutsi as outsiders, *inyenzi* (meaning cockroaches), "Hamitic" foreigners, RPF accomplices, and, most importantly, a danger to the Hutu majority and accomplices, the anti-Tutsi propaganda campaign was conducted through print media (including *Kangura*, an anti-Tutsi weekly magazine), radio stations (especially Radio Télévision Libre des Mille Collines [RTLM]), and political events and gatherings.[48] The most infamous example of anti-Tutsi propaganda was the publication in *Kangura* of the "Hutu Ten Commandments."[49] The ten commandments displayed a specifically gendered anti-Tutsi rhetoric in pronouncements such as "we shall consider a traitor any Hutu who marries a Tutsi woman, befriends a Tutsi woman, or employs a Tutsi woman. . . . Hutu women, be vigilant and try to bring your husbands, brothers, and sons back to reason." Chillingly, it also declared, "The Hutu should stop having mercy on Tutsi."[50]

Various forms of propaganda were central to the transformation of Hutu politics into a brand of ethnic nationalism. Ethnic nationalism, in the form of Hutu domination, was framed by hardliners as the solution to Rwanda's larger problems: hunger, overpopulation, fear, and uncertainty. Nationalist ideology (i.e., Hutu domination) entailed the normalization of exclusionary ideology to such an extent that the moral landscape was altered to frame lethal violence as a viable solution to the nation's problems.[51] This transformation involved Hutu hardliners monopolizing media outlets, diffusing fear, and practicing genocidal violence on a smaller scale than the massacres documented in 1994.[52] Anti-Tutsi massacres, unheard of since the 1959 revolution, began in the early 1990s, fueled by arguments by proponents of ethnic nationalism that problems could be solved through the elimination of Tutsi.[53]

During this time, militias expanded on all fronts, with the Rwandan army enlarging its forces to include a civilian defense program and MRND developing a youth militia called the Interahamwe. The Coalition pour la Défense de la République (CDR, Coalition for the Defense of the Republic) had its own youth militia, Impuzamugambi (which means "those with the same goal"). As Scott Straus notes, "the government incorporated civilians into war—which set the stage for civilian participation in the genocide."[54] Wealthy elites used their international connections to import weapons from France and Belgium.[55] Rwanda also received assistance from China and Egypt to purchase machetes, rifles, and grenades.[56] Between 1992 and 1994, Rwanda was sub-Saharan Africa's "third largest importer of weapons, with cumulative military imports totaling $100 million."[57] The majority of households in both the rural and urban sectors owned a machete or hoe tools that were used as weapons during the genocide.[58]

In early 1992, as fighting escalated, France, the US, the Vatican, and Belgium pressured the MRND and the RPF to begin peace talks and halt the violence. After five months, in June 1992, both agreed, and peace talks were facilitated by Tanzania and held in Arusha.[59] Because of the recent democratization efforts, the new multiparty government represented Rwanda in the peace talks and managed to quickly advance tentative agreements on power sharing, unification, and political cooperation by the end of 1992. A sticking point in these discussions centered on the percentage spilt of the two armies (RPF and the Rwandan national army), including the percentage of command positions— as both parties insisted on having the majority.[60]

Unfortunately, "these talks constituted a classic case of empty words short of real negotiation. While the talks were in progress, an extremist movement of northern Hutu elites was building its capacity to constrain the negotiations and their implementation."[61] With the training of the Interahamwe militia well underway by Hutu hardliners (MRND), tensions escalated in 1993 when episodes of violence again erupted, garnering international attention and concern.

The UN Security Council adopted Resolution 872 on October 5, 1993, to assist in the implementation of what became known as the Arusha Accords in order to facilitate a peace process between the RPF and government of Rwanda.[62] The UN Security Council sent peacekeeping troops to Rwanda under the leadership of Force Commander General Roméo Dallaire, a Canadian lieutenant.[63] This mission established the United Nations Assistance Mission for Rwanda (UNAMIR) with 2,500 peacekeeping soldiers.

On October 21, 1993, Burundi's first democratically elected Hutu president, Melchior Ndadaye, was assassinated by the Tutsi army. Hutu hardliners, including a social circle of Hutu extremists called the Akazu, exploited this event to showcase how dangerous Tutsi were, arguing that if Tutsi could assassinate a democratically elected president, they could destroy anyone and anything.[64] This kind of argument helped stoke the fear and anger needed to incite violence among ordinary citizens.

In early 1994, Dallaire received information from a confidential informant, known as "Jean Pierre," that the Interahamwe was preparing a "killing machine," training young men to kill one thousand Tutsi in twenty minutes' time, and that mass violence was imminent.[65] General Dallaire responded by writing a fax, later termed the "genocide fax," to Kofi Annan, who was directing the UN peacekeeping office in New York on January 11, 1994. The letter warned of militants' plans to murder the recently arrived Belgian UN troops along with Rwandan Tutsi.[66] The UN responded to Dallaire by insisting he provide information about the Interahamwe's plans to President Habyarimana and denied Dallaire's request for authority to raid the suspected arms caches to which "Jean Pierre" had alerted him. When Dallaire spoke with the Habyarimana regime about the extermination plans, he essentially alerted the regime to the information on the "killing machine" that Dallaire was privy to, allowing them to quickly distribute all their weapons to the Interahamwe.[67]

In the days leading up to April 6, President Habyarimana was in Dar es Salaam, attending meetings with heads of state to discuss a path forward after the failure of the Arusha peace accords. During these meetings, President Habyarimana agreed to form a transitional government to end the civil war in Rwanda. No such plan was implemented, for on the evening of April 6, 1994, Burundi's new president, Cyprien Ntaryamira, along with President Habyarimana and others, was killed when missiles shot down their plane near the Kigali airport. Parts of Habyarimana's plane wreckage oddly landed in his very own backyard.[68] To this day, experts debate who carried out the assassination: the Akazu, the RPF, or the *genocidaires*.[69] What is known is that in the hours, days, and months following the plane crash, a well-organized genocidal campaign unfolded, claiming the lives of an estimated eight hundred thousand Rwandans in less than four months.[70]

Within hours of Habyarimana's assassination, roadblocks were set up throughout Rwanda, preventing people from leaving their homes or escaping the country.[71] In the first twenty-four hours, many prominent opposition members, the majority Hutu, were murdered, leaving the country without government leaders. In the first five days of the genocide, more than ten thousand Rwandans were killed, mostly Tutsi and moderate Hutu, including the prime minister, Agathe Uwilingiyimana.[72] Uwilingiyimana, who was next in line to be president, was planning on communicating via radio to the Rwandan public to stay calm and safe. However, she was never able communicate this message as she was brutally murdered, along with the ten Belgian UN peace officers in charge of protecting her, as she surrendered outside her house in order to save her five children, who were hiding inside.[73]

The murder of ten Belgian UN soldiers had significant ramifications for Rwanda's future. With the 1993 catastrophe in Somalia fresh in the UN personnel's memories, on April 12, 1994, the Belgian, French, and American peacekeepers withdrew from Rwanda, and days later the UN Security Council, against Dallaire's fierce protests, voted to reduce the peacekeeping troops.[74]

In hindsight, this action was one of the most catastrophic failures of the international community, allowing the deaths of hundreds of thousands of Rwandans to occur under the watchful eyes of both the international community and the UN.[75]

Various scholars debate the extent to which the genocidal violence was planned prior to 1994.[76] However, scholars have documented how many moderate Hutu politicians were killed within twenty-four hours of the president's assassination, leaving a leadership vacuum of mostly Hutu hard-liners in place.[77] In the first few days of the genocide, targets for the various militias (the Interhamwe, Impuzamugambi, and Presidential Army) were named on the radio station RTLM, including details of where they lived and what they looked like. When Rwandans attempted to escape, they faced roadblocks guarded by a heavily armed militia. Civilians were required to show their identity cards, and if they were Tutsi, or someone who was friendly with Tutsi, they were killed with machetes, shot, tortured, and/or raped. Those with resources were sometimes able to negotiate for their lives with bribes.

The killings in Rwanda were intimate affairs: people murdered those they knew, parishioners executed those they had sat alongside in church just days earlier, schoolmates murdered families of schoolmates, and sometimes family members even killed their own, either willingly or because they were forced to do so.[78] The intimacy of the killings during the genocide lacked the "bureaucratic efficiency of mass extermination," which was previously documented in the Holocaust and past genocides.[79] The speed at which the genocide unfolded was also unlike prior atrocities.

The typical perpetrator was an ordinary man with an average level of education and no prior history of violence.[80] While the genocide was planned and facilitated by Hutu hardliners, ordinary citizens carried it out.[81] Between 175,000 and 210,000 people actively participated in genocidal interpersonal violence.[82] While civilian participation was central to advancing the genocidal agenda, it is likely that a relatively small percentage of the total perpetrators undertook the majority of the killing, and trained militia members murdered far more individuals than did civilians.

The timing of violence across the country varied from region to region. As the RPF counterattacked from the north, they drove the militias south in all directions. However, once genocidal violence began in an area, it rapidly spiked, with the majority of deaths occurring in the first days of the onset of violence.[83] Meso-level variations also shaped how violence unfolded. These factors included the number of Tutsi in an area, political party dominance of the region, the level of interethnic cohesion in a given community, and an area's proximity to the capital, which was the epicenter of the violence.[84]

The physical landscape of Rwanda was an advantage for perpetrators as they could position themselves on the hilltops, gazing below to see where civilians gathered or fled, and instruct the militia accordingly.[85]

Churches, considered safe havens in previous episodes of violence, no longer provided sanctuary. Because the church was so connected to political life in Rwanda, churches were instrumental in the killings. *Genocidaires* forced victims to congregate in churches (and some victims sought refuge in churches because they had been safe places in previous episodes of violence) in order to more efficiently murder crowds of civilians with grenades and machetes.[86] Church leaders and congregants not only followed the orders of genocidal militias but also gave killing orders themselves.

Gender-based violence was a defining feature of the genocide. While some estimate that 350,000 women were raped during the genocide, the real number is unknown.[87] *Genocidaires* often publicly humiliated or tortured women and girls before killing them, mutilating women's bodies by cutting off their breasts, cutting fetuses out of pregnant women's uteruses, and inserting objects into women's vaginas.[88] Both Tutsi and Hutu women, along with some men, were gang raped, with their family members forced to watch or participate. Murdered naked bodies were often left in public spaces to terrorize any remaining community members. Some assailants spared women's lives while others captured women and forced them into sexual slavery.[89] Stories emerged after the genocide of women begging to be shot.[90]

The brutality of the genocide remains inconceivable: infants were killed by being thrown against walls or into latrines; children were mutilated in front of their parents; and some Tutsi were forced to kill their own spouses or children.[91] As Alison Des Forges notes, "Victims generally regarded being shot as the least painful way to die and, if given the choice and possessing the means, they willingly paid to die that way."[92] Anyone who looked Tutsi was killed, and any Hutu who had intermarried or who refused to participate in genocidal violence or looting was also slaughtered. Militias massacred in schools and hospitals, sometimes with the assistance of hospital staff, even in maternity and pediatric units.[93]

On July 4, 1994, the RPF gained control over the capital and announced that it intended to form a new government. Once it had seized power in the capital and most of the country, it declared a ceasefire, swearing in a Hutu president and prime minister—Pasteur Bizimungu and Faustin Twagiramungu, respectively—on July 19, 1994. Even though Bizimungu was president and Twagiramungu was prime minister, it is generally agreed that Paul Kagame, the vice president and minister of defense (and currently the president), held the real power in the new government. The RPF's acquisition of power and process of securing control over the country entailed significant human rights abuses, such as the killing of civilians. These actions contributed to a colossal refugee and humanitarian crisis.[94]

The Great Lakes region suffered extraordinary destabilization during and after the genocide and war. People in neighboring countries recall finding bodies in Lake Rweru and Lake Kivu. The ecosystem in Lake Muhazi, located within Rwanda, was particularly affected by the human remains that were dumped in its water, poisoning fish and other lake life.[95] The contamination from the blood and bodies made fishing in most surrounding lakes impossible for months. As a Congolese Rwandan explained to me, "The bodies just kept coming. We would pull them out of the river and try to bury them, but there were so many it became difficult."[96]

In addition to the approximately 800,000 dead in Rwanda (between 10 and 15 percent of the population) and thousands of displaced persons inside Rwanda, more than two million people escaped to neighboring countries. One million of these refugees fled to the Kivu province in the Eastern Congo, bringing violence, chaos, and ethnic tensions with them.[97] Displaced persons in neighboring Democratic Republic of the Congo (then Zaire) endured horrific conditions in refugee camps: starvation, illness, and violent attacks by the RPF. Some camps were heavily armed, such as those in the Kivu region. Locals feared violence by the Interahamwe who sought refuge in the area. As refugees moved west into Congo, attacks from the RPA and allied Congolese Tutsi continued, with estimates of 233,000 deaths, mostly Hutu.[98] Some Congolese Tutsi opted to trek in the opposite direction, heading back into Rwanda. Within two years, many more followed, totaling more than one million people who returned to Rwanda.[99]

The years following the genocide were marked by continued violence both inside Rwanda and in the refugee camps located in neighboring countries. Human rights abuses by the RPF and its army were reported in early 1995 and 1996 but were suppressed by international organizations hesitant to critique the precarious situation and newly formed government after a genocide in which they were passively complicit through their own inaction.[100] One of the most brutal episodes of violence on internally displaced persons (IDP) camps was the Kibeho massacre.[101] On April 22, 1995, Australian soldiers were serving as part of UNAMIR on a mission to support the RPF government when "more than 4,000 unarmed men, women, and children died in a hail of bullets, grenades, and machete blades at the hands of the Rwandan Patriotic Army (RPA)."[102] The new Rwandan government saw this camp as a safe haven for *genocidaires* and announced prior to the massacre that all IDP camps were to be closed in order to serve justice to those who participated in the genocide and to relocate genocide survivors to their communities. However, Australian soldiers observed little attempt at relocating survivors and were traumatized as they witnessed the brutal massacre of civilians (mostly women and children). Kevin "Irish" O'Halloran, a platoon sergeant at the time, remembers "a whole crowd of people were running down the hill and the RPA were firing after them and the whole hillside was littered with different colored clothing as they lay dead on the ground. The RPA just stood at the top of the hill and picked people off as they ran away."[103]

The RPA defended its actions by claiming that the violence was minimal and justified for national security. The RPF independently investigated its own crimes, ruling that none of its actions had been criminal.[104] The European Union (EU) suspended aid after the Kibeho massacre, but the US and UK did not, setting a precedent that continues to the present day. Reports by the UN and human rights organizations documented the continued killings of civilians in Rwanda and then in the DRC throughout the late 1990s.[105]

For those who managed to cross the border into Rwanda or to leave the Rwandan IDP camps, they walked into a decimated nation. I have been told by those who were in Rwanda during this time that it is impossible to overemphasize the destruction that Rwanda's institutions and civil society experienced in the aftermath of the genocide. Institutions that kept children and adults protected and nurtured were destroyed, including kinship networks that were torn apart because of death, torture, or the flight of family members trying to escape the violence. Hospitals, schools, and churches were demolished not only physically but also symbolically, because of the unspeakable atrocities that occurred in these spaces that had previously served the public. Infrastructure throughout the country was damaged and destroyed by grenades or splattered with blood from machete killings. Human remains lined the streets, filled churches, and covered hillsides. Survivors report the penetrating stench of rotting human bodies and a lasting revulsion to dogs after having witnessed them feeding on the deceased.[106]

Genocide survivors endured extreme economic hardship resulting from looting, destruction, and having to bargain for their lives during the genocide. This added to their already destitute state in the wake of the civil war and financial tumult of the early 1990s. Because of the severe institutional devastation, few employment opportunities presented themselves to those who were physically and emotionally able to work. Many suffered extensive physical injuries, such as head wounds from machetes and missing limbs. In addition to physical wounds, Rwandans endured significant trauma that has continued to haunt them more than two decades later.[107] Post-traumatic stress disorder (PTSD), depression, and anxiety plague the majority of those who were in the country during the genocide, with long-term effects on their well-being.[108] Many survivors saw their family members murdered, and others did not know where their families were and still held out hope that they would eventually find them alive or be able to recover their remains and properly bury them. Today, many survivors live under the cloud of still not having located the remains of their loved ones (this is a common theme throughout this book).

Kinship networks were decimated, leaving children to suffer the brunt of this loss. An estimated 400,000 children, more than 10 percent of all of Rwanda's underage population, were orphaned as a result of the genocide or the deaths of their mothers from HIV contracted through genocidal rape.[109] In a study of adolescent and child survivors, researchers found that more than 90 percent had witnessed killings and/or had their lives threatened, 35 percent had lost immediate family members, 30 percent had witnessed rape or sexual mutilation, and 15 percent had hidden under corpses.[110] Many children had their families, peers, and people close to them murdered, often in front of their own eyes. Not only did children suffer from severe psychological problems after surviving such atrocities, but they also lost their caretakers, homes, and all their belongings.

Thousands of children ended up living on the streets or in foster care, and some were exploited by families, serving as live-in domestic labor in exchange for shelter and food.[111] Many orphans created child-headed households (CHH), in which the eldest orphan cared for the younger children in the house.[112] Some of the younger children were biological siblings, but sometimes they were orphans adopted into the family. There were so many CHHs that in some cases they made up entire villages, and many such households are still present in Rwanda today. United Nations International Children Emergency Fund (UNICEF) estimated in 1998 that there were more than 300,000 children living in CHHs and that these households experience significant challenges, such as social isolation, feelings of despair, and even suicide.[113] Children in CHHs, especially those under five years of age, also had poor physical health outcomes.[114] The prevalence of HIV/AIDS among orphans and widows has been a particularly devastating postgenocide health problem.[115] Children with HIV report being treated poorly by their peers and excluded from the community.[116] Women with HIV also face discrimination and report social isolation, loss of employment, and barriers to medical care.

Women faced significant hardships after the genocide: many were widowed or HIV positive, and many had husbands in jail for genocide crimes or criminal accusations and had lost not only their families and children but also their homes and property.[117] Rape survivors have reported social rejection and continued humiliation when their rape survivor status was revealed.[118] The disproportionate death, displacement, and imprisonment of men rendered women the majority in much of the country, and women mobilized in the midst of the widespread destruction.[119] Women's organizations stepped into leadership roles to "remedy the lack of state services, filling the void left by governmental collapse."[120] Women's active participation in community organizing led to the centrality of gender equality in Rwanda's new constitution and one of the highest percentages of women in parliament in the world.[121]

The beginning of the twenty-first century marked a change in governance for Rwanda; Vice President Paul Kagame became president in 2000 after President Bizimungu resigned. Kagame remains in power as of the writing of this book, prioritizing order, stability, and national security.[122] For some Rwandans, Kagame's rule has led to significant nationwide advances in health, with Rwanda now reporting some of the lowest infection numbers for malaria, tuberculosis, and HIV.[123] This is thanks to the implementation of health programs by the national government and its partnerships with international NGOs and government organizations such as UNICEF, United States Agency for International Development (USAID), and Partners in Health (PIH). Many aid programs focusing on development and health rave about their experience working in Rwanda. One woman working in Rwanda for a women's health and family planning NGO explained to me, "We pilot our programs in Rwanda because it is so easy to work with people here and they are so receptive to health programs. If a program doesn't work in Rwanda, it sure won't work elsewhere."[124] Such assistance has led to noticeable outcomes: a steady decline in the birth rate, a national commitment to family planning (facilitating a rise in contraceptive use), and an increase of educational attainment among girls and young women. The average Rwandan family in 2014–15 had three to four children, with motherhood beginning on average at age twenty-three.[125] Rwanda continues to be a youthful nation: in 2018 more than 90 percent of Rwanda's 12 million people were under the age of fifty-four, and the median age for both women and men is nineteen.

Despite the headway Rwanda has made in many areas of social life, most advancements have failed to significantly change the living conditions for the rural poor, and some policies have made their lives even more difficult.[126] Many of the impressive advancements in health, development, and technology are tempered by the government's political consolidation and imprisonment of political opponents for violating an ambiguously defined law prohibiting "divisionism."[127] Severe restrictions on free speech have limited the operations of independent news outlets and human rights organizations.[128]

One of the government's approaches to facilitating coexistence has been the implementation of "solidarity camps," known as *ingando*, and civic education efforts, known as *itorero*, where sections of the population (politicians, prospective university students, returned refugees, and released prisoners) undergo political reeducation and paramilitary training.[129] Reeducation efforts on multiple levels (e.g., national narratives, school curriculum, and *umuganda*— obligatory community service work) are mandatory and closely controlled by the regime, facilitating a specific historical narrative about the past that does not include acknowledgment of violence or wrongdoing by the RPF.[130] This means that survivors of RPF violence are rarely recognized as victims or survivors in public memory campaigns or judicial processes.[131]

Shortly after the genocide, the new Rwandan government had decided to prosecute all those accused of taking part in the genocide, including those committing nonviolent crimes such as looting and bribing. Prosecuting so many people, including individuals only involved in property crimes, was a daunting but urgent undertaking. The jails in Rwanda were not nearly large enough to hold the 200,000 to 300,000 suspected perpetrators of interpersonal violence (let alone those accused of property crimes). At the time, Rwanda had minimal resources to manage a myriad of suspects, not only because of the lack of physical space but also because much of the legal community was killed during the genocide, leaving only a handful of judges and approximately fifty lawyers in the entire country, many of whom refused to defend those accused of genocidal acts.[132] The international community was willing to assist, given its donor history and guilt over negligence and inaction during the genocide.

In November 1994, the security council of the UN voted in favor (thirteen to one, with Rwanda voting against and China abstaining) of forming the International Criminal Tribunal for Rwanda (ICTR) to investigate allegations of genocide and pervasive violations of international humanitarian law.[133] Many scholars believe that the ICTR was created to ease the guilt of the many nation-states who idly stood by and permitted the genocide to occur. Postgenocide, the UN stated that genocide constituted an "international threat to peace," and thus those who committed crimes against humanity needed to be punished.[134] While international criminal punishments were taking place in November 1994 for the ICTY,[135] mass international punishments and judgments had not taken place on this scale since the 1945 Nuremberg trials, which are often regarded as the focal precedent for international trials for mass atrocity. When the Nuremberg Tribunals finished, the recently established UN debated creating a permanent international court. This International Criminal Court (ICC) did not materialize until after the tribunals for Rwanda and the former Yugoslavia. Thus, because the ICC did not yet exist, in the wake of Rwanda's genocide it was a special tribunal, the ICTR, that had the jurisdiction to try the highest level of genocide suspects.

The ICTR was located outside Rwanda in Arusha, Tanzania, and aimed at punishing those who committed the highest criminal acts of genocide, including genocidal rape, organization of genocidal killings, and executing plans of mass killing. In the first years of operation, the ICTR suffered from major logistical and political problems. The UN Security Council did little to help the ICTR succeed: it failed to provide the courts with even the most basic supplies needed to run a courtroom, such as pencils and paper.[136] With poorly trained tribunal staff and judges who knew little about Rwandan history or culture, the courts proved to be both severely damaging and traumatizing for witnesses, especially rape and sexual torture survivors.[137]

Many Rwandans critiqued the ICTR for failing to inform local Rwandans about the proceedings. What occurred in court was rarely reported or disseminated to Rwandans, with the exception of those who were highly educated and living in urban areas. During the tenure of the ICTR, the majority of Rwandans did not know the status of ICTR cases or even how they were managed. The ICTR's Tanzanian location made many Rwandans feel disconnected from its process and prospects. It was difficult for witnesses to travel to Tanzania to testify and almost unimaginable for a poor or middle-class family to attend a trial of a suspected killer, even if the victims were family members. Rwandans who lost everything sometimes objected to the ICTR's refusal to punish genocide leaders with death. On the opposite end, some Rwandans felt the ICTR did little to offer any type of restorative justice and primarily focused on retributive justice.[138] Another point of contention was the ICTR's exclusion of human rights abuses committed by the RPF from the trials. Finally, the ICTR lacked the time required to prosecute suspects. Nevertheless, it did make legal history in 1998 when it handed down the world's first convictions for genocide and genocidal rape, which would significantly impact legal precedent in international courts for years to come. When the ICTR closed in 2012, ninety-three individuals had been indicted, resulting in sixty-two sentences.[139]

Amid the slow judicial process of the ICTR, Rwanda sought additional judicial processes through its national court system. However, it soon became apparent that the national court system did not have the capacity to try such a massive number of suspected perpetrators; the government of Rwanda then implemented an innovative local court system called *gacaca*. Gacaca is primarily based on an assumption that civic involvement in restorative judicial processes are vital for reconciliation in Rwanda.[140] Prior to its implementation postgenocide, gacaca was a judicial system used before colonial rule to solve disputes over land, marriage, and local conflict. On a specified day of the week, an elder (usually an older man) called together all the necessary parties in the disagreement. After hearing the debates, witnesses, and evidence, the elders made a decision.[141] Traditional gacaca was informal as it would litigate problems mainly between family members and neighbors and was based on the assumption that such disagreements were pertinent to the community as a whole, not just the individuals involved.[142] The goal of gacaca was to restore social harmony and reintegrate the wrongdoer into the community.[143]

After much debate in 1998 and 1999 by relevant government bodies, on October 12, 2000, a law was adopted allowing gacaca courts to try all but some tiers of category one crimes.[144] Since the implementation of gacaca, hundreds of thousands of lay judges have tried almost two million cases on hillsides, in community centers, or on soccer fields.[145] Nearly every week, perpetrators offered confessions in exchange for freedom, reduced sentences, or community work, and survivors made accusations and provided testimony. Gacaca challenged traditional notions of justice by vehemently insisting on a local and participatory process.[146] Gacaca occurred in every community across Rwanda.[147] These hearings served in some cases as a form of truth-telling, where survivors gained information on when, how, and where their loved ones were murdered.[148]

Like all judicial actions, gacaca faced several challenges. Victims' participation as witnesses in gacaca hearings was intended to be cathartic but was often traumatizing. This was especially true for women who had survived rape and in many cases were infected with HIV/AIDS; for these women, truth-telling could be a signficant risk.[149] Gacaca also raised debates throughout the international community about the importance and implementation of due process and the need for legal representation, which was nonexistent in gacaca.[150] False accusations for purposes of revenge or reprisal occurred in the form of fabricated testimony, which damaged relationships and eroded already fragile social trust. And, while gacaca was intended to be a "Rwandan Solution to a Rwandan Problem," no crimes committed by the RPF were included or allowed. The exclusion of RPF crimes represents what some have called victor's justice, perpetuating a transformation from community courts to ones inextricably linked to the state's interests.[151] Gacaca has drawn the attention of scholars from diverse disciplines because of its ambitious jurisdiction and its implementation of aspects of restorative justice that are vastly different from international tribunals.[152]

The information uncovered in both gacaca and the ICTR about the crimes committed and the pain inflicted on victims during those four gruesome months significantly contributed to the development of memorial projects throughout

Rwanda. In less than two decades, memorials were erected by citizens and the government of Rwanda in every community throughout the nation, from small burial markers to polished museums. These sites of memory provide physical places to bury the remains of victims and bear witness to the unfathomable pain and atrocity people experienced. At this particular historical moment—when gacaca and the ICTR have ended their unprecedented tenure, and when fountains and roundabouts dot the Kigali landscape while dirt backroads still exist behind the scenes—this book's story begins.

2

Memory Landscapes after Human Rights Violations

When I first visited Rwanda in 2009, *ibuka*, meaning to remember, was one of the first Kinyarwanda words I learned. Angel, a survivor of the 1994 genocide against the Tutsi, said to me later that it's probably the most important one.[1] I had heard a similar sentiment expressed years earlier when studying third-generation Holocaust survivors. Janet, a grandchild of Holocaust survivors, said, "I don't think antisemitism has affected me as directly as Jewish memory and Jewish suffering." Janet asserted that Jewish suffering, and remembrance of that suffering, shaped her identity far more than fear of antisemitism or antisemitic experiences. Following the genocidal violence in Cambodia, a Cambodian NGO began the development of the Documentation Center of Cambodia in Phnom Penh, with an aim to record and research the violence that occurred during the period 1975–79. The director of the Documentation Center of Cambodia, Youk Chhang, told a reporter, "They say that time heals all wounds. But time alone can do nothing. You will always have time. To me, research heals. Knowing and understanding what happened has set me free."[2] Survivors of mass atrocity and other human rights violations can carry a preoccupation with memory: drowning in memories, they struggle to keep their heads above water and gasp for a breath of fresh air to "set [them] free."

Two decades after the genocide, the demand to remember penetrates every aspect of life during Rwanda's mourning period. The annual time of mourning lasts for three months, from April 7 to July 4 (liberation day), marking the approximately one hundred days of the 1994 genocide against the Tutsi. In the years immediately following the genocide, survivors explained that all joyful celebrations ceased for the one hundred days of mourning: "No birthday celebrations, no weddings, no parties, no public joy," Gloria, a survivor, explained. Eventually, this became unsustainable for the growing nation, and while many survivors commemorate well into July, present-day commemorations on the national level are concentrated during the first week. It's not uncommon for survivors to refrain from work, or for children to stay home from school to attend commemoration events with their families. During this week, the TV stations and radio stations run twenty-four-hour news cycles on commemoration events. This news coverage runs in households, bars, and restaurants. Flowers and purple ribbons are sold at the side of most busy roads in cities or major towns for people to buy and place on graves, or wear in solidarity.

On the first day of the official nationwide commemorative week, more than five thousand survivors, tourists, government officials, and young people gather at the national stadium to sanctify the onset of the mourning period, honoring those killed. During the morning stadium program, attendees listen to survivor testimonies, performances by famous Rwandan pop stars singing about genocide and hope for the future, poetry from survivors or well-known writers, and concluding remarks in a much-anticipated speech from Rwanda's commander-in-chief, President Paul Kagame.[3]

While the mourning period, particularly the first week, is the busiest time for commemorating and memorial visits, remembrance rituals occur all year long. Some survivors visit memorial sites on a daily or weekly basis; they go there to socialize, receive resources such as legal advice or counseling, and remember their loved ones. Employees working at memorials, who are often also survivors, remark on the constant flow of visitors coming to grieve or learn about the country's past. The volume of visitors to these memorials changes throughout the calendar year, with more intense times of grief during April and May and international visitation during popular tourism months.

Anyone traveling throughout Rwanda is sure to encounter numerous memorial sites commemorating those who died in the 1994 genocide. There is no need to look for these memorials: one would be hard put to drive more than fifteen miles outside the capital city without seeing one at the side of the road. White and purple ribbons catch the eye, and signs feature the exhortation *ibuka*. Banners declaring "never again" and marked with white crosses alert visitors to burial sites and commemorative spaces throughout the country. In a nation slightly smaller than the US state of Maryland, these memorials are literally inescapable; in 2017 the commemorative sites numbered more than 500 and in 2019, more than 750.

The memorials take a variety of forms: some comprise mostly gravestones or markers at former schools, hospitals, or communities; others are marked with small and simple signs, plaques, or ribbons accompanied by brief commemorations of those who died. Other forms of remembrance include formal massacre sites, extensive museums, or displays of mass graves that included testimonies.[4] There are walls listing victims' names and sites incorporating historical evidence from the region. The seven large national memorials represent only a small part of the spatial structures dedicated to those who perished in the genocide. These structures range from small plaques to graveyards to memorials in churches, schools, or community buildings. It is hard to overstate the all-consuming nature of Rwanda's mourning period. Having been in Rwanda during commemoration week in 2012, I can hardly convey the emotional intensity of feeling the presence of memory in every aspect of everyday life: the billboards, conversations, events (burials and commemorations), purple clothing, road signs (stating "we will remember you always"), talk radio, TV, and music—all focused the mind constantly on Rwanda's past atrocity.

The Politics of Memorials in Rwanda

Scholarship on Rwandan memorials highlights how such spaces are used as an instrument of the state to restrict the range of narratives about the genocide and its aftermath and to suppress national memory of certain kinds of victims and violence. Scholars argue that memorial sites can exploit the suffering of genocide survivors for political and economic gain. As Jennie Burnet explains, in the last decade, nationalized mourning has constructed only one type of victim and "minimizes and even denies the multiplicity of truths about the genocide."[5] Constraining constructions of victimhood means that the vast majority of victims who are remembered in public commemorative events are Tutsis who were murdered or otherwise victimized by the genocidal militia in 1994. Those disregarded are individuals killed by the RPF and Hutus killed by the genocidal militia. Ignoring these deaths has the effect of reducing the nation's collective memory to a singular account that marginalizes citizens who do not fit into the designated categories.[6]

Scholars assert that Rwanda's singular narrative of victimhood is partially directed at global actors and seeks to "convert international feelings of guilt and ineptitude [because of the international community's inaction in 1994] into admissions that the [RPF] deserves to have a monopoly on knowledge construction."[7] Drawing on the guilt of the international community for political and economic gain allows governmental supporters and elites to maintain control over power and resources. From the government's perspective, then, remembering the past furthers their political agenda of justifying their policies and politics.

Scholars have expressed concern that the current government's administrative control over many memorials, including all seven national sites, seeks to "constrain, not encourage, democratic discourse."[8] A lack of open dialogue within and about memorials could diminish their power to serve as a mechanism for transitional justice and as a means of promoting human rights. For memorials to foster human rights, "we need a way to think of rights as a force that destabilizes rather than secures social relations . . . not national redemption, ethical imperative or norm building."[9] Destabilizing social relations with regard to memorialization entails challenging power dynamics and privilege. Memorials that strive for unified national redemption thus do so at the risk of human rights promotion and protection, as they often ignore present-day injustices of current regimes. This is a common critique of many state-sponsored, post-atrocity memorialization projects.[10] As Paul Connerton writes, "The relationship between memorials and forgetting is reciprocal: the threat of forgetting begets memorials and the construction of memorials begets forgetting," for memorials can obscure the past as much as they expose it.[11]

While theoretically and empirically justified, theories on the damaging impacts of powerful nationalist narratives can overlook the meso- and micro-interactions between survivor communities and memorial spaces that can foster productive dialogue. As Jay Winter argues, even when memorials are employed for nationalist agendas, they can also promote mourning and honor those who were killed.[12] Rachel Ibreck asserts that memorials "are not simply a tool to serve political interests; they are also shaped by the distinct concerns of Rwanda's genocide survivors, the largest group of active contributors to the manufacture of genocide memorials."[13] While memorials often serve national interests, they can also simultaneously offer communities a site for discussions of the past, a place where survivors can tell their own personal stories to those who will bear witness and educate publics on the dangers of exclusionary ideology.

Even when political regimes, like those in Rwanda, hold disproportionate power over memory and commemoration politics, the diverse communities that engage in state-sponsored remembrance rituals also resist their hegemony with counter-memories and counter-rituals. Such resistance can emerge from within or in response to the process of remembrance, including memorials and commemorations.[14] Ibreck suggests that survivors, not the government, have led the development and implementation of memorialization, thereby gaining a powerful political platform for their voices to be heard in both memorials and commemorative events. This was especially true in the early days of memorialization.[15]

Commemoration entails the exchange and "interaction, not just attendance, creating opportunities to challenge the dominant public memory."[16] Memorials require interaction and dialogue, though it is unclear how, or how much, is possible when memorials also aim to sustain national unity and uphold state interests. In Rwanda, dialogue in response to memorials can be seen among survivors who live near and attend local memorials, and also between guides and members of the public, many of whom are also survivors. It can also occur on an individual level, as discussed in the following chapter, in which survivors remake the meanings of national narratives into ones that validate their own experiences and mourning processes.

Like almost all governments, the current regime in Rwanda uses memorials as instruments of state-building and power consolidation by creating a singular narrative of perpetrator and victim.[17] In addition to being used as a tool of the regime, monuments are also spaces the local population can use for its own needs. Based on interviews with survivors, this chapter examines the physical and logistical functions memorials have had for them, including providing substantial material benefit to their surrounding communities. In general, the survivors with whom I spoke were not eager to criticize the government's role in memorialization because of their own social location, experiences during the genocide, and involvement in memorial projects. Most of the criticisms I heard from survivors were that they felt ignored during memorialization processes because of the type of violence they had experienced (i.e., sexual and gender-based violence) or because they lived in poverty. These dynamics are discussed further in chapters 4, 5, and 6. Overall, even those interviewees who felt marginalized by the memorialization process nevertheless emphasized the good that memorials were doing, both physically and symbolically, to survivors and the larger communities in which they resided.

In the aftermath of the genocide, the memorials filled an immediate and critical role in housing bodily remains and evidence of genocidal violence. Memorials were constructed in response to public health and social welfare problems directly after the genocide, becoming not only burial sites but also meaningful spaces that cultivated much-needed civic engagement, social networking, and survivor services. In the following pages, I unpack what memorials do for survivors and how they cater to these multiple functions.

Memorials as Burial Sites

The first memorial was constructed on November 13, 1994, in Muyumbu, where four thousand bodies were laid to rest. The Muyumbu memorial was an effort supported by the new government and launched by survivors living in Muyumbu. It served as a response to the significant loss that Muyumbu had experienced and also provided a logistical solution to the problem that bodies were being discovered on a daily basis: "Of priority to them [Muyumbu residents] was to urgently find the remains of their loved ones and accord them dignified burial. The country was grieving. Bodies were strewn in the streets, farmlands, hillsides, landfills, and across villages. Many others had been dumped in mass graves."[18] While the symbolic and emotional memory work memorials do is central to survivors, these spaces started out as physical and logistical solutions to material problems. The problems included public health and social welfare concerns that arose from the magnitude of decomposing bodies and the lack of information regarding who had died and who had survived the genocide. Survivors shared stories of how after the genocide human remains were "everywhere." It was thus urgent to start memorial construction immediately after the genocide. Memorials began as sites where remains could be housed but afterward developed into sites of community engagement, civic work, networking, resource allocation, and survivor services.

The story of the creation of Rwanda's first genocide memorial in Muyumbu is representative of many memorials in Rwanda that house remains, whether exposed or buried.[19] When I spoke about the functions of memorial spaces with Robert, an older man at the Center for Memory, Survivors, and Reconciliation (CMSR), he said, "After the genocide, there were so many bodies; they were everywhere. It was overwhelming, and we just kept discovering more and more every day. So that is why we decided to bury victims at the memorials. They could be places to mourn and grieve and eventually Ibuka [the umbrella organization for survivor services] and other organizations also came to the memorials so survivors could mourn and get other things we needed." Memorials in Rwanda operate as both burial sites and places to receive resources, ranging from formal services such as counseling, legal assistance, or support groups to informal resources, such as community meetings and social networking. These services were vital in reestablishing basic civil services such as roads, schools, and public health.

During the genocide, Rwanda's infrastructure was destroyed; in the aftermath, buildings stood riddled with bullet holes, damaged schools could not reopen, and decomposing bodies lined the streets, with mass graves discovered almost daily. Some survivors reflected on the challenges of caring for the deceased because they lacked the expertise to exhume human remains in a respectful, safe, and healthy way. Mugabo explained, "The beginning was difficult, because we didn't have the skills and no method, no technology, anything." Nicole remembered being handed gloves and a mask when a mass grave was discovered in her community: "We just had to begin lifting the bodies out, identifying them, and then cleaning them so we could properly bury them."

The development of burial sites into memorials took years to evolve. Although survivors across all three sites in this study emphasized the importance of memorials as "a home for the dead," the process of cleaning and developing burial sites took different forms based on their varied locations (whether rural or urban), the availability of international funding, the state of the site (whether it posed a public health concern), and community needs (e.g., whether the site would serve the community of victims or others such as tourists and schools). It took years after the genocide to begin the development of many of the national memorials and several more to implement the plans that are being created today.[20]

The Center for Commemoration (CFC) was not cleaned and developed until 2006 because preparing the memorial as a home for the dead meant getting the bones ready for display and putting the remains back in the same area where they were found. At this site, survivors separated the clothes from the bones, cleaned the bones, and then organized them carefully on shelves in the church where the victims perished more than a decade ago.[21] Prior to 2006, there was no protective covering over the memorial (now there is a tin roof), and, while bodily remains were cleaned up, bones were stacked in piles. Now the bones are organized by type (skulls, femurs, etc.), and victims' clothes hang from the ceiling instead of lying piled up on the floor. The bones at the CFC were never buried but remained in an area similar to where the victims were killed. This practice has come under heavy criticism because it was developed after the genocide and is not part of Rwandan culture.[22]

At the CMSR, mass graves were discovered in late 1994, along with the unburied bodies of victims executed by the militia in a nearby forest. The first burial of these victims took place in 1995, but because so many bodies were involved and they were buried quickly and without expertise, the bones surfaced after the rainy season the following year. In the lower level of a building on site, community members retrieved the bones, cleaned them, and organized them by type. Clothes were again separated from bones to allow survivors to search for their loved ones' attire. This was of particular importance since victims were taken from other locations to be killed at this site. Thus, it took the family members of these victims longer to find and identify their loved ones than was the case at the CFC, which is located in a smaller rural community in which the majority of people died in or around the local church. After the bones and clothing were separated, the bones were kept on waterproof tarps in the lower level of the building and often shown to visitors during historical tours of the area. The reburial of these bodies, more than five thousand in total, took place in April 2012. Unlike the CFC, this memorial has not placed the bones on display as all remains have been buried.

The Center for Genocide Prevention and Education (CGPE) opened as a burial place in 2001 when eight mass graves were constructed to hold 250,000 bodies. The graves consist of nine-foot-deep concrete crypts, each filled from floor to ceiling with coffins. According to the memorial, "the coffins rarely contain the remains of an individual victim, and can even contain the remains of up to 50 victims because of the impossibility, in many cases, of ensuring that the remains of individuals are kept intact."[23] No massacres occurred at this site in 1994, but bodies were brought here from the surrounding area. The first set of mass graves filled faster than anticipated, and the memorial opened and filled three additional graves. Some bones are on display at this memorial in the museum area, but the majority of remains have been placed in graves.

At the CFC and the CMSR, survivors remarked on the importance of separating clothes from bones in the reburial process. The clothes are placed in piles that survivors rummage through in hopes of identifying the attire of their loved ones and thus confirming the location of their final resting place. Locating the remains of loved ones was a central theme across discussions of healing, reconciliation, trauma, and recovery.[24] Discussed more in chapter 6, missing persons—and by extension, missing confirmed remains of those presumed dead—are a significant barrier to reconciliation and healing as survivors continue to search, falsely hoping for loved ones to return and thus feeling trapped in the past and unable to move on.

This searching was still ongoing when I was in Rwanda in 2012, especially at the CMSR, although by that time many of the victims had already been identified by loved ones. During one interview I conducted there, a woman was searching through a pile of clothes set aside by the exhumers who were preparing remains for reburial by separating the bones from clothing, jewelry, and tissue. At one point the woman began screaming and memorial workers and exhumers surrounded her. After several minutes, Rose, a counselor whom I was interviewing at that moment, explained to me that the woman had found the shirt her husband had been wearing eighteen years earlier.[25] Because the bodies had only recently been exhumed and had clothes separated from them, a wave of survivors who had still been unable to locate their loved ones frequented the memorial to search for identifying clothing or jewelry before burial ceremonies took place during commemoration week. When we resumed our interview, Rose shared with me a story about another survivor who had found her grandmother's necklace in the pile of clothes the previous week. Relieved to "know where her [grandmother's] remains were," she had asked the memorial authorities for permission to keep the necklace.[26]

The situation I witnessed, and the scene Rose had observed the week before, represents the answer to many survivors' prayers. Nearly all the individuals I interviewed mentioned either how much better they felt knowing where their loved ones' remains were located or how much better they would feel if they knew. Siboyintore expressed certainty that survivors' trauma levels would decrease if they could all discover the locations of their loved ones' remains: "If we could have the relatives be buried at the memorial . . . at a certain time, the traumatization would reduce." Ada, a counselor, reported that in her widows' support group, three women who had lost their husbands and not yet found their remains told her, "We wish we could see the remains, and then take them to the memorials, at least their remains could be living with other remains of the memorials. Then we could begin to be okay." Bodies continued to be discovered as the city expanded and gacaca court confessions increased. Honorine explained that a city initiative supported burials "because there were bodies of the victims around Kigali City, and no one was there to bury them. And all those bodies were being discovered progressively as they were digging for new homes, new houses, expansion of new other things." The discovery of bodies meant the continuation of burials at memorials and graveyards.[27] According to the survivors I spoke with, knowing where their loved ones' remains were located brought the possibility of closure and ritual while also allaying their fears the remains might have been thrown into the river, eaten by dogs, or buried without a marker.

Memorials Housing Evidence

Because memorials hold not only the bodies of genocide victims but also the weapons used by perpetrators and remnants of the violence (e.g., blood on the walls at the CFC), burial sites also function as spaces where evidence is housed. As survivors point out, displaying proof of what "really happened" is key to the role of these sites in presenting the realities of the genocide in a visceral way to future generations, thus combatting possible counternarratives that deny the genocide. The evidence and information are available for prosecutors to present in court cases or gacaca trials.

The CFC emphasizes in situ evidence, with most of the destruction from 1994 left almost completely intact. The weapons used to torture women are on display, the wall at which babies were thrown remains stained with blood, and bones line the former pews and areas previously used for worship. The CMSR housed remains prior to 2012 and erected a wall naming those killed at that site. The CGPE is by far the most extensive in its housing of evidence, including an archive of testimony about the genocide (from both survivors and perpetrators), a full inventory of physical evidence, a three-story polished museum of Rwandan history, and digital archives accessible in multiple languages.

At the CFC, visitors are presented with evidence of horrific brutality against women, children, and infants. In seeing so many bones on display and piles of clothes from the rural village, visitors are left to imagine the magnitude of the genocide. They learn how grenades were used; how churches were manipulated into presenting themselves, falsely, as safety zones; and how innocent lives were taken. At the CMSR, visitors experience a guided narrative in which they learn how the inaction and failures of the UN led to the deaths of thousands upon the very grounds where the tour was taking place. Many leave with feelings of frustration and anger at the ineffectiveness of the international community in preventing and intervening in the genocide. The CGPE offers a carefully guided and structured experience, with numbered landmarks, specific places to stop and reflect, and a museum, which includes a room dedicated to children who died. Since this site has by far the most extensive resources and evidence, many visitors (domestic and international), researchers, and prosecutors visit for information and research.

During interviews, survivors I spoke with shared the importance of preserving evidence and keeping it safe within memorial spaces. But evidence such as human remains has seldom been used in court cases because the institutional capacity and organizational partnership needed to conduct forensic archaeological and anthropological work that could identify bodies or analyze geospatial and temporal patterns (to locate possible sites for investigation such as mass graves or former massacre sites) are simply lacking. As Erin Jessee notes, Rwanda conducted three exhumation phases, with the second phase taking place in 1995. The effort in 1995 was spearheaded by the Office of the Prosecutor for the ICTR, who charged Physicians for Human Rights (PHR) with the task of unearthing mass graves in two Rwandan cities. The effort failed for a series of reasons, and "the investigations were short lived and far from exhaustive."[28] The lack of DNA identification processes and partnerships with organizations such as the International Commission for Missing Persons (ICMP), present in other postgenocide cases, has meant that even two decades later, many survivors have not been able to locate their loved ones' remains.[29] The failure of these processes in Rwanda has presented a major barrier to reconciliation and healing and is discussed more in chapter 6.

Sites of Resources

In interviews, survivors pointed out that in addition to housing remains and important evidence, a central function of memorials is to provide resources to survivors and their families.[30] The CMSR has become the headquarters for a range of survivor services, such as psychological counseling, legal aid, and financial assistance. Mitaako, a young man at the CMSR, explained that the memorial is for "those who can't get school fees, so it connects the survivors with the other organizations, [and] pays school fees for them." Many survivors at this site primarily take advantage of the resources offered in offices at the memorial, sometimes without visiting the burial sites themselves, which are located meters away from the offices. While providing services at a memorial site has the potential to disrupt those who visit the site for the purposes of grieving and healing, or force those who are seeking services to memorialize, the survivors interviewed saw these services as more of a benefit than a drawback. When commenting on this unusual setup, some survivors welcomed the ability to obtain services while also "greet[ing] their loved ones" or "pay[ing] their respects" to those buried at the memorial.

Employees, especially counselors (who were also survivors), pointed out that the close proximity of counseling offices to the memorial aids in the grieving process. Counselors commented in interviews that they often used the memorial in their sessions with clients. For example, they might help survivors visit a memorial for the first time or encourage them to spend less time at the memorial if the counselors believed those visits were hindering the healing process. As counselors explained, healing works best somewhere in the middle of a continuum between obsessively visiting memorials and avoiding them. On one end of the spectrum are those clients who, as Immaculee explained, "avoid memorials" and "haven't cried in seventeen years." Survivors who fall on this end are encouraged through counseling to slowly begin visiting memorials and allow themselves to cry and feel pain. On the other end of the spectrum, counselors have found "mostly students who spend their prep time near the graves," "attend[ing] every commemoration."[31] These survivors are often described as "living with the dead" and are encouraged through counseling to slowly decrease the time spent at memorials. Survivors on both ends of the spectrum come to this site with additional problems, from psychological trauma and property disputes to the challenges arising from living in poverty. The CMSR can often address these problems with resources that include full-time staff members, detailed and extensive protocols, and a variety of departments. However, in some cases survivors' needs are so profound that these services are of little help, and in these instances the memorial workers may be left feeling devastated and responsible.

Although the CFC does not have resources as extensive as those of the CMSR, it provides informal resources for those who live near and work at the memorial. Survivors explained to me that memorial staff often help them with their problems, facilitate conflict management among those in the village, and keep in close contact with counselors at the local hospitals who can help residents whose trauma interferes with their daily life. Survivors spoke of the memorial as a place where they could talk with other survivors and find out what is happening in the community. I would often see groups of young women gathering in front of the memorial before or after school or on weekends. Groups gather in the road in front of the memorial to talk, meet to walk to school together, or pass the time while they await a decision from the local authorities located across the street. The memorial's close proximity to the office of local authorities and a community of CHHs, though they are now adults, facilitates its use as a social networking site. Anitha explained that the memorial "psychologically can help us to overcome, because we talk, we share, we forgive, we do everything here."

Survivors interviewed at the CGPE also pointed to providing resources as a central aspect of the memorial's existence; however, at this site the delivery of services is different from what takes place at the two memorials just discussed. The CGPE provides educational resources and services for schools in the area and large tour group opportunities for church groups, returning refugees, East Africans, and international visitors.[32] Their education program consists of workshops for students in secondary schools in the greater Kigali area, and their social program provides financial assistance to a small, selected group of survivors from vulnerable populations (orphans, widows, or rape survivors). However, such resources are not well known to many of the survivors outside this memorial, and participants I interviewed were unclear how the memorial allocates the money from the social program to survivors. At the CGPE, the resource they emphasize the most, and frame as the best method for uplifting the community and preventing future violence, is education.

What memorial spaces accomplish materially after atrocity depends on the physical needs of the community, the level of political consolidation of the state, survivors' social locations and mobilization efforts, and the availability of resources (financial contributions, human capital, and scientific tools such as forensic and spatial data analysis). In Rwanda, survivors use the resources and physical functions of memorial spaces in ways that better their lives through social networking, obtaining formal services, or visiting the memorials just as one would pay respects at a cemetery. While these resources are far from enough, as survivors remain in poverty (this is discussed in chapters 4 and 5), those I interviewed nonetheless responded positively when asked about the potential for memorials to eventually provide additional resources to survivors and for the spaces to become more engaging. For example, participants at one of the sites consistently remarked on how they dreamed that the site would eventually have a wall of names of those who perished and that the wall would include pictures so that their loved ones would not be forgotten among the thousands who died.

While participants made clear that the government of Rwanda now tightly controls memorial spaces, they noted some of the benefits of this state control, including securing public health (by recovering decomposing bodies); removing eminent trauma triggers (shallow mass graves, blood, bodily remains); and, with the assistance of survivors, deciding which civic spaces should or should not return to their previous function (e.g., churches that have become memorials). These initiatives by the government were often lauded as necessary for rebuilding under unprecedented conditions and as impressively swift and efficient for a country with little access to DNA technology and with a shortage of scientists and data analysts (since many of these professionals were the first to be killed in the genocide).[33] Memorials straddle these somewhat paradoxical spaces between reburial and display, remembering and moving forward, and individual and collective mourning. Wrought with the highest of stakes (public health and safety, providing dignity to murdered innocent lives, preventing future violence), memorial spaces operationalize power in contradictory ways: for while memorials (in Rwanda and elsewhere) may legitimize political consolidation and stratify already struggling communities, they also have the capacity to bring much-needed hope to survivors of atrocity.

3

 The Role of
Memory Work in
Violence Prevention

I come here to remember my parents. This is their home now, and I miss them
every day.

Gloria, Center for Commemoration

In sharing the history of our past, we can head towards a brighter future.

Habinana, the Center for Memory, Survivors, and Reconciliation

We educate others, so hopefully we will never see violence like that again.

Sonia, the Center for Genocide Prevention and Education

In the previous chapter, we saw that memorials not only serve survivors and communities as commemorative spaces. They also fulfill a physical, practical function as burial sites and repositories of evidence. In this chapter, I build on that insight to examine the ideological purposes these memorials serve. As the above quotes from Gloria, Habinana, and Sonia reveal, memorials function as sites of meaning-making. For these three women and others, memorial spaces—and processes of remembering more generally—are inextricably linked to the prevention of future violence. This narrative of violence prevention is the dominant one espoused by the state, too, and survivors with whom I spoke echo this agenda with remarkable unanimity.[1] Yet, even though these sentiments could easily pass as state propaganda, on a personal level, conceptualizing memorials as spaces that promote a path to a better future has helped each of them find a sense of peace in the years since the genocide. In this chapter I examine how survivors have actively created their own accounts, making this narrative of violence prevention their own, and in so doing have significantly eased their suffering in the aftermath of atrocity.[2] Survivors have appropriated aspects of the state narrative to serve their own ideological interests, creating meaning and purpose in their post-genocide lives.

In this chapter, I analyze this process. In general, I find two distinct ideological paths that lead Rwandans to see memorials as preventing violence.[3] First, some survivors understand the function of these memorials as holding various social actors accountable for past violence by asserting particular narratives of Rwandan history. For these survivors, memorials help them articulate (and sometimes even relive) the history of the genocide and continue identifying those they consider responsible. These survivors believe that by holding perpetrators accountable, memorials help prevent future violence. An additional or alternative narrative focuses on memorials as spaces for honoring the innocent people who died in the genocide. Many survivors believe that honoring the innocent and acknowledging the harm their loss of life has done to society may prevent future violence from unfolding. While there are key differences in how these two ideological narratives frame and remember the past, ultimately, they both conceptualize memorials as serving the same purpose: preventing future violence. Thus, in a political climate that does not tolerate debate or discussion about Rwandan history, this chapter shows that survivors both embrace and contest state narratives, making such narratives personal through their own ideological processes of meaning-making.

Meaning-Making

I conceptualize survivors' meaning-making as their approaches to understanding situations, events, objects, and discourse in light of their experiences and interpretations of the world around them. To analyze processes of meaning-making around memorials, I rely on my interviews as well as my observations of how survivors engage with memorials. Such ethnographic observations were vital to understanding how survivors find meaning in memorials because I was able to observe how daily behaviors enacted the particular views of memorials articulated in the interviews.

Meaning-making is articulated through language and organized through narratives; language, and thus narrative, brings together the various parts of meaning-making processes to create a transmittable social construction of one's reality. People create meaning by gathering social facts and finding ways they fit together—a process that decentralizes abstract notions of objective reality because, in point of fact, this process is centered on the individual: meaning-making diminishes reliance on established historical facts and bends toward a narrative that serves the needs of the teller. This is particularly true after severe trauma, when world beliefs are shattered.[4] Thus, meaning-making after trauma is not born out of truth, per se, but out of the human desire for order and understanding because, for survivors (as well as nations), the reality of both the past and the imagined future is understood and articulated through the lens of the present.[5] This process of meaning-making is of particular importance in the aftermath of mass atrocity and collective trauma, when survivors string together actions, objects, rituals, and memories in an effort to reassemble disorder and trauma into a comprehensible narrative.[6] This process facilitates survival by helping individuals reimagine their world—and a future in it—after witnessing or enduring the unimaginable.[7]

This process of meaning-making after traumatic events, such as genocide and mass atrocity, has captured the attention of social psychologists, psychiatrists, and social scientists alike.[8] The violence that took place in Rwanda devastated the social and psychological structures on which people depend to build a meaningful life (family, education, ritual, religion, etc.), making the effort to create new structures (or fix old ones) critical for survival in genocide's aftermath. As Marilyn Armour writes, "The need for meaning-making is essential when perilous conditions such as those that occurred during the Holocaust violate core assumptions about how the world functions and shatter beliefs about a person's security, invulnerability, and sense of predictability."[9]

Grief rituals have been found to help in the aftermath of significant or unanticipated loss.[10] Anthropologist Renato Rosaldo, reflecting on the unexpected death of his wife, explains that ritual has been inaccurately "defined by its formality and routine; under such descriptions, it more nearly resembles a recipe, a fixed program, or a book of etiquette, rather than an open-ended human process."[11] The "open-ended human process" of grief rituals is reminiscent of the dialectical nature of narrative creation, where survivors draw on a range of available cultural tools in order to create meaning. Creating meaning and narratives from grief is an ongoing process in which the meaning and story change over time through engagement with others, rituals, and cultural/religious resources. For survivors of genocide, their experience of grief and loss comes in the wake of such an extreme event that no corresponding rituals or social practices to overcome this trauma are known to them. When an individual dies from accident or old age, there are rituals, processes, and social norms by which a society responds, but the brutal murder of an entire generation—of entire lineages—events like those have no such norms for grief and trauma. This chapter focuses on how the rituals of narrative-telling and remembrance have helped create meaning after the Rwandan genocide. However, before delving into the two narrative pathways (one focusing on guilt, the other on innocence) that have led to survivors' unwavering belief that violence prevention depends on remembrance and intentional memory work, I first turn to a brief overview of the state's narrative about the genocide.

Memory, Nationalism, and Rwanda's Official Historical Narrative

As James Young states, "The motives of memories are never pure."[12] Narratives of war and mass atrocity particularly lend themselves to intentional and inadvertent forgetting because of the inevitable complexity and chaos associated with the events, accompanied by the desperate desire to transition to peace after conflict. When states and social actors "remember" or retell historical narratives, impartiality is impossible since such stories always serve an interest. Some of these retellings may be fully justifiable, but others may serve to further stratify already fractured communities with a mix of accuracies, inaccuracies, and omissions.[13] In memory projects that are state-sanctioned, such as the national memorials in Rwanda, remembering past atrocities occurs through the lens of present-day politics, with collective remembering often supporting present-day political administrations and agendas.[14] Often, after political conflict, "the new power holders shape what is remembered and what is forgotten with their choice of narratives about the past being informed by their objectives for the future."[15] Rwanda is no different. The memorialization of the 1994 genocide against the Tutsi helps construct a version of history that validates the current president and his administration, orchestrating a political climate where narratives of the past are tightly controlled.

In the state's narrative, precolonial Rwanda is described as a kingdom of social harmony, where Rwandans shared the same culture, language, and values. Despite vast research that has demonstrated the inequality inherent in the social, political, and economic structures prior to colonialism, the state's narrative emphasizes that colonial powers were responsible for bringing stratification and exploitation to Rwanda.[16] In the state's story, ethnic division was the legacy of German rule from afar and later Belgian rule, solidified through a range of social policies and laws, including the introduction of mandatory identity cards. Colonial powers promulgated a false assertation that Hutus, Tutsi, and Twa migrated to Rwanda in a particular order: "Forest-dwelling Twa arrived first, Hutu cultivators came next, and Tutsi herders, whom the colonials regarded as superior, conquered the other groups."[17] Divisionism advanced into a violent Hutu nationalism in the postcolonial era, culminating in genocide.[18] In this narrative, those to blame for the violence that unfolded, including genocide, include colonial actors, "bad government" (i.e., Habyarimana's rule), and, later on, the international community for not intervening in 1994.[19] On July 4, 1994, the genocidal violence ended when the RPF liberated the country, ultimately eliminating ethnic division and rebuilding unity among Rwandans through state security, development, and justice.[20] A key implication of the official narrative is that Rwanda's episodes of violence did not stem from divisions in race, tribe, or ethnicity but from outside ideological manipulation. Thus, the key message that the Rwandan government conveys is that "this process can be reversed and un-made in order to promote unification" by dismantling ethnic divisions and disentangling Rwanda from colonial powers.[21]

The state narrative, particularly in its indictment of colonialism's horrific legacy in Rwanda, is not entirely inaccurate. Like origin narratives across the globe, it ignores the nuances of the nation's history in the interest of advancing state policies while constricting discussions on complex historical realities. Scholars have extensively documented the official narrative of Rwanda's history, which has been disseminated in Rwanda through civic education programs, mandatory camps, speeches, guided reconciliation activities, and the public education curriculum.[22]

Narratives That Result in Violence Prevention

When survivors at all three sites spoke about why memorials mattered to them and what purposes they served, two types of narratives, structured by notions of guilt and innocence, emerged with some consistency. The first focuses on assigning culpability for the 1994 genocide against the Tutsi, and the second focuses on the innocent individuals who perished.

Narratives Focused on Culpability

In my interviews, survivors at all three sites repeatedly stated that a primary reason for memorials is to "remember our country's history." Remembering the history of the genocide and violence leading up to it countered what survivors feared would be a forgetting of Rwanda's bloodshed. As Louise stated, "Memorials contribute a lot in providing the history of Rwanda, because if the memorials didn't exist, maybe the history of Rwanda would come to an end, and people will forget about the history of the country." Anne described the loss of so many great minds in the genocide, but, with the memorials, "the history of Rwanda cannot perish."

Remembering Rwanda's history prior to the 1994 genocide against the Tutsi illustrates how historical narratives of a difficult past can simultaneously vary by social location, align with state interests, and serve as a process of meaning-making for survivors of violence. Survivors from diverse social locations—who differed by age, gender, and proximity to past violence—sifted through Rwanda's complex history to place culpability for the 1994 genocidal violence on different social actors. They identified three divergent points of culpability: colonialism, the emergence of Hutu extremist militias in the 1950s, and the swift mobilization of extremists in the 1990s.

The first culpability narrative reaches furthest back in time, situating the original divisionist ideology in the nation's colonial period, when colonialist goals aligned closely with those of the state. According to this narrative, divisionist ideology extended through independence, peaked in the 1990s, and culminated in the 1994 genocide against the Tutsi. As Joseph explained, "After colonialism, [colonists] came and they told us, 'These ones are bad for you, don't live with them.' And this one, 'It's your enemy, do not live with them.' These were indications of the genocide to come. Then the genocide ideology develops from '59." In Joseph's narrative of Rwanda's history, peaceful coexistence was the general rule prior to colonialism, during Rwanda's social order of kingdoms. Gloria echoes Joseph, explaining that "originally, Rwandans— Hutu, Tutsi, and Twa—were not three different people, but they were made to be three. . . . Before colonialism in Rwanda, people were united . . . but the colonialists came with their ideas and plans to divide Rwanda, where they used this divide and rule system." Gloria was not alone in her historical retelling, for Honorine, Immaculee, and others who lived miles apart shared almost identical stories, and these narratives in turn resembled the official state narrative. In telling the history of divisionism in such a way, these survivors emphasize that divisionism did not emerge from timeless ethnic wars, but rather from a power structure that was carefully crafted and cultivated by external colonial powers.

The subset of survivors who ascribed to this particular narrative envisioned the era of the Rwandan Kingdom as one of unity, intermarriage, and social harmony. However, as scholars have documented (and as people I interviewed acknowledged when pressed), Rwanda's kingdom was not a realm of bliss for all. Instead it was highly stratified, with those at the lowest social rungs experiencing forms of indentured labor and extreme poverty.[23] Social categories varied according to wealth, belying present-day state narratives that seek to romanticize this time.[24] Still, this powerful historical narrative offers a way to imagine life prior to colonialism as a period of social harmony, destroyed by colonialists, to which Rwandans one day could return.[25]

The people most dedicated to the narrative of colonial fault are, not surprisingly, those employed as memorial guides, educators, or general staff. In interviews and guided tours, they echo state discourse by amplifying a belief in a peaceful indigenous past and a possible return to this model of social stability.[26] Having been trained to relate this story, and having themselves told it repeatedly, this subgroup of survivors naturally becomes invested in the official narrative and sees it reinforced when present-day experiences are curated by the frequent interactions that support it.[27] This account also asserts a not-so-distant time in Rwanda's past when Tutsi, Hutu, and Twa coexisted in peaceful harmony. When blame does shift to Rwandans, it is placed on "bad leadership" and "bad government" for carrying out colonizers' blueprints for rupturing Rwandans' close relationships. In emphasizing "bad government," present-day leadership is implicitly hailed as "good leadership" that distinctly opposes those who supported the divisionism that led to mass atrocity.

The second subset of survivors using memorials to identify culpability for the genocide points to the 1950s, not the colonial era. David explained that "in 1961 or 1962 . . . Tutsi were brought by force to go live in [the area outside the city], and there were many, many problems of health, the Tsetse—the insect of malaria." Rugira explained that there were mass killings in "this region in '59, '73, '67, but the difference was that no one was killed inside the church during those times." Some, like Mahigo, understand the uprisings in the 1950s and 1960s as preparation for the genocide: "In 1961, 1963, 1973, all that period, Tutsis were killed the most. The perpetrators killed the Tutsis in the same way as they killed them in 1994."

Survivors over the age of thirty-five who were not employed by a memorial (as a guide, educator, director, etc.) most often tell this narrative, likely because their parents experienced significant violence during this time. Survivors of this generational cohort explain that in the early 1990s their parents told them about the massacres that had occurred in the 1950s. Additionally, a few of the oldest survivors I interviewed were young adults in the 1960s and 1970s, and many of them related vivid stories about loved ones who had been killed, tortured, or taken from their homes in the middle of the night, never to return. For this group, these are the memories that mark the beginning of the violence in Rwanda. However, the narratives among this subset of survivors differ as to whether any peaceful times, such as the precolonial period as imagined in the first narrative, ever returned after 1959. Some survivors explained that in certain regions nonlethal coexistence returned after the uprisings, while other interviewees felt that after the 1959 massacres, coexistence without fear was no longer possible. On the whole, this subgroup longed for the social dynamics they experienced in the early 1950s. This narrative, unlike the first, does not fault colonizers but blames groups of perpetrators who rebelled against the government that was in place prior to Rwanda's independence in 1962. Here, the perpetrators are nameless: a non-Tutsi, nebulous group of rebels who rose up against the government.

Blaming non-Tutsi extremist rebels neglects several important social actors in the 1950s and early 1960s: individuals (primarily Hutus) who were oppressed under Belgian colonial rule when resources and opportunities were concentrated among Tutsi, predominantly Tutsi militias who waged armed attacks on exiled Rwandans in neighboring countries, Belgian colonists who simultaneously enforced identity cards and electoral representation, Pan-Africanists who facilitated state independence across the continent, Banyamalenge (Tutsi refugees who fled to Congo), and Catholic Church leaders, among others.

Also absent from this narrative are complex social and political dynamics, such as social movement mobilization in colonial emancipation efforts; a shift from kingdom to republic; the development of political parties; resistance movements; the loss of social, economic, and political power for Tutsis; and relationships between institutions like the Catholic Church and the state.

The third subset of survivors using memorials to identify culpability for the genocide locates the origin of the violence in Rwanda in the 1990s, with the publication of the infamous "Hutu 10 commandments." This subset is roughly the same generation, relying on childhood memories of the violence in the 1990s. Isabel shared the following memory: "Children like me, I was observing in 1990. Sometimes [the militia] came to my home, one day they took my father, they tortured him and they brought him back home, along with the other Tutsi men who were our neighbors. The Interahamwe did the same to those people too."

Survivors under the age of thirty-five, the majority of whom were also orphaned by the genocide when they were between the ages of five and seventeen, are the most committed to the 1990s narrative because that is what they personally remember or are told to remember by their surviving siblings. Many of these survivors lack elders in their lives who could share with them longer historical narratives of violence in Rwanda. For some of these survivors, the 1994 genocide against the Tutsi came out of "nowhere" and felt like a "shock." These survivors often reported hearing indirectly about violence that occurred prior to 1994 or having fuzzy memories of their parents whispering or seemingly suppressing their fears to protect their young children. Women in this subgroup tended to blame propaganda during the 1990s for the high prevalence of sexual and gender-based violence on a massive scale amid the chaos of genocide. These women survivors shared the most vivid stories of men being taken from their villages and killed, leaving majority-women communities to care for children and older adults for the remainder of the civil war and during the genocide.

The omissions that help stabilize or make sense of a particular historical event provide insight into both the storyteller and broader societal dynamics. In the three narratives of guilt, survivors' social location (their age, gender, proximity to violence, and connection to the state through factors such as working at memorials) shapes how they tell the story of a difficult past—in many cases going back to events they themselves did not witness. Survivors draw on cultural and political resources such as family and personal memories, state-sanctioned narratives, and historical artifacts to tell a story that makes sense to them, to place blame outside of their own communities, and to make a peaceful future feel possible. While the culprits varied across these three narratives of blame, all survivors interviewed believed that memorials equipped with visual evidence from 1994 would prevent future violence in Rwanda and beyond.

Rwandan history is taught at memorials. As Rebecca poignantly asserted, "I feel memorials teach about the Rwandan history, and it teaches about the dangers of genocide, and it teaches more what happened, cannot happen again, not only in Rwanda but in the rest of the world." Oliver reflected that remembering Rwanda's history could assist in recovering from violence in postelection Kenya, or from the genocidal aftermath and ongoing conflict in Sudan. In explaining how memorials might be pertinent to Kenya, Shema explained, "Do you remember that instance of Raila Odinga versus Kibaki during the elections? The Kenyans now, when they visit Rwanda, they say, 'This is real, this is where we were going to go.' So, we hope now, whenever they get conflicts in their countries, they find a means of solving them immediately." For these survivors, Rwanda's memorials were cautionary physical reminders of what happens when violence escalates and is not immediately addressed. While memorials may not perfectly align with their own versions, they were better than no acknowledgment of the past, which they knew was also possible. As Isabel stated, "It could be much worse. Look at America, where you come from, where there are no memorials to slavery or other injustices that Americans have done."

Narratives Focused on Honoring the Innocent

While survivors parse out who is to blame for the genocidal violence, they simultaneously emphasize memorials' function of honoring the innocent: those who had died and barely survived. Survivors stressed in interviews that they were remembering the innocent, who, Isabel explained, "couldn't defend themselves" or thought the "church would save them." As Louise emphasized, "First of all, they have to remember the innocent people who have been killed. They were innocent." This narrative was particularly salient among women, likely due to the fact that many of the women interviewed had survived killings in churches where mothers were murdered with their children and infants were thrown to their death against church walls. Remembering, honoring, and grieving for individual loved ones was particularly salient at the CFC and the CMSR—spaces that housed the remains of people who had died at those very sites. All three memorials cultivated practices of honoring these victims by providing a space where survivors could gather, tell stories, and reflect on the cherished lives that had been lost.

At all three sites, survivors spoke in general terms about the importance of "honoring our loved ones" who died unnatural deaths without the possibility of being memorialized as the violence was still unfolding. Most survivors agreed that remembering their loved ones helped them heal. As Patrick shared, "The most important aspect of the memorial is to give respect to those people who died in the genocide, and we have that slogan that we will never forget them, which is most important to survivors because whenever they feel like they've thought about their parents, they just go [to the memorial], they cry, I mean they feel those emotions, and then they come back when they're better." However, some visitors, rescuers in particular, commented that remembering their loved ones is still very painful. As Jacob, who rescued three families during the genocide, commented, "I think [memorials] are very important because they remind people of the relatives that they lost during the genocide and they remind me of the neighbors and friends I had who I loved, who I lost."

One of the primary ways that orphaned survivors said they honored their parents was by leading lives that their parents would have been proud of. Some expressed the belief that honoring innocent lives can translate into violence prevention and a brighter future for Rwanda. As Ismael described it, "What survivors have to remember is about their parents, about how was the society before the genocide, because it's not enough to say my father was courageous, while yourself, you're not courageous . . . it's not enough to say my mother was kind, while yourself, you're not kind." Ella echoed this sentiment by stating, "What survivors have to do is capture the best qualities from our parents. What we have to do is to try our best, to protect the good from our parents." Protecting the good in their parents translated into actions that improved their country, such as rebuilding homes that were destroyed in the genocide. In the years that immediately followed, David worked to rebuild his family's house: "Our family house was destroyed, but I tried my best after genocide in poor conditions, to rebuild another house at the same place, because I feel it's the pride of my family. And I feel it's the best gift I can give to my parents, is to build this house at the same place, and live there as a good representative."

For some, being a positive family representative meant caring for survivors who were less fortunate, particularly orphans. A handful of survivors I interviewed had adopted orphans. Jane, for example, had taken in eight orphans, expanding her already full family of four biological children (her husband was killed during the first week of violence). Oliver had adopted three orphans to care for, in addition to his biological children. The vast majority of survivors at the CFC were orphans who raised and continued to care for their surviving siblings to support their families' roots and legacies. As Carene, who had cared for her younger brother and sister since she was twelve years old, explained, "It is what our parents would have wanted, for us to be together." Isabel argued, "The best way to remember [my parents] is to care for the orphans, to look after orphans, after widows, and to look after these memorials, cleaning them—and always commemorating them every month."

Like Isabel, many survivors cited cleaning and tending to memorials as another way to honor their loved ones. The aesthetic of the space mattered. Since "imagined communities . . . come to be attached to imagined places," a future vision of peaceful communities had to be mapped onto the physical space of the memorial.[28] This sentiment was pervasive in interviews at the CFC, where the majority of memorial gardeners and cleaners had family members buried. As Emmy said, commenting on the women who care for memorials, "It is in this spirit that women care about the memorial sites, and they are so touched—that we have our parents, our sister, and brothers within the memorial sites, and by taking care of the memorial site they give honor to those buried."

The appearance of the memorial has profound importance. Allowing survivors to create a sense of order, timeless beauty, and peace in a space that figured so prominently in the chaotic and violent events of the past is crucial to the healing process. Rebecca explained her dedication to maintaining a memorial site's pristine beauty: "It is everybody's wish to have a beautiful or a nice-looking memorial, such that all those people who were killed in genocide, they could rest in a place which is very beautiful." Cleaning these memorials orders the visual representation of these spaces, which feature immaculate and picturesque landscaping whose beauty serves to honor loved ones. These deliberate acts of creating order and beauty help survivors accept the reality that their loved ones are truly gone from earth and that it is now time to look toward the future.

Survivors explain the processes of mourning and remembrance the memorial facilitates by helping them "face the reality" of all they have lost. Ava, a counselor, became emotional, tears welling up in her eyes, as she explained to me the difficulty some of her clients had in coming to terms with the magnitude of their loss, which sometimes included several loved ones or even entire families: "People are needing more and more time to grieve as time passes, because now, finally survivors have said, 'OK, I am not going to find my mum now, it had been too long.' So now they can grieve, now that they are safe and they know their beloved ones who haven't been found, probably won't." This idea of the elasticity of time, of catching up to the grief of the past, emerged when survivors explained how they had now entered a time of grief and not just "physical survival." As Angel explained, "People should remember, they should always remember their beloved ones, especially when they visit these memorials, because that's when they can get time to remember them deeply, because in the time of the war, when it was happening, they didn't get enough time."[29]

Mass graves that contain nameless dead provide a particular challenge for survivors who have not yet located the remains of their loved ones. Anitha, another counselor, recalled that a client of hers had said, "I never got the chance of getting the flowers to [place on] the graves of my parents." Anitha told her client that she would assist with this task by finding some beautiful flowers to place on one of the mass burial sites. Her client returned the following week for a counseling session. Anitha brought flowers for her client and supported her in placing them on one of the mass graves. Anitha's client felt much better and said to her, "I feel like you are giving value to my beloved people who I lost, which is good for me." Anitha told me that she felt comforted in being able to provide her client the opportunity to grieve in the present, even though ideally this type of grief would have occurred years ago, since this allowed her client to move on and finally "have a future."

Some memorial spaces lend themselves to remembering innocent loved ones who perished, and others are more effective at recalling Rwanda's history. At the CFC, rural survivors most often emphasized remembering individuals, as one may expect, for the memorial contains the clothes, bones, and belongings of those murdered there almost two decades ago. The building is unrenovated, and it is not a space that would be conducive to extensive reconciliation or education programs. It is meant as a reminder of the past and a final resting place for so many of those killed in 1994. While the memorial may not be ideal—some wished for a wall of victims' names, a more modern building, a visitor center, fewer bones on display—the survivors with whom I spoke intentionally created meaning in the circumstances that were available to them for memorialization. Unlike in other memorials throughout the country, where bodies were brought to the memorial from other sites or reburied at the memorial after the discovery of a mass grave, at the CFC the memorial is personal: it is home to beloved parents, siblings, and community members.

When I interviewed Emmy, she said, like so many, that she works at the memorial near her home because the best way to honor her parents is to live a life that contributes to violence prevention. Emmy asserted that memorialization is absolutely vital to violence prevention. When I probed Emmy more about this assertion, she defended it with certainty. During my first interview with Emmy, I wondered whether she was telling me about the importance of memorialization and the horrors of colonial divisionism because she thought that was what I wanted to hear. Or perhaps she felt that this was the story she should tell, knowing that I was reporting back to a Western audience and given the lack of safe spaces in which Rwandans could tell a more complex story.[30] I knew that not all survivors engaged with memorials and wondered what made these spaces so significant for some of those in my sample. Had her beliefs about the function of the memorials been instilled in her during her few years of school? Or were these beliefs internalized from listening to memorial guides employed by the present-day government? Was she invested in memorialization as a citizen devoted to the regime's economic growth and development? After interviewing Emmy three times, I was invited to come see her work at the memorial to better understand her point of view. As she explained, I might be able to appreciate the memorial's importance to her, despite its flaws, after spending time chatting with her while she worked there.

Emmy is a gardener at the CFC who spends most days tending to the grounds. She does not lead tours or share stories of her survival with visitors. She arrives early in the morning to sweep the pathways with a broom made of thin sticks bound together at the top, which Emmy bends over to use to clear pathways and garden areas. The memorial is immaculate. Not a dead or brown flower is anywhere to be seen; the bushes are meticulously shaped into perfect circles; luscious green lawns are neatly cut by hand with a machete; not a single weed peeks out from the dirt path or in between planted flowers. Emmy talks while she works, emphasizing the pride she takes in caring for the physical grounds of the final resting place to so many people she loved.

Emmy's dedication to the site demonstrates to her community and the world how significant it is. In Emmy's view, the beautiful physical space she tends to reflects the image she has of those who died: making this space picturesque honors her loved ones while simultaneously creating a space that outsiders value. As she sees it, this place of beauty and order ultimately leads to violence prevention, for if visitors value the site, then they will never engage in or passively observe genocidal violence in their lifetime. As she explains, "How could anyone think violence is the solution after coming here?"

Emmy's historical narrative about Rwanda is riddled with some of the same inaccuracies and absences featured in other narratives related in this chapter. She asserts that violence erupted out of nowhere in 1994 and that colonialists were solely responsible for divisionism because prior to their hegemony, Rwandans lived in harmony. After multiple interviews with Emmy over the course of a year and days spent with her at the memorial, I came to see that even though she echoed sentiments from the official state narrative, she had nevertheless repurposed this narrative and memorial space for herself. She wasn't particularly invested in the performance of nationalism or reverberating a sentiment that reflected positively on her government, and indeed, there were aspects of the regime with which she fiercely disagreed. Instead she was reclaiming the memorial space, and the historical narrative, to support a belief that sustains her. After the horrors she had experienced, maintaining her belief in a future without genocidal violence was an act of resistance. Even though the memorial space is a grid onto which the government maps its authoritarian rule, it is also a space where survivors invest their time and energy to honor their families and ensure the end of genocide. Even survivors who experienced shattering devastation—such as the loss of an entire family, sexual assault, AIDS, or bodily mutilation—were able to find hope in the idea that remembering the past directly correlated to attaining a better future.

There is no hard evidence that efforts put forth by survivors who live by and work at memorials will prevent future instances of mass violence in Rwanda or elsewhere in the world. Of course, these narratives that survivors construct about violence prevention are just that: stories. But they are powerful ones. Their memory work allows them to gain a sense of control over an uncontrollable past and future. The group of survivors with whom I spoke at that particular time shared aspects of a historical narrative told by the state but also carried out their own memory work (telling stories of the past, remembering the innocent, tending to the physical space). The meaning they derived from the official narrative about remembering the past was the notion that they might be able to prevent the pain they endured from ever becoming someone else's reality. The possibility of preventing future anguish made the heartache of their own families' brutal murders slightly more bearable. Such hope also meant that they had power and agency, even in a constrictive political climate, unlike when they were children running for their lives or hiding under the dead bodies of their neighbors. Memorials offer survivors not only the imagined possibilities that sustain resiliency but also a page on which survivors can write their stories of hope for a less violent future.

4

Trauma and the Stratification of Collective Memory

Angel and I sat in the living room of her two-bedroom cement home that she shares with her brother and sister. As is true in many other homes and in banks and stores, a framed photo of President Paul Kagame hangs on the wall. The photo on Angel's wall covers part of a crack that runs from the ceiling to the corner on the opposite side of the room. Angel lives in a child-headed household (CHH) village, a community of orphans who came together after the genocide to create families. They live in homes across the road from the church where five thousand people in the community were killed in April 1994. On this particularly warm day in April, Angel and I sipped orange Fanta sodas bought from the tiny storefront located about a half mile down the dirt road. We talked about the upcoming commemoration event that would be held in the memorial across from her house.

I asked Angel—knowing her story of survival—if she would ever be interested in sharing her story as one of the testimonials featured in Rwandan commemorations during the annual mourning period. When Angel was fourteen years old, genocidal violence erupted across her country and village. Separated from her parents and siblings while fleeing to the swamp after the genocidal militia arrived in her community, Angel hid alone. Her mother and sister sought refuge in the local church, where they had been safe during previous episodes of violence. Unfortunately, the church could not offer refuge on this particular day in mid-April 1994; they perished along with five thousand others when they were locked in the church by the militia and killed with machetes, bullets, and grenades.

Angel spent the days after her mother's and sister's deaths in the nearby swamp with others from her village but was eventually discovered by the militia and raped along with several other young women. One evening, she made a run for her home, hoping to find her father, brothers, and cousins, only to be shot in the back. A smooth raised patch of skin, shaped like a nickel, still scars her right shoulder. She not only survived but also rescued another young girl, eventually reuniting with the only other surviving member of her family— her younger brother, who was twelve years old at the time and with whom she lives today. Stories of resilience and unfathomable strength are not uncommon among Angel's community of orphans, who endured dire conditions and continue to experience trauma and extreme poverty. The women and handful of men who live near Angel cite "luck" or the "grace of God" for their survival. In many ways, Angel's experiences represent key facets of the Rwandan genocide: brutality, the loss of entire communities, and sexual violence—but also strength, persistence, and courage. At the same time, Angel's experience embodies the central challenges that many survivors face in present-day Rwanda: poverty, new family structures, and mental health challenges.

With Angel's survival and life story in mind, I was compelled to ask if she had considered speaking at the upcoming commemoration.[1] Angel raised the orange Fanta soda to her lips, took a sip, and shook her head as she slowly lowered the glass bottle to the coffee table in front of her. "No," she said, avoiding eye contact. I pressed her a bit: "Why not? You have such an incredible story." She responded, "They would never want my testimony." Angel explained that the government preferred to avoid commemorative events that caused "traumatizing" in response to reliving their own painful experiences. Here she referenced an English-language term Rwandans use to describe a distinctive involuntary response to intense trauma triggered by memories of the genocide. Angel's powerful story would be certain to trigger this kind of response in others, and because Angel was poor, had never finished school, and had her children taken away from her because of her declining mental health, she further reasoned that she would not be the type of survivor from whom the public would want to hear.

As Angel explained the concept, "traumatizing is what happens to survivors when we remember too much." Although the experience of at least one symptom of trauma—such as lack of sleep, headaches, anxiety, depression, or trust issues—is common for many Rwandans, Angel explained that not everyone has the kind of extreme response she and others in Rwanda call "traumatizing," when survivors have flashbacks of 1994 and experience physical symptoms such as convulsions, screaming, and loss of consciousness. Because experiencing or witnessing this response is so upsetting, not just for the individuals experiencing it but for the community as a whole, Angel explained that the government tries to prevent it from occurring during commemorations. The commemorations that Angel referenced include both large gatherings (of five thousand people) and small ones (of fewer than one hundred people) consisting of survivors, tourists, international leaders, East Africans, and Rwandans. These omnipresent commemorations of the Rwandan genocide occur during the mourning months, from April to early July, every year at every major memorial site on specific anniversaries (of massacres, acts of resistance, or memorial dedications) and for burials or reburials (prompted by discoveries of mass graves or improper original burials). Commemorations are supported by the government and almost always include public testimony by one or more genocide survivors. However, as Angel points out, not all survivors are welcome to speak at these events.

My conversation with Angel reveals how trauma and the behavior she calls "traumatizing" manifest themselves during public remembrances of the 1994 genocide against the Tutsi.[2] Traumatizing is inextricably linked to genocide memory; throughout my interviews, survivors and commemoration planners alike expressed a preoccupation with this phenomenon as it related to memory rituals. As Angel elaborates, planning and implementation protocols for commemorations hinge on planners' ideas about the kinds of testimonials that are counterproductive to healing because they incite trauma. In order to fully understand how the dynamics of creating a collective memory can be stratifying through the planning and implementation of commemorations, it was essential for me to understand what the planners of these events identified as triggers of traumatizing.

Angel's story—and its marginalization—illustrates how public commemorative processes and rituals are classed and gendered, excluding some populations' experiences from the collective memory of past events. Marginalization of narratives of atrocity is not unique to Rwanda as states across the globe work to reconcile memories of mass atrocity with present-day stakes in economic growth and political power. In South Africa, stories of black women's experiences have been left out of archives.[3] In international literature on the Holocaust, the experiences of Roma victims have been considerably underrepresented.[4] Rwanda is representative of a modern global challenge in which states confront moving forward in ways that cultivate development and progress after mass violence and loss. Policies and official attitudes around the phenomenon of traumatizing in Rwanda allow us to better understand the rifts within commemoration, which serves as a method of remembering the past in order to move on. Looking more closely at official views on traumatizing at commemorative events can illuminate how stratification begins with micro-level decisions that lead to macro-level outcomes.

In the pages that follow, an account of the systematic exclusion of stories like Angel's demonstrates one of the unanticipated consequences of actions by planners and government officials to avoid further harm to survivors and the greater community during commemorations of the genocide. To better understand how collective memory becomes stratified, I examine the actions of survivors and the staff responsible for organizing and conducting commemorations based on how they conceptualize three factors: the nature of trauma itself, appropriate treatments for trauma, and the social needs that should drive the process of constructing a collective memory.

Creating a collective memory for a nation is both a process (involving truth-seeking, mobilization, and survivor/expert testimony) and an outcome (involving the creation of new symbols, a dominant narrative, and nationalism). What I term the "stratification of collective memory" is the process whereby certain memories are elevated while others are marginalized in an attempt to create a more unified national narrative (as an outcome). Stratification, in this sense, is borrowed from the sociological concept of social stratification as a hierarchal system that has "predictable rules behind the ranking of individuals" and "implies some form of legitimation of the ranking of people and the unequal distribution of valued goods, services, and prestige."[5] In order for social stratification to remain stable over long periods of time, people have to believe in the hierarchy and be able to justify inequality. Justification must also be present for the stratification of collective memory to function. In Rwanda, the stratification of collective memory occurs at both a structural level (through government-run commemorations) and a sociocultural level (through individual perceptions concerning who experiences trauma and what should be done about traumatizing). By analyzing how social actors understand the mental health phenomenon of these public displays of extreme trauma—and how the phenomenon of this response is itself stratified because women, young people, and the poor are disproportionately affected—we can see how a collective memory of a violent past is created and disseminated.

Traumatizing in Context

The prevalence of trauma in postconflict societies like Rwanda is undeniable. Researchers have found trauma responses and PTSD, along with a series of other mental health challenges, to significantly characterize postconflict life in communities throughout the world.[6] Mental health workers have struggled to find effective practices to treat such trauma.[7] Treating trauma is especially challenging in a setting characterized by extreme infrastructural and cultural destruction, which are all too common in the aftermath of political violence, mass human rights abuses, and genocide. Children, adolescents, and young adults (the majority of those who survived the genocide in Rwanda) are found to face particular challenges in the aftermath of mass atrocity, with some studies demonstrating that trauma responses and symptoms can actually increase, rather than decrease, over time.[8]

Humanitarian missions, supported by the World Health Organization (WHO), the UN, and nongovernmental organizations, especially from the West, have donated millions to Rwanda for the training of mental healthcare providers and the treatment of trauma. For example, following the genocide, in October 1994, UNICEF developed and began implementing the Trauma Recovery Programme (TRP) in collaboration with the Ministry of Rehabilitation and the Ministry of Health.[9] The TRP was a nationwide effort focused on helping children and various caregivers "cope with the psychological harm associated with the 1994 Genocide through the use of trauma counselors trained in elementary psychosocial methods of trauma alleviation."[10] It is important to note that the TRP was built on the assumption that posttraumatic stress reactions do not resolve naturally without some form of external intervention. The program entails some form of talk therapy (i.e., recollection and expression of the traumatic event and trauma feelings).[11]

While in the US the contours and validity of PTSD as a diagnostic tool are not often questioned, and cognitive and talk therapy are standard treatments, some scholars argue that Western approaches to mental health treatment may not be the most appropriate solution for contexts such as Rwanda.[12] Derek Summerfield stresses that for "the vast majority of survivors, posttraumatic stress is a pseudo condition, a reframing of the understandable suffering of war as a technical problem to which short-term technical solutions like counseling are applicable." These survivors may gain little benefit from the kinds of interventions foreseen by "Western agencies and their 'experts' who from afar define the condition and bring the cure."[13] A recent report on Rwanda's TRP found no symptomatic difference between those who received treatment from a professional trained by the TRP and those who did not, arguing "limited evidence of benefit and non-trivial evidence of harm for psychosocial interventions in postconflict, humanitarian settings. . . . These findings, therefore, dramatically underscore the dangers of scaling up and incorporating these interventions into the recommendations from national ministries of health and mental health, absent any attention to effectiveness or safety."[14] While the TRP might have been more effective in a less catastrophic situation, these studies point to the importance of interrogating Western notions of trauma and trauma treatment in terms of their effectiveness in the context of Rwanda after the genocide.

Participants in my interviews had diverging views on trauma treatment but largely agreed about the nature of the trauma experienced by survivors of the 1994 genocide. Hundreds of thousands of Rwandans experience some form of traumatic response each year, with significant repercussions. Long-term effects include damage to survivors' social ties; their inability to care for their children or seek resources; and physical symptoms such as headaches, stomach pains, and sleep difficulties. Trauma extends beyond the survivor population to affect perpetrators, counselors, and even members of the next generation, some of whom were born after the genocide. However, in Rwanda, the dynamics (symptoms, demographics, onset) of traumatizing are not stagnant, nor do they comprise a singular trauma response, but rather reflect an ongoing temporal process that is deeply connected to genocide memory.

Trauma responses linked to memory are not unique to Rwanda and are common in survivors of genocide and wartime violence more generally. Collective trauma has been found among Holocaust survivors, Bosnian genocide survivors, and Vietnamese civilians who witnessed wartime atrocities. However, what is unique to Rwanda is the concern of commemoration staff that such trauma responses occur in public spaces at high rates, especially during the mourning months.[15]

As I began to inquire more and more about traumatizing (who traumatizes, when, where, and how), I started to understand its central place in Rwandan commemorations throughout the mourning months (April to early July), and in survivors' lives throughout the calendar year. The phenomenon, as it was explained to me and later confirmed through my own observation during commemorative events, occurs when a person relives in the present-day moment the violence and fear experienced during the genocidal violence in 1994. Traumatizing manifests when individuals respond to their flashbacks of trauma by crying, moaning out loud, and shrieking in terror and pain.

During my research, I observed this phenomenon a number of times. The first time was on April 7, 2012, while attending a commemoration. It was there that I bore witness as a survivor shared details of her ordeal. She described how smells of her survival still haunted her because her senses would "play tricks on her" and all of a sudden she would remember what it was like to hide in a pile of rotting bodies, pretending she was dead in order to survive. As she recalled how her body remembers, a woman three rows in front me started to "traumatize." Watching this was like nothing I had ever witnessed before in my life. The traumatic response began with a cry and then escalated into shrieking and moaning followed by screams in Kinyarwanda of "They are killing me, they are killing me!" and "Save me, please, save me!" The survivor was noticed immediately by trauma counselors and carefully removed from the commemoration;

her eyes rolled back into her head and her body seized up on the way to the trauma tent, where she would stay until she had recovered. Moments later, a man two rows behind me had a similar response, followed by another woman in my row and another woman at the end of the section I was sitting in—all within minutes. I watched as I saw how pain, fear, and trauma can literally disable the body. It was at this moment that I started to understand traumatizing's contagious nature and why it is such a central concern to commemoration planners.

Since trauma can spread through groups of people witnessing the behaviors of those in its midst, memorial and commemoration staff try to contain those who are traumatizing. As Ada, a counselor, explained, "Most of the time when one person traumatizes, it affects the whole community and the whole community can begin to traumatize. We learned about this in the early years as it can get out of control and dangerous very fast." Not only can traumatizing be exhausting, frightening, and harrowing for the person traumatizing, but it can also lead to unsafe actions such as running into traffic or trying to harm oneself or others.

Of those who traumatize at a commemoration or memorial, the majority generally return after fifteen or thirty minutes of rest, hydration, and time in a quiet space, according to information reported to me by Ibuka. Officials told me in 2012 that more than 75 percent of those who traumatize at commemorations are successfully cared for in large white trauma tents set up in close proximity to commemoration events and staffed with volunteers, medics, beds, and water. When someone is traumatizing intensely or needs care beyond what can be provided in trauma tents, that person is taken by ambulance to a local hospital to be sedated and receive medical attention. However, even with a rate of fewer than 25 percent of those affected needing hospital care, there have been cases of commemorations, such as one I attended in 2012, during which so many people were taken to a local hospital that the facility had to stop receiving patients. Ambulances were forced to take the traumatized patients to a hospital in another sector.

The highest incidence of cases requiring trauma tents and care by medical staff occurs during the mourning months at commemorations, memorials, or funeral or burial services. The reasons for this may be the large number of such events during the mourning months and the fact that it is more acceptable during this time to mourn in public. In addition to large-scale commemorations, smaller, less public ones occur during the commemoration months in, for instance, CHH villages or tight-knit communities that have experienced significant trauma. In recent years, village leaders have invited staff from hospitals, mental health centers, NGOs, and the commemoration commission to attend their gatherings and assist people who traumatize during the events.

Everyone I interviewed, including survivors, government workers, and counselors of all levels (e.g., psychologists, head counselors, and Red Cross counselors), reported that cases of severe trauma have been steadily increasing over the past ten years across the country. The increase in trauma is surprising as commemoration staff have attempted to curb it in recent years by avoiding violent images, films, and intense testimonies. As more people attend commemorations, more seem to traumatize during them. There are several possible explanations for this increase, including better diagnostic procedures for trauma (leading to more instances of treatment, but not necessarily more people experiencing trauma) and, because commemorations are more widely attended, a larger number of survivors exposed to situations that might trigger their trauma. These are not the explanations survivors gave in interviews. Instead, most stated that their lives had continued and become more orderly, giving them more time to relive horrific memories of the genocide: "In 1996 people were still surviving, trying to get food, trying to find homes and bodies, and in 2012 those same people have a home or food, they can think back and say, 'Oh, how did I survive? I survived in hiding under bodies and my mum was killed and this and this.' See how one could traumatize years later as you remember? Because remembering is a luxury: it is not something you always had." As Nadene, a survivor in her forties, explains, remembering is a "luxury," because many did not have the opportunity to remember when they were trying to survive in the most basic ways. This comment is of particular interest because memory studies assume that societies must create collective memories in order to counter forgetting, which is assumed to occur as time progresses from the specific event. In the case of Rwanda, fully remembering is considered a privilege by some: it is not something that naturally occurs after an event but a process that begins only after other essentials in life have been taken care of. Furthermore, remembering is not reserved for specific physical places or moments in time: it continues as an ongoing process after the restoration of life's physical necessities.

Although the most visual trauma incidents occur during the mourning months, counselors consistently reminded me that survivors in particular traumatize all year round. The most common time outside the commemoration period to traumatize is during life cycle events, such as births, deaths, marriages, or other significant temporal markers (e.g., matriculation at school or the breakup of a marriage or relationship). Such events can serve as triggers or reminders of those who are no longer alive. Joseph, who lives with his older sister, explained that when his sister gave birth, she thought about how her mother was not there to witness such a blessing. She traumatized soon after and needed to be hospitalized and sedated. This trauma affects the lives of survivors by shaping not only life cycle events but also critical junctures and decisions that affect them for years to come.

Traumatizing and Stratification

In Rwanda, survivors report particular patterns or configurations to which certain social groups are more prone to traumatize than are other groups. This is an indication that trauma shapes the lives of some more than others. The population generally referred to as the "vulnerables" includes those with minimal social capital and power, such as "the poor, the orphans, the widows, the people who have the least," as survivor Fidèle notes. When describing the demographics of those who traumatize, Rwandans emphasized four main factors in the likelihood of this response: (1) gender, (2) age, (3) socioeconomic status, and (4) past history of psychological counseling or treatment. According to counseling staff I interviewed, these factors correlate with actual incidences of traumatizing. More importantly, though, perceptions around the demographics of those most at risk of traumatizing factor into decision-making about memory projects.

According to survivors, the majority of those who physically survived the genocide were women because men were targeted and killed in the early stages of the genocide, and around 300,000 children were killed, making them almost 40 percent of the total number of victims.[16] While men tended to be targeted in massacres in the early days of the genocide and women were not targeted for death in the same way, women were subject to sexual violence on a massive scale. Thus, gender and age significantly shaped the experiences of all survivors. As is true of previous genocides, women were often with their children when they made life-and-death decisions about where to hide or how to negotiate with perpetrators to secure their own or others' survival. Men were often killed away from their homes or churches because many kept watch on the hillsides to monitor militia movement in the valleys below and calculate how best to protect their communities.[17]

Men's and women's differential treatment during the genocide no doubt influenced their perceptions and actual experiences concerning their own trauma. According to counselors, many of the women in trauma center tents at commemorations are rape survivors. Still, despite clearly gendered patterns of traumatic experiences, common explanations for the different kinds of struggles experienced by female and male survivors tend to revert to gender stereotypes. For example, Eugene states: "In our culture, men are not supposed to be like women. . . . You may find out that when they don't talk about the problem, it keeps on piling up on themselves, so at a certain point they explode, and it tends to affect them so much." Here, gender roles are used to explain the barriers to seeking help that male survivors often face, with the likely result that their trauma intensifies further.

At all sites where I interviewed, survivors, including trauma counselors, reported that women traumatize more often than men.[18] The interviewees differed on why this may be the case. Some claimed that women have "softer hearts" or are "weak" and therefore unable to handle the stress of commemoration or the flashbacks they experience during these events. In this argument, because women are not equipped to handle these situations, their minds have "too much to handle," and they traumatize. As Fidèle, a memorial guide, explained, "Most of the women traumatize in large numbers, because they are weak. . . . For men they are at least strong emotionally, they don't traumatize as much as women." Here Fidèle implies that some men do in fact traumatize. In fact, Marie, a counselor who works with survivors, argues that when men traumatize, it is often much more severe: "Women just cry and that's why the level of traumatizing is increasing in women and children, but for the men they just say that you need to be patient and you need to be strong . . . but that doesn't mean that there's no men; when we see men traumatize, it is much more severe." Marie attributes this observed difference between male and female survivors to men's reluctance to address their feelings with peers or professionals.

Other survivors argue that the reason women traumatize more than men has less to do with innate gender differences than with their particular experiences during the genocide, including sexual assault and witnessing the killing or torture of children, spouses, and other loved ones. Oliver, a survivor and human rights lawyer in his fifties, explained, "Those who were not violated, [perpetrators] killed their sons and daughters and husbands while they [were] watching. . . . Those who were not raped, at least they observed everything . . . the killing of their parents, their husbands and their sons." Others reflect on how rape during or after the genocide causes certain women to "traumatize a lot." As Claudine, a survivor and counselor in her late thirties, explained, when a rape survivor "comes to commemoration week, they tend to traumatize, and most of the times they end up in a hospital. They remember their rape and think it's 1994 and they are getting raped." This situation in particular can trigger a trauma response for those around the traumatizing woman, including her children, if she has any.

Those who work with trauma survivors also report that young people (those under twenty-one) traumatize more often than adults. This observation situates young people, including those born after 1994 and those orphaned by the genocide, among the "vulnerable population" of survivors. Young people who were not alive or present during the genocide but have observed their peers' trauma or heard family members' narratives can experience secondary trauma that may lead to traumatizing. As Carene, a tour guide, explained, "Because as you see and you have heard, these crying people just traumatize. When we have students in the viewing room and they hear these traumatized people, they can also be traumatized." The contagion of trauma is exemplified in the case of young people observing their parents traumatizing. As Martin, a man who was ten when he survived the genocide, reflected about a commemoration held in his village earlier that week, "Trauma is increasing year by year because the children of the survivors also tend to traumatize year by year, because when these women produce kids and then when it comes to commemoration, you may find that when they [the women] traumatize, their daughters or sons, they also traumatize when they watch their mum traumatize." Contagion happens when children (and others) experience empathy and fear when witnessing others undergoing a severe traumatic response.

Orphans between the ages of fifteen and thirty were reported to traumatize at high rates; some were born after the genocide and experienced their mothers, who had been victims of genocidal rape, dying of AIDS. Counselors theorized that young people may imagine how their lives might have been had their parents not been killed; it is also likely that they experience flashbacks of their parents' deaths. Valentine, a counselor who works with orphans, explains the situation of an orphaned girl she worked with who was adopted after the genocide: "When she recognizes this is not her real family, she starts imagining how the next years are going to be, and this family—she wishes to get something from the family, like more of their affection, and she feels like she's not getting their affection as she would have gotten it from her original parents." As described by Valentine, this young woman imagined the affection she would have received from her biological parents, and this triggered her trauma response. This illustrates how, even in the absence of flashbacks, the profound sense of loss that genocide orphans experience can create significant posttraumatic symptoms.

For other orphans, remembering the violence their parents endured can also spark trauma. For example, young people in CHH villages often gather together to remember their loved ones who were killed in 1994. Fidèle, a survivor from one such village, described the remembrance rituals in his community: "Survivors remember and then gather in a circle around a fire, and then they start asking things, like for example, 'How do I remember my father? Who was my mom? How was my mom killed?' And then talk like give a testimony, but around a fire you know, I would remember my father being raped—my mom being raped, I remember someone chopping them up or something. That was something that was getting people traumatized." Here, Fidèle explains that orphaned children regularly remember the particularly brutal ways their parents died.

In addition to gender and age, counselors also perceive poverty to be a significant indicator for trauma. Poverty often tracks with the severity of trauma responses because poor survivors lost not only their families but also their livelihoods. However, it is difficult to disentangle poverty from gender and age, for in present-day Rwanda some of the poorest populations are women (widows in particular) and orphans. These specific populations live in dire conditions, often because of the genocide. For example, Patience, a survivor living in poor conditions, explained that, prior to the genocide, she and her husband had a "very nice home," were quite comfortable, and had two "lovely children." During the genocide, Patience's husband, the primary earner of the family, was murdered along with her two children, and she was raped. She now lives in a home with dangerous toilets (uneven terrain surrounds the toilet, which has no doors for privacy) and cracked walls, in a poor village with other widows and orphans. Patience has a child who, now eighteen years old, was conceived from rape. She said that when she reflects on what her "life could have been," she can easily traumatize.

Counselors also reported that those living in extreme poverty have the highest chance of traumatizing outside the commemoration months. Immaculee, a counselor, told the story of a typical orphan: "And that poverty [the orphan experiences] is because she lost or he lost their parents. That problem is brought by because he or she lost his parents and relatives. So, when it comes to April, he or she just thinks, 'I have this poverty just because I lost my parents or my relatives. If it was not for the genocide, I would be living a happy life.' So, those poems and songs, they remind them of their families, they lost their parents, they lost so much." Even with government assistance to aid in orphans' education, counselors and survivors alike feel that it is not enough to prevent traumatizing. Clause, an orphan survivor, said this: "Even if they try themselves to earn their capacity [through government organizations like FARG], the problem of the life, that is remembered, that they lost all things during the genocide, and after genocide, it was not easy for each and every one to follow others. For example, some of them don't have houses. They don't have people or any family or relatives. They have some problems, physical problems caused by the genocide and psychological, and it's a lot of things." Clause further explained, "And that condition predisposes them to be traumatized. And even if the government has tried to help some of the vulnerables, it is not enough."

Finally, those who have not sought psychological counseling or opportunities to talk about their experiences were described by survivors as at high risk for traumatizing because they have not let "their emotions out" and can easily experience a full-blown traumatic "crisis" in response to mourning or a significant life event. As Rose, a counselor, elaborated, "When you find that they never talked about that [the genocide], because they had no one to help them psychologically they kept those things, those events in their history private and they would pile and pile and pile up. So, then year after year—so you may find that when it comes to commemoration, that's when he or she explodes. And then he or she lets them out, and it leads to traumatizing."

These perceptions are socially constructed as they are understood within an existing system of social norms about gender, age, and socioeconomic status. Even so, the perceptions about who traumatizes are still significant in that they shape behaviors and reactions, which, given the contagion processes at work, can impact the actual incidences of traumatizing.

Trauma has a myriad of effects on survivors' lives, impacting physical (headaches, inability to take care of themselves) and emotional dimensions. Traumatizing, and trauma more generally, interrupts the ability to function in everyday life. Those who suffer from traumatizing explain that it interferes with attending school, taking care of their children, and at times leaving the house. In many cases the ability to seek treatment depends upon the presence of loved ones who can intervene and the availability of resources in the particular geographical location.

In Rwanda, several free and low-cost services, including psychological and medical treatment, are available to those experiencing trauma. However, in rural areas, people generally have to travel or walk great distances to access these resources. Beth, an orphaned young woman, explained that it took her "over half of one day to get my medication, and when I visit with the doctor it can be much longer and I need money for a moto."[19] Unsurprisingly, respondents report that those who seek and receive services are also the ones most socially connected in their communities. Talk therapy as a means of addressing trauma was not readily available to many survivors because this was a relatively new practice and most often centered in Kigali, the capital. Those who attended group services for rape survivors often traveled even greater lengths in order to maintain anonymity. Furthermore, counselors reported being overburdened with cases and often called upon elders in the community to help both in their offices and in the homes of people who did not show up for their appointments.

Trauma is often a source of tensions in kinship relations. In one particular community populated entirely by orphans, life became difficult when the head of one household was taken to the hospital, sometimes for several days at a time, for treatment. Angel's brother, Clovis, decided to drop out of school to care for Angel when she was traumatizing frequently. Eventually, Angel's child was taken away from her by children's services to a nearby convent for permanent care because her trauma was so severe that she no longer could properly care for her baby. Angel agreed that this was in her daughter's best interest, even though she "[missed] her deeply." At the time of the interview, Angel was receiving care provided by the state in hopes that one day she and her daughter would be reunited (and that did happen—years later).

Ranking Traumatizing Narratives

While most survivors' I spoke with generally agree about the nature of trauma from past experiences and who is most vulnerable to suffering from trauma, there is notably less agreement about trauma's role in the healing process. Some feel trauma is a necessary aspect of healing, while others feel that it does not promote healing yet is necessary for the purpose of preserving memory. Others argue that giving expression to devastating pain and traumatizing should be avoided entirely. Surprisingly, these starkly different opinions do not appear to alter the general belief that, regardless of whether trauma is helpful for individuals or the country as a whole, traumatized individuals and their families are deserving of services to support their physical and psychological journeys of recovery postgenocide. Furthermore, these understandings of trauma structure commemorations, memorialization projects, and rituals.

In my interviews, three distinct narratives emerged on the subject of trauma's role in the healing process. In the first narrative, survivors argued that traumatizing heals, and for that reason some survivors continue to engage in commemorative rituals despite the extreme emotional pain they experience at such events. In the second narrative, interviewees described traumatizing as pain worth enduring for the greater good that commemorative rituals bring to their lives. In the final narrative, interviewees argued that trauma is detrimental and should be avoided at all cost within the contours of commemorative events, which are otherwise beneficial occasions for remembrance. While beliefs about trauma certainly diverged, none of the interviewees questioned whether commemorations should continue: all believed in the importance of memorials and remembrance rituals. But a clearly unintended effect of these competing narratives about trauma is that they served to stratify the survivor community by marginalizing specific groups and experiences in the process of addressing the aftermath of genocidal violence.

The first narrative, shared mostly by survivors (some of them counselors) in rural areas, asserts that traumatizing is a process that occurs as part of the healing journey when people begin to understand the magnitude of what happened to them in 1994. Rural counselors may have echoed this narrative more than urban counselors because they interact less with government workers, who on the whole feel traumatizing should be avoided. Women were more likely than men to express the view that traumatizing could be therapeutic and occurred when people "didn't talk about what happened to them and it all exploded." After such an "explosion," the traumatized individual benefited because he or she "felt better and released those emotions." Chanise, a rural survivor in her forties, echoed this sentiment: "It is normally good for whoever was in the genocide, to hear about the testimony, to hear those poems, to hear those songs, because it is very good if you have something on your heart and then you let it out. It helps you in becoming strong, because if you don't let it out [i.e., traumatize], that's when you might find someone with headaches that are nonstop or ulcers."

Like Chanise, Anne, a survivor and trauma counselor in rural Rwanda, explained the not uncommon notion that expressing trauma is inevitable and therefore needs to occur and "come out" in order for the body and mind to heal: "It is very good for them to hear those songs and testimonies and poems, so that they give out what they feel and if it is to cry or if it is to talk about what they saw, that is really good even if it leads to traumatizing. Because then it will be less in the future." For Anne, traumatizing led to healing not only by releasing emotions but also by mitigating the effects of future traumatizing. Other interviewees pointed to the role of trauma in paving the way to proactive behaviors that helped survivors. Some counselors, including Audrey, noticed that after a trauma crisis, individuals often received counseling or other support that "made things improve after because they started going to group or counseling."

Although a significant portion of people with whom I spoke felt that traumatizing could be helpful, the majority of them did not. One alternative narrative, shared mostly by survivors, portrayed traumatizing as "difficult and bad for [the individual] and the community" but also something "that happens after genocide and after someone sees so much," as Audrey explained. According to this narrative, trauma should be prevented whenever possible, and those experiencing it should be cared for, but other important dynamics of postgenocide life, such as commemorating, were also at stake. Some survivors expressed anger at the thought that certain testimonies should not be shared because of the possible risk of trauma. For them, "telling the truth is most important, yes, people might traumatize but they are traumatizing from truth, not lies and we must honor those who did not survive with the truth," as Garuka, a survivor in his late thirties, illuminated.

Paul, a tour guide, cited a particular instance that he felt was "worth" taking the chance of inciting trauma. He explained that he felt obligated, when guiding groups of visitors, to teach about genocidal rape and the particular human rights violations women experienced: "When you reach . . . this section [on rape], you have to explain to them those horrible things. You also tell them because you're a teacher, so you have to be free, saying that even if they can get some problems from knowing, they get those emotions; others can get traumas, trauma cases. But it's the only way to show, to tell what happened even if it's hurting. We have to share about the women. . . . It's important for people to know." Several tour guides echoed this sentiment regarding how valuable the information or "truth" is, even if it causes trauma.

Others expressed the concern that, if measures are taken to avoid trauma altogether, it could lead to a dismantling of the commemorative events and months altogether; Nadege, a woman in her fifties living in Kigali, remarked: "Of course, we cannot stop commemorating because it brings trauma. Of course, when we are remembering, we are not watching a football match; we are not in entertainment. That is why people should show their emotions, crying, or traumatizing, they are letting it out for the commemoration. Even if people get traumatized, that's okay, because that is the only time they get to cry, and people mourn for them, so I don't see any problem with people traumatizing, because that is the only time they have for mourning in public." Nadege echoed the essence of the second narrative, that mourning or commemorating is too important not to do, even if it means people will traumatize. These first two narratives also help explain why survivors who traumatize at commemorations continue to attend even when they experience (or witness) a highly upsetting trauma response. For if they feel traumatizing can be beneficial, healing, or a process that leads to a greater good, it becomes reasonable and rational to assume that they would continue attending commemorations even if they experienced adverse emotional responses.

The third narrative differs quite significantly from the other two and is shared primarily by those who work for memorials or at commemorations. They find traumatizing to be a disorder that causes harm to the individual and those around them. As Shema, a counselor, clearly expressed, "Traumatizing is not a part of healing, it's a part of a disorder, a mental disorder. I think that when someone is traumatized, he can verbalize what was happening, but that is anxiety. That is a sign of anxiety and not part of healing." Those who asserted that traumatizing was damaging often had vivid memories of a time before Rwanda had educated so many counselors, when people were traumatizing without access to any sort of psychological care. Survivors remembered these times as scary, dangerous, and chaotic.[20]

Commemoration staff and urban counselors who worked closely together during the mourning months to plan and curate remembrance events tended to share in this narrative. In the urban areas, counselors are often consulted about what they perceived as trauma triggers and put communities in touch with government staff about these findings. It was unclear how closely rural counselors worked with commemoration staff. In the rural areas, it appeared that counselors and government officials managed separate domains, and that may explain the differing views between urban and rural counselors.

The people with whom I spoke who worked in urban areas, and a few men in rural areas, argued that trauma disrupts daily life and should be treated and avoided at all costs. The emphasis here was on prevention, even with the agreement that treatment is essential. These survivors pointed to the chaos and danger caused by traumatizing at crowded events, a particular point of concern during the commemoration months. Traumatizing was viewed as something to research and observe for the purpose of making commemoration organizers fully aware of what causes trauma so that they could steer clear of practices that trigger these reactions, not only for the safety of the individual but for that of the community and nation as a whole. While not deliberate, this narrative steeped in goals of public safety has the unintended effect of excluding certain material that may cause trauma from public commemorations and memorials, resulting in the stratification of survivor testimony and historical narratives of the country's violent past. Of the three competing narratives about trauma, the idea that trauma is detrimental has become the prevailing view because those with the power to control commemorations hold this belief, which in turn is reflected in mnemonic practices.

The Stratification of Collective Memory

The phenomenon of traumatizing affects the physical setup at commemorations, where exits are left clear, tents are available for immediate care, and ambulances stand at the ready to take the afflicted to local hospitals. Another way in which traumatizing impacts commemoration is that the content of the programs is structured according to beliefs about the nature of trauma. For example, those who believe trauma is detrimental to society and should be prevented censor certain narratives from public commemorations in order to prevent the audience from experiencing trauma. Others, who believe experiencing trauma is part of the healing process, support showing films, music videos, and images that may increase trauma during commemorative events.

More than any other group, those on the planning, implementation, and protocol staff have the power to structure commemorations according to their views. While survivors disagree about the extent of damage trauma can cause and how it should best be handled, those the government employs to develop and manage annual commemorations appear to be unified behind the view that building and maintaining meaningful and safe spaces for remembering depends upon keeping traumatizing at a minimum. Thus, in seeking to reduce traumatizing, especially at large-scale public commemorations, committee members review the previous years' events and try to avoid aspects of commemoration that triggered trauma. As Ismael, a survivor in his fifties, explained the thinking: "What we do . . . is try to discuss what happens, what was going on, what was difficult for us, and what we plan to do next time. . . . The framework has changed over time. It's like research action, but we try to do something, we try to discuss our need, next year, we change and we try our best." Macro changes that occur as a result of the evaluation of previous events include increasing the availability of counseling and mental health services in order to prevent trauma year-round.

However, the majority of changes discussed by those who coordinate commemorations were ways to prevent trauma. These precautionary efforts included: (1) encouraging smaller gatherings (under one hundred people) and shortening the overall time people spend commemorating, and (2) regulating commemoration content such as testimonies and videos.

Smaller gatherings, such as those within a CHH village or among widow association groups during commemoration, used to occur during the mourning months without any outside communal support. However, it came to the attention of the commemoration staff that these small personal commemorations would often "get out of control," with the entire community beginning to traumatize and no one available to care for them. As Bisangwa explained, "The person himself or herself was crying, and then it affected everyone who was listening. So, those things are not being done, because you end up by everyone in that area getting traumatized. Those things, they're trying to minimize, and that doesn't mean that it is a solution, but I think it is one of the ways to protect people—some people." While authorities attempt to decrease the number of small commemorations, staff from local hospitals, NGOs, mental health organizations, or the commemoration commission are available to support those that continue.

Counselors from nearby hospitals and community centers are now available to provide care to those participating in small commemoration gatherings. For example, Jean Claude explained that in his village (a child-headed community), a commemoration was planned for the first Tuesday of the official week of mourning. For the past two years, he has contacted the local hospital, not far from the village, to let them know traumatizing would be occurring, and they now send two counselors out each year. Jean Claude remarked that "this helped greatly because when people traumatized it did not spread like three years ago. It spread a little but not to everyone." Even though the trauma was contagious at this event, Jean Claude felt that it was helpful for people to have counselors there to help deal with emotions and limit the spread.

In addition to decreasing small gatherings and providing support to these events to prevent trauma, commemoration staff aim to make remembrance events shorter than in prior years. As organizer Gilbert specified, "We also try to have people organize commemoration ceremonies [so that they] do not take long hours, because the longer it takes, the more traumatized people become." Memorial staff at one site attempted to do this by holding a burial early in the day for people killed in 1994 but never properly buried and another evening commemoration several hours later. Commemoration staff felt this would allow people time to go home and rest, preventing trauma. However, during that particular evening commemoration, which I personally witnessed, such high rates of trauma occurred that poems, speakers, and testimonies were cut short, ambulances filled with patients, and the trauma staff were overwhelmed with survivors. Commemoration staff did not consider this a success, and when asked about the incident, one of the organizers, Frank, reflected, "It was too much for one week, they were organizing the bones one day, then washing them the next to prepare for burial, then the burial of their loved ones, sometimes for the first time and then an evening commemoration, the first for this site, and five thousand people came. You saw, all the chairs were filled. That is why we had to cut some parts short; it was too much, too, too much for one week." As Frank explained, even though the event itself was meant to be on the shorter side, because there were so many events preceding the commemoration, the trauma accumulated and the end result was a commemoration that was "too much" and needed adjustment.

Commemoration staff portrayed cutting testimony as a desperate yet unavoidable choice, since testimony is considered an essential aspect of commemorating. Testimonies not only tell the history of the particular area during the genocide; they also serve as a mechanism to combat genocide deniers. A testimony is thought to be helpful not just for the one sharing his or her story of survival but also for those bearing witness, listening, validating, and acknowledging what occurred in a public venue.[21] However, for commemoration planners and staff, not all testimonies are created equal in their ability to heal and to structure a meaningful remembrance experience for attendees.

Commemoration staff emphasized two central components needed for these events to serve as ideal narratives for pubic remembrance rituals: they must avoid "strong language" or details of the genocide that could upset the audience, and they must end with a positive message about survival, resilience, and Rwanda's future. "Strong language" includes details of killing, violence, or rape. David, a commemoration staff member, elucidated: "You see, for example, [if a testimony is strong] it will traumatize many people and you can't have them say it for a big commemoration . . . like 'I was violated by one hundred people . . .' you see, everybody will be traumatized. So, you look for another person who has less trauma." Here, David explained that if someone is interested in providing a testimony, commemoration staff must first vet their story. As demonstrated in the above example, testimonies about rape do not fit the ideal narrative for a commemoration. Men who succeed postgenocide in receiving an education or who are successful economically or socially comprise the majority of shared public testimonies I attended. As a result, women sexual assault survivors I interviewed often complained that their experiences were rendered invisible because they were denied a public forum where they could share them. A few commemoration staff members commented on the lack of "strong testimony," with Mahigo saying, "We know it's not perfect to silence strong testimony, but we don't have enough trauma counselors to have them speak." This real concern underlines the fact that support for "strong testimony" requires resources. In effect, the ability to allow raw testimony is a luxury that not every community can afford.

The marginalization of women sexual assault survivors takes the form of not only erasing their experiences from commemoration testimony but also preventing those without a hopeful message from presenting their stories publicly. Jean Pierre, for example, a young man who takes care of his younger sister and lives in a CHH, nonchalantly revealed, "It wouldn't ever be me there [giving a testimony]." This assumption is confirmed by Anne, a commemoration staff member who said, "The idea here is to commemorate, but at the same time to lay a foundation for the future, to look forward." Anne detailed that commemoration committee members "try to look for those survivors who went through, of course, that experience, but who after all have done something to develop themselves and . . . who come forth to give their testimonies, how they survived, how they suffered, but how also they have overcome, and how they are building their dreams—joining others to you know—to . . . come from darkness to light, the idea is to have hope." The intention behind this specific genre of narrative is to fill survivors and other attendees with hope that they can go on in the face of sadness and loss, ensuring that people leave commemoration events feeling sad but not traumatized. This intention excludes those survivors whose stories would leave one feeling not inspired but defeated or angry.

Some survivors comment in passing about feeling disappointed at the lack of "strong testimony" and film clips at commemorative events. Based on the level of trauma films have caused in the recent past, commemoration staff for the 2012 commemorations chose to include few visuals. Nicole, a staff member, clarified: "Because every year we try to find out [new ways in which] we can minimize trauma. For example, last year there was a film that was shown in the evening at National Stadium. Many people got traumatized. So, this year we decided that we shall show fewer films, which are not so scary and not too strong or violent." Another staff member, Emmanuel, explained that, practically speaking, showing films was "not possible": "We exclude these films because we don't have enough counselors. If the number of people who attended the commemoration is very large, and we don't have enough counselors we have to be careful. What they must consider is: Do they have enough counselors? And also which hospital people will go to if they traumatize, if you don't have enough space in the hospital, then you decide not to show the movies, which will decrease the number of people who are traumatizing." Several members of the commemoration staff defended the decision not to show films as one of practicality and care, for they felt that films increase trauma to levels that do not allow for proper treatment for traumatized individuals.

While people are aware of the commemoration staff's reasoning for not showing films during commemorations, the majority disagreed with this decision, asserting that, in Charity's words, "I know the government realizes how people feel or how people react after watching these movies and seeing these films, like the number of people who are traumatizing could really increase . . . but I don't agree with the government decision, because if we are remembering or trying to remember . . . we want to see what was really happening." This widespread reaction reflects the belief that people should "see" what "really happened" during the genocide and that traumatizing is a step in "the way to healing." After a commemoration at one site that did not include photos or films, survivors in the surrounding village felt angry that no film had been shown and complained that the "government was controlling remembrance" and not letting people see "what really happened." As they pointed out, the films were not just for them but also for the non-survivor attendees at commemorations who did not know "[what it] was like in 1994."

While survivors didn't mention the political and economic stakes of a particular vision of remembrance and memorializing, the notion of an ideal testimony does not occur in a vacuum. Rather, it exists in a globalized political climate in which Rwanda is one of the most aided countries in the world partly because it projects an image of itself as a model developing country that has succeeded against the odds.[22] Investment funds, tourist dollars, and state economic development projects are all on the line when presenting Rwanda as a country that has overcome its calamitous past despite the global community's failure to intervene in the genocide.

Scholars have documented that how a society chooses to remember its past structures how it reacts to present-day conflicts, creates policy, and supports particular educational reforms or curricula. This means that a country's choices about how to narrate its past matter in everyday life. In the case of traumatizing, the manner in which survivors, commemoration staff, and government employees perceive this psychological phenomenon structures the kind of narrative that becomes central, public, and recognizable at national remembrance events and memorialization projects. Public commemorative testimonies shared at the national level are not only witnessed by survivors; they are also observed by tourists (some of them high profile) and televised, transcribed, or documented for years to come. Quite literally, the testimonies and material shared during commemoration events become a recorded history of Rwandan memorial practices and, in many ways, a recorded history of what occurred during those violent months in 1994.

When no space is made for women's experiences of sexualized violence or survivors' struggles in the genocide's aftermath—stories like Angel's—legitimate fears arise that these narratives will be forgotten. Survivors like Angel express trepidation about how future generations, who will be more removed from the genocide, will understand (or misunderstand) the dynamics of the genocide and its aftermath. This raises questions: How might the stratification of collective memory affect future policy decisions or survivors' expectations if testimonies primarily comprise success stories? How will future generations understand the full extent of the genocide when current commemorations leave out stories of mass rapes and gender-based violence? In the absence of brutal images and testimonies of survivors who still struggle, will future generations be able to account for the long-term consequences of the genocide? Who is silenced and what remains unsaid when only tales of flourishing survivors are shared? These are questions that haunt Rwandan survivors but are unfortunately not unique to Rwanda.

Leaving out disturbing narratives of rape and orphanage may indeed ease immediate suffering. However, survivors and their children know all too well what happened during those hundred days, and the silencing of their voices becomes another form of violence. This symbolic violence occurs when vulnerable populations are told to suffer in silence without the possibility of telling their stories and having their experiences and continuing struggles validated. The symbolic violence of marginalizing those who have been traumatized by excluding films and images of the events from commemorations also has the potential to allow the past to be forgotten or ignored. In the case of Rwandan survivors in the US, some refugees have explained that detailed (and sometimes violent) survival narratives were helpful in their recovery as they worked to combat the cognitive dissonance that occurs when the veracity of the brutality they witnessed is questioned.[23] However, a central difference between the survivors in Rwanda and those Rwandan survivors in the US is the legitimate concern over the physical safety and care of traumatized survivors. Having a stadium filled with people experiencing the peak moments of trauma and believing their lives are in danger can be frightening and potentially harmful when there are not enough trained professionals or hospital beds to accommodate those in need. Commemoration personnel, based on the assumption that traumatizing is a psychiatric pathology, trust that it is in the best interest of their country and its citizens to prevent such chaos by balancing truthtelling and commemorative practices.

As we have seen, the different perspectives on trauma are not equally weighted because the views of those with power are the ones that prevail. The official perspective on public displays of trauma is that they are detrimental, and the resulting stratification of survivors' memories of their experiences can have immeasurable implications for reconciliation and civic engagement. If survivors like Angel cannot locate themselves in national memory projects, they may choose to disengage from civic projects or reconciliation programs, which serve the vital function of enabling postgenocide coexistence. A survivor in Angel's village, Emmy, said to me after a commemoration, "Yes, I attended the commemoration but no one like me spoke. They have forgotten about me because I did not do well after the genocide. So why should I be part of their reconciliation agendas? They don't remember me when it's time to honor my family." For survivors like Emmy who suffered some of the most horrific violence and still live in dire conditions, the stratification of collective memory exacerbates social inequality and makes official narratives about the past unrecognizable. In the next chapter, I explore how the stratification of collective memory functions during guided tours at memorials, focusing on the inclusion or exclusion of a specific part of Angel's story: sexual and gender-based violence and genocidal rape.

5

Gendered Violence and the Politics of Remembering and Forgetting

> I saw my neighbor beg the killers to kill her after her sister was raped publicly
> and bled to death. They did not kill her and she is alive today, but she is dead
> inside. If you look at her you will see, she is no longer alive.
>
> Ella, genocidal rape survivor

During the 1994 genocide against the Tutsi in Rwanda, rape was used as a weapon to destroy individuals and their families. Like other dimensions of the genocide, the legacy of mass sexual and gender-based violence (SGBV) still haunts Rwandan communities, individual survivors, and, in many regards, the nation as a whole. However, unlike other dynamics of the genocide, SGBV and its aftermath are not consistently discussed in memorial tours or commemorations dedicated to remembering those violent months in 1994. This is no reflection of the prevalence of this kind of violence: in 1994 it was the rule rather than the exception, and approximately 350,000 women were victims of rape.[1]

From the perspectives of military decision makers and as many feminist scholars have documented, women have long been considered casualties of warfare and state-sanctioned violence and treated as enemy property that can be destroyed through rape and sexual terrorism.[2] Theorists have argued about the pervasiveness of genocidal rape in recent decades compared to the past, but few deny the phenomenon's historical ubiquity. While rape has been present in every documented genocide and war, it was only since the mass atrocities in Rwanda and the Balkans that genocidal rape has been acknowledged as a distinct weapon of genocide, reflected in the judgments of ICTY and ICTR.[3]

SGBV such as mass rape and gendered torture (i.e., the mutilation of women's breasts or buttocks, or men's penises) is used as an attack on family bonds and lineages; it aims to destroy communities and nations.[4] And it is effective: mass rape humiliates victims and their families, thereby damaging familial bonds.[5] Survivors and their family members report many lasting effects of SGBV on kinship networks years after genocidal violence. These include the unintentional isolation of rape survivors from the family and fractured familial relationships due to the trauma of gendered torture and rape, both resulting in the disruption of social networks and traditional exchanges of care. All this negatively impacts the entire family.[6]

It has been argued that wartime and genocidal rape constitute a crime to destroy the self aimed especially at children born out of acts of sexual violence.[7] For in Rwanda, and in a range of other cases, women have been raped so that they will bear children with the rapists' ethnic (or national) identity.[8] In these cases, rape has been described as a tool of biological warfare in the spread of sexually transmitted diseases and forced impregnation.[9] Mass rape "deals a significant blow to a victimized cultural entity by breaking up families, robbing raped women of access to marriage and reproduction in the future, condemning them to refugee life, and otherwise intimidating the community into fleeing. In a strongly patriarchal society, rape alone is powerful enough to interfere with the reproduction of the group because it marks the rape victims as unmarriageable."[10]

On a macro level, the rape of both women and men during episodes of political violence obliterates the gendered and paternalistic assumptions upon which many nation-building efforts are built (however inaccurate they may be): that women and children must be protected, that men should defend their families and communities, and that sex is sacred and meant for heterosexual marriage.[11] Nationalism scholar Anne McClintock warns, "All nationalisms are gendered, all are invented and all are dangerous . . . in the sense that they represent relations to political power and to the technologies of violence."[12] McClintock highlights the impacts of nationalist projects, including genocidal campaigns, on women's bodies and lives, for women are often regarded as reproducers of the state. In a biological sense, women's reproduction, which produces citizens for the state, has been at the center of nationalist projects, shaping national pro-/anti-natal and immigration policies and laws.[13] In a cultural sense, women produce citizens in their roles as mothers, educators, and caregivers.[14] And in a symbolic sense, state propaganda often depicts women as embodying or representing community, the national collective, and territorial boundaries.[15]

This preoccupation with women's reproductive role coincides with national anxieties over racial and ethnic purity, paving the way for eugenic ideologies and practices.[16] Because of women's material and symbolic function in the nation-state, the rape of women, especially public sexual assault and torture, common in war and genocide, can be a tactic of invading territory, harming national identity, and destroying the possibility of cultural and biological reproduction. Mass extermination effectively destroys generations, cultural practices, family lineages, and social life; however, as the pervasiveness of rape during times of political unrest suggests, communities are also torn apart by acts of sexual domination and violence. It is precisely the brutality of rape—the devastation it inflicts on social relations, communities, and the psyche—that makes it a timeless mechanism of annihilation and domination during genocide and war. Such acts of violence and aggression are often mobilized around the supposed creation of a greater nation, which requires nationalist propaganda and ideology that "involves a revival of patriarchal values and attitudes that work to legitimize male control, sexual entitlement, and power."[17] In legitimating the state or nationalist project, SGBV decimates undesirable communities.[18]

All these horrors unfolded during the 1994 genocide against the Tutsi, and decades later, survivors describe the genocidal rapes and SGBV as the "hardest to forgive." This chapter analyzes the ways memorials in present-day Rwanda deal with the challenge of commemorating the crimes that were "the hardest to forgive." Centering on interviews with memorial guides, rape survivors, and observations from multiple memorial tours at each site, it offers analysis of how memorial staff and memorial materials deal with information about SGBV, and it sheds light on the complicated processes of remembering gendered violence. These remembrance practices occur within a particular historical moment in which rape survivors still exhibit secrecy and feel shame about the violence inflicted on them, telling few people (in cases of remarriage, sometimes not even their partners) and traveling long distances to remain anonymous when receiving much-needed medical and counseling services.[19] Those known as rape survivors in their communities report feeling ostracized or, at best, ignored, while others are even accused of "having sex with the enemy."

Memorials and SGBV

From an outsider's perspective, the absence of material regarding SGBV and its lasting impact on memorials may come as a surprise. On the

Gendered Violence

macro level, Rwanda is often regarded internationally as a model for gender equality in Africa. Leading the world in the percentage of women in parliament and the number of gender-inclusive policies, one could justifiably hypothesize that these forms of structural empowerment must translate into the centering of women's experiences in national memorial projects. However, my analysis of commemorative practices in Rwanda suggests that the macro progress of women in the political sphere does not necessarily trickle down into an inclusion of SGBV narratives in national memorials. While the government of Rwanda has championed women's empowerment and gender equity, it seems to have allowed their experiences to be written out of memorial narratives, likely because the nationalist story is one of women's power and importance, not victimization.[20]

During my work in Rwanda, I found that memorial sites serve to do one of three things: enforce existing silence about SGBV, disrupt that silence, or react with hesitance (combining the two by enforcing and responding to silence about SGBV at different points in time). These three interconnected dimensions depend upon the following: the focus or aim of the memorial, the presence of social services, and the use of physical evidence (including mass graves). As table 1 demonstrates, one of these dimensions alone is not sufficient for creating an environment in which discussions on SGBV take place: only sites with a combination of these factors create an environment where the silence can be broken.

These three seemingly gender-neutral dimensions of memorials—their focus (commemoration, reconciliation, or education), their use of physical evidence (blood on the walls, survivors' clothing, exposed remains, weapons), and the presence of survivor services (e.g., counseling, funds or resources for

Table 1. Dimensions of memorials related to gender-based violence

Memorial name	Focus of memorial	Presence of social services	Presence of physical evidence	Gender-based violence discussed
Center for Commemoration (CFC)	Commemoration	No	Yes	Yes
Center for Memory, Survivors, and Reconciliation (CMSR)	Reconciliation	Yes	No	No
Center for Genocide Prevention and Education (CGPE)	Education	Yes	Yes	Sometimes

rape survivors)—have distinctly gendered outcomes, particularly in terms of suppressing or facilitating national collective memories of SGBV. In analyzing these dimensions, I answer the question of why the three memorials in this study—the CFC; the CMSR; and the CGPE—vary so significantly in their approach to SGBV within a seemingly gender-friendly political climate. All three sites commemorating the 1994 genocide against the Tutsi are funded and supported by the national government and located within a short distance of one another. My analysis of the approach to SGBV at each site focuses on the mechanisms by which gendered silences are broken or sustained in each context.

Understanding the mechanisms by which silences about SGBV are broken or sustained is imperative in four central ways. First, collective memory scholars have argued that the past is structurally remembered and forgotten by those in positions of power, through institutions, politics, or educational pursuits. Creating a collective memory is a contested and stratifying process involving multiple, interconnected power dynamics. Memory projects, like truth commissions, can assist in healing cultural trauma and repairing a divided community or nation, by acknowledging those who have suffered in atrocities and allowing their voices to be heard.[21] While testimonies are often a central tool in disseminating and creating collective memories, scholars have argued that it is imperative to evaluate whose memories are shared, and where and how. While we know that collective memory processes are contested and often exclude or marginalize women, scholars in this line of work have rarely talked with *people* about memorials. In fact, we know too little about how memorials commemorating a violent past come to include certain stories and not others. The dynamics shaping this process are not yet understood at the micro level.

Second, because Rwanda is not the only case in which SGBV is forgotten and silenced, it is especially important to understand how this occurs on a micro level, paying particular attention to moments when the silence around SGBV is broken and in what context. A nation's collective memory has profound effects on its present and future. Because tour guides, survivors, and political leaders so rarely support or take part in discussions about SGBV, it is particularly important to understand the mechanisms that allow this powerful silence to be broken.

Third, in discussions on human rights, violence, and memory politics, universality is often invoked by policy makers, politicians, and even scholars to explain women's absence. The rhetoric of universality translates to a form of gender neutrality in which the dynamics of sexism, specific forms of violence, and acknowledgment of inequality are subsumed within generalized narratives about violence or human rights. Efforts to remain neutral in considerations of rights or rights abuses result in men's experiences being treated as the norm. As Catherine MacKinnon reminds us: "Human rights have not been women's rights—not in theory or in reality, not legally or socially, not domestically or internationally. Rights that human beings have by virtue of being human have not been rights to which women have had access, nor have violations of women as such been part of the definition of the violation of the human as such on which human rights law has traditionally been predicated."[22] Also left out of human rights considerations have been children, especially those already marginalized because they were conceived during rape.[23]

The rhetoric of universality and neutrality dominates the entire spectrum of human rights discourse, from legislation and education on basic human rights to actions concerning the protection of human rights, human rights abuses, and the prosecution and aftermath of rights violations. The memorials in Rwanda (and arguably elsewhere) are a lens through which to view how the continuum of gender neutrality endures in the aftermath of mass human rights violations. The mnemonic practices of some Rwandan memorials, though created with a commitment to commemorate those who died and those who survived, uphold the systematic exclusion of women evident in broader human rights discourse and implementation.[24]

Yet the silences and resistance to silence must be understood within a climate where multiple conflicting dynamics collide. More women occupy seats in Rwanda's parliament than in almost any other country in the world. More memorials per capita exist in Rwanda than in any other country witnessing comparable levels of violence. A ministry of gender has been in existence for over two decades and is dedicated to "gender equality and women's empowerment."[25] An entire government body was created with responsibility for memorials and commemorations. And in Rwanda, genocidal rape was a defining characteristic of the genocidal violence that tore the country apart. The convergence of all these factors might lead to the hypothesis that Rwanda would be the most likely country to make SGBV a central part of its remembrances of 1994—especially in public, nationally funded, and government memorial spaces. And indeed, by comparison to memorials in other countries, those in Rwanda may focus more on SGBV when commemorating the genocide. Yet even so, memory projects in Rwanda fail to consistently engage with accounts of SGBV during the 1994 genocide against the Tutsi. This fact suggests that the number of women in parliament and the existence of gender-friendly social policies may not necessarily serve as strong indicators of the centrality of SGBV, or even gender considerations on the whole, in national memorial projects.

Gender Dynamics of the 1994 Genocide against the Tutsi and Present-Day Gender Relations

The genocide in Rwanda was structured along gender divides in a number of significant ways. Gendercide, the active participation of women in perpetrating violence, and the gendered division of labor were all features of the genocide.[26] Perpetrators made use of traditional gender roles and stereotypes in inciting genocidal violence and encouraging the participation of particular groups. Drawing on misogynistic notions of manhood and masculinity for the recruitment and retention of participants in the violence, those orchestrating attacks created a climate in which SGBV became a tool to exterminate communities. In early propaganda campaigns, Tutsi women were depicted as "unattainable untrustworthy temptresses who would give birth to the inyenzi of the future."[27] Rape and gendered violence were used as tools not only to destroy the victims and their families but also to prove one's commitment to the genocidal movement and to traditional masculinity and femininity more generally.

The 1994 genocide against the Tutsi took place during a time of economic turmoil in Rwanda. The civil war from 1990 to 1993 had consumed the majority of the national budget, while agricultural production declined because of displaced people, poor weather, a plunge in coffee prices, and lack of public assistance.[28] As reports argue, prior to 1990, young men had several economic options, including clearing new farmland on hills, acquiring land from elders, migration, or obtaining employment either from wealthier people or through the formal civil sector. Because of national and international policies enacted in the early 1990s, such as fiscal constraints imposed by the World Bank and woefully inadequate government assistance for the poor, nearly all options for economic mobility or sustainability were extremely limited.[29] The inaccessibility of land to young men was significant because it prevented them from marrying, moving away from home, or increasing their social status and wealth. The government blamed these hardships, which the majority of rural Hutu men experienced, on Tutsi. Later these accusations were used to encourage the 1994 genocidal violence.[30]

During its recruitment of killers to attack Tutsi men (and later women) as well as "Hutu moderates," the genocidal regime referred to the killing as "work" and a job for "strong men," who needed to protect their families, nation, and prospects for future wealth.[31] Men who failed to participate in genocidal violence were called cowards on national radio, treated as traitors, and sometimes killed. Furthermore, Tutsi women were sexualized and denigrated in the propaganda campaigns, which warned of their manipulative and hyper-sexualized powers.[32] Any men who married or interacted with Tutsi women were considered traitors. This climate no doubt contributed to the rampant sexual violence, in which rape was framed as the "appropriate form of retribution for their [Tutsi women's] purported arrogance, immorality, hyper-sexuality, and espionage."[33] Rape was intended to destroy and humiliate the Tutsi population and their sympathizers, and to reclaim the masculinity that was threatened during the early 1990s by constraints on opportunities for economic autonomy and advancement, including the ability to build a traditional family.[34] While the specific root causes of rape may be impossible to identify, the contentious climate for gender roles in the early 1990s contributed to the gendered frames used to encourage and justify SGBV.

Survivors with whom I spoke emphasized that rape was used as a weapon to humiliate Tutsi women and men, and to ruin their lives if they survived the rape. For example, Ada explained, "Some women during the genocide, who tried to escape, at the barriers they were arrested and raped—or brought [to the perpetrator's home], for one or two month [*sic*], raped by several persons . . . rape was used as an instrument to humiliate women." SGBV was also used as a weapon to damage familial roles that had previously assured safety and security, especially when men were forced to rape the women they loved. Mihigo related that "during genocide, some men were forced to sleep with their own daughters, or other men were forced to sleep with their mothers during genocide. They still have that problem on their heart. . . . It can never be solved." Mihigo's story emphasizes that sexual violence was intentionally used to destroy familial bonds, to stymie feelings of masculinity or femininity, and to humiliate. Rape and other forms of SGBV were most commonly perpetrated in public spaces rather than in private homes to convey a message of terror and to further humiliate victims.[35] The feelings of shame after SGBV were often cited by survivors as the most destructive vestige of the violence.

Charity spoke of her friend "who was raped during genocide and she was impregnated, so she feels like that child, that she gave birth to [is] not her real child, because she was forced." Charity continued that her friend has "an inferior [*sic*] complex that everyone recognizes her [as someone] that was raped during the genocide." Angel emphasized that those who were raped were "damaged forever" and could not get married. As she explained it, "That is why many women did not tell anyone." Women I interviewed who had borne children out of rape would tell me about their children and their ages, and then explicitly state, "This one was born after the genocide." It was in these "meta-silences" that I would come to learn of both rape and forced pregnancies among participants (see the appendix for discussion on listening to silences when interviewing survivors of SGBV).[36]

Rape was also used as a means to kill. As Beth explained, "There is an intention of rape or sexual assault during genocide, because people were killed—and women raped in the same time period, and the intention was not just humiliation, but also to kill . . . sometimes slowly—several have HIV today." Neza emphasized, "The way rape or other sexual crimes were committed, it is in the same way people are killed with intent to destroy, intent to destroy the group." Because sexual violence during the 1994 genocide against the Tutsi held the same intent as murder (to annihilate families and communities), survivors hailed the judgments by the ICTR and ICTY that rape had been used as an international crime of genocide and a crime against humanity. These rulings had the effect of shifting the category of sexual violence during genocide to one of genocidal rape, which is a strategy of genocide and a crime against humanity.[37]

After large numbers of men had already been killed in the early phases of the genocidal violence, the highest-ranked officials commanded the rape and murder of girls and women.[38] Genocidal rape and SGBV has been documented in every prefecture of Rwanda, where women and girls of all ages were victimized.[39] Men were not spared sexual violence and torture, but far fewer survivors have come forward. In the case of Rwanda, as well as in other cases of genocide, rape was not simply a casualty or by-product of genocide but a strategic political tool and established policy.[40]

In the aftermath of this horrific violence, survivors of SGBV continue to experience trauma, shame, exclusion, and, in the case of those who became pregnant out of genocidal rape, ambivalent feelings toward their children, whose very presence serves as a reminder of the violence.[41] Scholars have found that impregnation from genocidal rape in Rwanda can often complicate the healing process as the child becomes a constant reminder of trauma and violation.[42] Some victims also experience physical challenges or sterility due to the mutilation and torture they experienced.[43]

Since the 1994 genocide against the Tutsi, Rwanda has been praised by both national and international institutions and leaders as a gender and development success story.[44] In 2003 Rwanda surpassed Sweden as the country with the highest percentage of women in its national legislature and maintained this position for several years.[45] In the last two decades, women in Rwanda have had increasing opportunities to serve in the national legislature and to participate in politics and leadership at all levels. Other changes have followed, including the development of a Ministry of Gender, a proliferation of women-led and women-serving NGOs and councils, and the passing of breakthrough legislation that ensures equal rights for women and other groups.[46]

Women's organizations in civil society have been incredibly productive and expansive, providing women and children with much-needed services and care. As Burnet explains, "While none of these changes happened overnight, women's organizations have indeed served the needs of thousands of individual women. The growth of women's organizations, as well as their mission to help the most vulnerable people in society (women and children), positioned them as among the most active sector of civil society between 1994 and 2003."[47] The impact could also be long-lasting: sociologists have demonstrated that increases in women's representation correlate to an increase in social policies, improvement in children's health through funding and legislation, and the passing of women-friendly policies more generally.[48]

While these welcome changes have produced tangible benefits for many Rwandan women, they were not as far-reaching as many had hoped, and they even created additional challenges. The engagement of women in the legislative, judicial, and executive branches of government had the unintended consequence of creating a leadership vacuum in local and regional organizations, whose women leaders left for government positions.[49] Burnet also found that some women in rural areas were not even aware of the existence of women's councils, initiatives, or development funds, and as a result, it is likely that rural communities have not benefited as much as they could have from these resources.[50] Furthermore, Timothy Longman cautions that "merely having women present in parliament does not mean that women's interests are truly represented."[51]

In my own interviews, participants often showcased with pride the legislative accomplishments of Rwanda when discussing gender equality but remarked that women still experience violence and an unequal division of labor within the home. For example, Louise, a woman in her late thirties, explained, "I have a very good job, a lot of power in my job to make changes for society, but you know what? When I come home, I still cook, and clean, and care for my babies the most. It is not equal in my home and that is the way it always was and my husband sees no problem with it." Louise's comment echoes Marie Berry's finding that "empowerment efforts and the rights women are granted in one social arena do not necessarily translate into women's increased power across all spheres."[52] While Rwanda's empowerment efforts mark a stark improvement over the conditions many women survived before, during, and immediately after the genocide, they also represent the limits of evaluating gender equity and equality through solely rights-based approaches.

Gendered Forgetting and Remembering

The three sites described in chapters 2 and 3, while sharing some patterns in their forms of remembrance (as seen in chapter 3), epitomize three different approaches to facing a past that includes SGBV: remembrance (disclosing narratives of SGBV), silence (the intentional institutional noninclusion of gendered violence that occurred during 1994 genocide against the Tutsi), and hesitance (intermittent disclosure despite reluctance). What puzzled me when observing tours at these three sites is that they were all funded and supported by a national government that includes a high percentage of women electorates, that they all commemorate the same event, and that they were all located within a short distance from one another. They also had other overlapping elements, such as services for rape survivors, space where evidence is housed, and mass burial sites. During observations and interviews, I became preoccupied with understanding what accounted for the significant variance in approaches to addressing SGBV. The answer to this question lies in the three sites' availability of material evidence of SGBV, the presence or absence of social services for rape survivors, and, most importantly, whether the site's focus was commemoration, education, or reconciliation.

A Site of Remembrance:
The Center for Commemoration

Ava, a memorial guide, led a group of Kenyan visitors through the CFC—a church-turned-memorial aimed at remembering the five thousand people killed there in 1994. Ava showed the visitors what remained of the former place of worship, detailing how women and children fled to this church for refuge, only to be killed in the most brutal ways. She called the visitors' attention to the spears and pointed sticks displayed on the walls, explaining that these weapons were used to publicly torture women. She further described how women were victims of specific forms of violence, such as mass rape, and emphasized that those who survived endure particular challenges, such as trauma, bearing children out of rape, physical disabilities, and AIDS.[53]

Today, the CFC emphasizes in situ evidence, with much of the destruction from 1994 left intact. The weapons used to torture women are on display, the wall at which babies were thrown to their death remains stained with blood, and bones line the former pews. At the CFC, visitors are meant to feel horrified by the brutality that was used against women, children, and infants. Visitors who see so many bones on display and piles of clothes from the rural village can begin to imagine the magnitude of the 1994 genocide against the Tutsi.

They learn about how the *genocidaires* used grenades, manipulated churches to act as false safety zones, and took innocent lives.

During the period of genocidal violence, in the village where the CFC is now located, women and men were generally separated, with mostly women and children gathering in the local church and surrounding area and men retreating to the hills to fend off perpetrators. However, after several days of warding off the militia, the men on the hills miscalculated the route the perpetrators would take, and while they stood watch on a nearby hill, the militia bombarded the women and children in the village—many of whom sought refuge in the church. Within the church compound, women and children witnessed and experienced horrific forms of violence: sexual assault, rape with foreign objects, mutilation (including the mutilation of pregnant women), the killing of fetuses, torture, and the throwing of infants to their deaths against church walls.

Unlike the other two memorial sites chosen for this book, the CFC is the only one where guides consistently included stories of SGBV in their tours. Memorial guides at the other sites often cited a lack of available testimony as one of the main reasons for the exclusion. Although the CFC lacked live testimony—that is, rape survivors willing to share their experience with visitors either in person or on video—guides used other resources, such as evidence of sexualized violence, to illuminate and facilitate the telling of such stories.

The murder and torture weapons and blood stains on the pews and walls at the CFC preserve the site's history and form an essential part of the tour; in many instances, this "evidence" has the function of initiating discussions about the violence that was inflicted on women, children, and some men. Guides explained to visitors, "You see over there, we have the sticks that were used to injure women's private areas, we kept the blood where babies were thrown in front of their mothers, over there." Habinana, a guide, then discussed how rape was used as a weapon to terrorize the community and humiliate women and children who were manipulated into congregating in one specific area, making it easier for perpetrators to kill them. Habinana also told me that once he has described what happened in this space, visitors often ask about the aftermath: "This gives me a chance to talk about AIDS, the widows, what is still happening in our village."

While the use of evidence to facilitate discussions only occurred at one site, guides at all three sites reported that supplementing historical information with physical objects from the past is the ideal way to pay tribute. Claudine, another guide, explained, "The best way to honor and share about these horrible things is to maintain the facts, the evidence that is right here." At the

CFC, the presence of evidence, a product of the site's focus on commemoration, aided those having difficult conversations about SGBV.

A Site of Silence: The Center for Memory, Survivors, and Reconciliation

At the CMSR, Oliver, a senior guide, directed a group of visitors through the memorial, explaining that people were murdered when UN soldiers abandoned the site in April 1994 during a moment of peak genocidal violence. Visitors looked up at the wall of names, bearing witness to those who were murdered. Visitors with their heads bent solemnly downward stood silently by the mass graves as Oliver shared the story of those who were killed in the very location where visitors stood: perpetrators killed victims with machetes, guns, and ultimately, grenades. He went on to describe the aftermath of the genocide: children were orphaned, schools lay in shambles, the entire societal structure was decimated, and human remains lined the roads. The remains of victims' loved ones were exposed "everywhere" whenever it rained for the first decade or more, washing away the little dirt that covered bodies, Oliver explained. Dirt was intentionally placed over bodies in a hurry, either by perpetrators to hide their crimes or by survivors and other victims in efforts to give their loved ones whatever ounce of a proper burial they were able to provide in the midst of trying to escape violence and save others.

Visitors would learn how the inaction and failures of the UN and the international community led to the death of thousands on the very land where they now walked. Visitors were encouraged to feel angry at the ineffectiveness of the international community in stopping the 1994 genocide. Oliver detailed how perpetrators roamed the streets and escaped to neighboring countries, and how Rwanda brought them to justice through a variety of courts and legal pursuits, including Gacaca and the ICTR. After expressing how Rwandans as a whole still suffered but were "heading in a good direction," he ended the tour, letting visitors look around.[54] Oliver is notably proud of Rwanda, and the picture painted in Western newspapers in 1994 of an underdeveloped country with "warring tribes" is a far cry from the Rwanda Oliver knows, where SUVs speed down paved roads to the suburbs and the economy is one of the fastest growing in Central Africa.[55]

During the tour described here, Oliver, like other memorial guides observed at this site, rarely if ever mentioned the aftermath of SGBV, including trauma, shame, children born out of rape (an estimated twenty thousand), or sexually transmitted diseases, such as HIV/AIDS.[56] It is particularly perplexing that this silence persists at a site dedicated to providing daily tours and a number of services to survivors, including counseling and support groups specifically for rape survivors and a variety of reconciliation programs. In fact, rape survivors come from all over the country to this very site to obtain services that include group and individual counseling and advice from employees who aid survivors in navigating various survivor resource networks and programs for medical care and legal assistance.

The central reasons for overlooking this particular aspect of genocidal violence and its aftermath, according to Carene, a memorial guide in her thirties, were the lack of available testimonies from rape survivors and an effort to appear gender-neutral on issues related to the genocidal violence. Bisangwa, a guide at CMSR, bluntly stated that he never discusses rape or SGBV on the tours because "we don't have any testimonies to share here about that." Survivors from this site provided testimony about how they had hidden, buried bodies, or been abandoned by international organizations, but as in other communities throughout the country (and arguably the world), few survivors of SGBV are willing to share their stories in public.

Other guides and memorial workers explained that the 1994 genocide against the Tutsi affected both men and women, and that women should not get their "own special ceremony." Here, men's experiences are considered the norm. Guides argued that women and men both deserved recognition for what they went through and, since the end result for most of them was death, what caused that death was unimportant. For example, as Clause said, "When you are dead you are dead. It doesn't matter what happened before that, because both people end up dead and their families end up alone." Here, Clause reflects on how both families "end up alone," whether or not gendered violence occurred prior to death. Another guide stated frankly, "If you died naked or you died burnt, you are still dead." Since rape and gendered torture here are not considered distinct experiences—or counted as experiences at all when the end result is death—the pervasive experience of gendered violence is silenced, subsumed under what is seen as the more important frame: killing and death.

This emphasis on gender neutrality impacted stories of SGBV not only among the dead but also among the living. In the view of some survivors, albeit not many, it was unproductive to detail in public the problems that widows and women faced, "because every survivor has problems, and we don't need to explain all of them all the time." Often within the same response, participants acknowledged the high rate of HIV/AIDS for women genocide survivors and balanced such challenges against those of men who had lost their families and continued to suffer. Sonia, a guide and survivor, said that since "both men and women experienced violation, some men had their privates cut apart, so if you discuss one example, we have so many to discuss and that is not always possible." This argument that gendered violence should only be acknowledged if men and women are both discussed as experiencing equal destruction results in the silencing of SGBV narratives of all kinds.

The CMSR's focus on reconciliation in its programs and narratives further influences the disclosure of stories about rape and sexual violence. Mutuzo shared that "rape and all of those horrible things are the hardest to forget, sometimes forgiving those crimes is not possible." Because the memorial emphasizes reconciliation among Rwandans, in both its programs and narratives of UN culpability, avoiding mention of crimes against women and children may be strategically intended to facilitate reconciliation and promote Rwandan progress. SGBV holds a unique place in survivors' (and visitors') minds, as Mutuzo's comment suggests, because of sexual assault's ability to not only transmit lethal diseases but also symbolically destroy the family and nation. It is precisely the brutality of these crimes and the lack of language available to discuss rape and torture that make silence over this particular aspect of the past a desirable choice for CMSR. Naming the most "unforgiveable crimes" could endanger reconciliation and the legitimacy of their reconciliatory programs. Here, the physical and historical dynamics of the site, the tours of the grounds and discussions with visitors about UN abandonment, take precedent over the social services on site such as rape survivor counseling groups and resources for HIV/AIDS survivors, and that factor leads to silence around SGBV.

A Site of Resistant Disclosure:
The Center for Genocide Prevention
and Education

During one of my visits to the CGPE, Jean Claude, one of the senior memorial guides, escorted a tour of visitors through the site. He described the upcoming projects for the memorial, including an expansion of the archives, a mobile education program that can travel to rural areas, and an increase in funding for the social program. Jean Claude then paused and asked the visitors if they had any questions. A visitor raised her hand and asked, "What does the social program do?" Jean Claude responded, "During the genocide, many women were raped. Because of this, those who survived can have AIDS, or many problems. Our social program aims to help those women, one family at a time."[57]

The CGPE is one of the most frequently visited memorials in Rwanda. On display is a detailed history of Rwanda, the 1994 genocide against the Tutsi, and its aftermath. It houses the remains of thousands of victims and written testimonies about the mass graves discovered in the area. Unlike the CFC, which consistently commemorates SGBV, or the CMSR, which does not, the CGPE occasionally makes direct and indirect references to SGBV. During a visit to CGPE, information on SGBV was most often verbally discussed during a guided tour. The brevity of Jean Claude's description of the social program was intentional, designed to encourage visitors to ask questions. This is a technique that several memorial guides use as an "appropriate way" to incorporate information on SGBV. The CMSR and Jean Claude's memorial, the CGPE, both have a "social program," but only the CGPE uses the program as a mechanism to discuss SGBV and its aftermath. Social programs at both sites assist widows or female orphans who are HIV positive as a result of genocidal rape. The program at the CGPE helps a small group of women or a couple of families by assisting them financially with HIV medication, job training, and counseling. As Nadege stated, "The social program is most especially for the ladies who were raped in the genocide, up to now if they can be able to talk about that experience, and they can get things which help them to be healed."

For this memorial site, social programs not only assist the families who are the direct recipients of such services; these programs also help launch discussions about SGBV with visitors to the memorial. Emmanuel, one of the supervisors at the CGPE, when asked how guides discuss SGBV if they choose to do so, responded, "They [the guides] don't talk about it [rape] specifically, but they do talk about the social program." I inquired further about how social programs help elucidate SGBV to memorial attendees, and he responded: "We can say, 'We have a program that helps vulnerable people,' and the students ask, 'What makes someone vulnerable?' and one way is HIV contracted through rape." While discussing the creation, implementation, or upkeep of the memorial, guides described to tour participants some aspects of social service programs beyond the traditional bounds of remembrance rituals and events, focusing on the specific program that assists rape survivors. Therese revealed that they tell visitors about how the memorial has some "programs for ladies who have troubles," and memorial attendees respond by asking, "Why do you have a program for ladies? What are their troubles?" and that question gives the guide the opportunity to say, "Many ladies were raped during the genocide and it caused this and that and then I explain more." In this way, the social programs offer memorial guides a chance to include factual information about the aftermath of SGBV in the form of answering a question, which absolves them of the responsibility to initiate such difficult conversations. As tour guides revealed, it also helped them to keep their references to SGBV broad: "We don't talk about [SGBV] specifically, but we just do it in general terms." This means that "sometimes I mention about the aftermath of genocide, like HIV, widows, orphans, vulnerable people." For guides, references to HIV, widows, and vulnerable people within the context of genocide's aftermath function as codes for sexual violence, allowing them to refer to SGBV without explicitly identifying it. Guides say they feel more at ease when they can address violence in "less direct" terms, through a description of health and social aftereffects.

This notion of the generalizability of violence highlights how guides consider certain types of violence as appropriate or inappropriate within the limits of public discourse. Understanding certain types of violence as appropriate (i.e., nonsexual physical violence) and others as inappropriate (i.e., sexual violence), they develop coded language to address SGBV, such as framing it in health-related terms with reference to HIV/AIDS. Additionally, directing attention to the "problems of trauma" among women survivors provides another opportunity for attendees to ask questions about SGBV.

Those at the CGPE who did not discuss SGBV revealed that in large part their reason was a lack of available live narratives about this experience. Guides have a general script they follow in the tour, but they also have a choice regarding which details they include, and some of them described their decision-making around discussing SGBV. For example, Jean Bosco explained that it depends on the degree to which the people he is guiding appear to be receptive to such information: "I look to see if the visitor is ready to hear about that stuff, if not, then I don't elaborate on how people got HIV." Jean Bosco's statement exemplifies the hesitancy that was a defining feature at this site. Narratives of SGBV occupy a precarious position at CGPE, where guides rely on the audience to ask specific questions or "look" as if they are receptive to such stories; this approach is emblematic of the reluctance to break the silence around violent sexual crimes.

These three memorial sites' foci fundamentally influenced whether and how gendered violence is remembered, forgotten, or shrouded in partial silences. By analyzing the dimensions and processes that shape whether and how SGBV is included in discussions of the past, we can begin to see how collective memory is generated and how that process drives gender considerations to the margins. The memorials that focus on education and commemoration, for example, are significantly more likely to discuss SGBV by drawing on the evidence housed in the memorial or social programs for rape survivors. However, unlike the CFC, the disclosure of genocide narratives that include SGBV at the CGPE is wholly contingent upon visitor questions. Stories of gendered violence remained untold unless a visitor asked about them directly—even when the structure was in place to encourage these types of questions. At the CMSR, by contrast, in order to maintain a focus toward reconciliation, a rhetorical divide was created between a past of SGBV and Rwanda's bright future, imposing a silence on stories of rape, gendered torture, and its aftermath. This silence, intended to make reconciliation more attainable, was grounded in the idea that confronting the past should be gender neutral.

While each memorial site's focus was the driving force in shaping how it addressed gendered violence, other factors were also at play: the presence or absence of social programs, whether those social programs were discussed during tours, and whether displaying evidence played a central role in advancing the memorial's aims. All these variables, however, function within a dialectical interaction between the guides themselves and the memorials at which they work, for, while they follow a semistructured script written by the memorial staff and the national supervising commission, guides also have agency in deciding what to prioritize when talking to the public. Although we may not see much variation in tours within a specific genre of memorial (e.g., commemoration or reconciliation), this could change over time with a societal- and cultural-level shift in discussions of SGBV.

Why does sharing narratives of SGBV matter? Because memorials and memory culture play such vital roles in present-day Rwanda, these stories determine whether women's experiences of victimization and survival are included in the larger collective memory of the 1994 genocide against the Tutsi. In writing of her 1993 visit to the US Holocaust Museum to research women's experience of genocide, Andrea Dworkin describes the harmful effects of excluding women's experiences:

> Women were apparently neither known nor unknown, a common enough condition but no less heartbreaking for that. . . . In the museum, the story of women is missing. . . . [Perpetrators of genocide] do not ignore the specific meaning or presence of women, nor how to stigmatize or physically hurt women as such, nor do those who commit genocide forget that to destroy a people, one must destroy the women. So how can this museum, dedicated to memory, forget to say what happened to Jewish women? If this genocide is unique, then what happened to Jewish women was unique; attention must be paid. If not here, where?[58]

As Dworkin elucidates, Rwandan memorials have had few models on which to base an inclusion of women in stories of genocide. While the specific details of the memorials described in this chapter may be unique to Rwanda, mass rape and SGBV during war and genocide are not, for we know that these gendered dynamics occur in every studied war and genocide.[59] However, by understanding how these acts of gendered terrorism are remembered or forgotten sheds light on gender roles after social change and extreme violence generally, across diverse cases in the US, the Balkans, or Sudan.[60] The instances of defiance in the face of these silences provide us important contexts to analyze, in which women's absences are disrupted using the memorial and museum physical space (such as the use of evidence) or services provided within the memorial.

Understanding the processes by which SGBV becomes marginalized in survivor narratives, and also the ways in which some have resisted that marginalization, has important implications for other postconflict zones. Knowing how silences around SGBV can be broken could help countries that are seeking to commemorate a more expansive version of violence and the aftermath of mass atrocity. However, investing in the inclusion of SGBV in a nation's collective memory requires analysis of institutional, cultural, and social power dynamics that make the public disclosure of SGBV challenging at best.

Memorials are important spaces and symbols of healing that provide an opportunity for survivors—loved ones and strangers alike—to bear witness to those who died. They are "a gesture of defiance and resistance against the absorption into the present and against the desire to forget or conceal."[61] The goal of genocide is to leave none to tell the story, but memorials, even though their versions of the past are incomplete and designed to promote those in power, "resist the solvent-like power of time and becoming, to attempt to ensure the persistence of a truth, of justice, of a person and to work . . . against death by denying its capacity to reduce all to utter silence and unending absence."[62] Silence around SGBV reaffirms genocide's power as a type of violence that "drives a wedge through a community, . . . shatter[s] a society [and] destroy[s] a people."[63] Silences, along with other social processes that stratify collective memory, have profound effects on reconciliation efforts, which are the subject of the next chapter.

Gendered Violence

6

Survivors' Lived Experiences of Reconciliation

In a village outside the capital city, a CHH community resides across the road from a memorial. Charity, who was orphaned as a child, now lives with her brother and daughters three homes down from one of the individuals who perpetrated violence in her village during the genocide. The perpetrator was released from prison years ago, when the prisons were overcrowded, and he now lives in the home where he lived before the genocide. During my first interview with Charity, I asked what "reconciliation" meant to her. In answering, Charity explained that the perpetrators must verbalize their understanding of the wrongs they have committed, sharing any information that would aide in finding missing persons (or missing persons' remains), and ask for forgiveness. In turn, the victims can choose whether they will grant forgiveness. Given her detailed explanation of this process and her assurance earlier in our conversation that reconciliation is occurring in Rwanda today, I assumed that Charity had experienced such a process. But I was wrong. "Has this happened to you, Charity?" I (NF) asked. "No," she answered.

NF: Have you witnessed this process?
CHARITY: No.
NF: Did anyone you know experience this process?
CHARITY: No.
NF: If this has not happened, and you feel reconciliation is still occurring, then what does reconciliation mean to you? What does it look like?

Charity gave me a very different answer this time. "My neighbor will take me to the hospital if I need to go, even if he is a different ethnicity than me . . .

and there are no longer laws about education [quotas or extra exams for certain ethnicities]."

Despite her initial affirmation of what I call "the reconciliation formula," Charity admits to a lived experience of reconciliation that does not conform to the process she had so carefully outlined.[1] In her lived experience, she finds evidence of reconciliation in different ethnic groups coexisting without violence. Charity's various articulations of the meaning of reconciliation reflect two key aspects of the lived everyday experiences of this ambiguous (and often contested) process in Rwanda: (1) a macro-level state-supported narrative, experienced by few, that depicts a utopian vision of what reconciliation should look like; and (2) a micro-level description of the more mundane ways that people experience reconciliation and interethnic coexistence on a daily basis.[2] While the macro narrative was typically the first one that respondents shared in my interviews, the second, more nuanced description of reconciliation usually emerged later in the course of more in-depth questioning, subsequent interviews, and my observations of their daily lives.[3]

This chapter examines this incongruity between Rwandans' ideal and everyday experiences of reconciliation. Like Charity, most survivors I interviewed said that they believed reconciliation was occurring in present-day Rwanda, and they recited the same "reconciliation formula," in which perpetrators admitted wrongdoing and asked for (and received) forgiveness. Yet, also like Charity, most of the survivors I interviewed had not seen this process in practice. In fact, none of them had personally experienced it, and only one participant had witnessed a version of this process after a gacaca trial.[4] This discordance between stated ideal and lived reality pushed me to inquire more deeply about the lived experiences of reconciliation. What did these experiences look, feel, and sound like in their everyday lives? How did their utopian vision of reconciliation interact with (or undermine) their lived experience? I asked survivors questions such as: What does reconciliation mean to you? How do you know when that is occurring? Is reconciliation, in any form, taking place here in Rwanda? Are you experiencing it? How does it feel? Who experiences reconciliation? Does it happen every day? Is it one big event? Can you give me instances of reconciliation that you have witnessed or experienced? Can you think of any examples of reconciliation that you wish would take place? In addition, I asked survivors about this "reconciliation formula," which emerged as a dominant theme in sixty respondent interviews. Do you believe this could happen someday? If this process were to happen, I asked, what would it provide you with that you do not have now? What are your hopes for this process?

This chapter focuses on how survivors narrate their everyday experiences of reconciliation. As suggested here, their answers fall into two broad categories:

a one-size-fits-all reconciliation ideal, in which reconciliation is defined by its end product (social harmony), and a micro-level description of reconciliation as a series of peaceful social interactions between ethnic groups in which reconciliation is a daily process. Yet I do not mean to suggest that the latter is the more "correct" definition of reconciliation and the former merely a state narrative that is meaningless to everyday people. To the contrary, I argue that both narratives of reconciliation are central to survivors' understandings and experiences of reconciliation in Rwanda today.

In this chapter, I examine these narratives of reconciliation and their multiple meanings for survivors in postgenocide Rwanda. Reconciliation is an extraordinarily complex social phenomenon. The seventy-two survivors I interviewed found themselves navigating between competing narratives of reconciliation and revising their articulations and understandings of these narratives (sometimes dramatically) over time. Attending to the nuance of the reconciliation process exposes how lived experiences are intertwined with a macro formulaic ideal and how the macro is connected to everyday interactions that signal coexistence for survivors.

Conceptualizing Reconciliation through Top-Down, Bottom-Up, and Narrative Analyses

Governments, international nongovernmental organizations (INGOs), and international organizations, such as the UN and World Bank, have developed a range of mechanisms to quantify reconciliation in order to make decisions about aid, policy, and other forms of intervention. These top-down approaches generally rely on large quantitative data sets. For example, the Global Peace Index (GPI) measures twenty-three indicators of safety and absence of violence (often called "negative peace") across 163 nations, allowing researchers to document and compare nations' "internal peacefulness" as well as their "external peacefulness."[5] In addition, the Human Development Index (HDI), used by the UN, synthesizes various indicators of population health, such as life expectancy, expected years of education, and overall standard of living.[6] By documenting changes in these dimensions of population health over time, particularly during reconciliation, researchers can track the often uneven success of reconciliation efforts.[7]

In recent years, researchers have developed more nuanced measurements of conflict and resolution through large-scale geotemporal datasets that disaggregate event-level conflicts. The two leading datasets in this vein are the Uppsala Conflict Data Program's Georeferenced Event Dataset (UCDP GED) and the

Armed Conflict Location and Event Data Project (ACLED).[8] Unlike the GPI and the HDI, these meso-level data allow researchers to measure the degree of violence against certain actors (i.e., civilians or military troops) as well as identify spatial-temporal patterns of where and when violence is likely to occur.

National reconciliation barometers capture another angle by using public opinion to measure reconciliation efforts.[9] By surveying marginalized groups (such as Aboriginals in Australia and people of color in South Africa) about their views on interracial and interethnic tensions, these tools reflect reconciliation from the perspectives of those who are living through it on the ground.[10] A benefit of reconciliation barometers is that these surveys can be adapted for individual countries and specific localities.

Taken together, these measures of peace, violence, and reconciliation provide an important, though partial, view of these dynamics. Indeed, any effort to measure social phenomena as complex as reconciliation will necessarily fall short. In particular, scholars note, top-down measures "do little to tell us what actual implications these events have on the relative peace and stability of a community, nor do they tell us about how these events have been perceived by communities, which may be a more accurate predictor of future events."[11] In recognition of this shortcoming, researchers and policymakers have called for more human-focused and locally situated analyses of peacebuilding and have recently begun to concentrate more on how those experiencing reconciliation measure coexistence in their own locales.[12]

Such measurements can be helpful in assessing events and opinions related to peace and conflict at the state and substate levels. Without speaking to individuals on the ground who are striving to live in peace after atrocity, top-down measurements provide only a broad picture of what is occurring and who is experiencing it, missing some of the nuances. In recent years, the growing recognition of this disconnect between the macro and the micro has brought an important shift in peace studies and peacebuilding programs toward a focus on local and bottom-up approaches.[13]

In this vein, Firchow and colleagues have developed what they call "Everyday Peace Indicators" (EPI), which measure community peace and conflict through markers such as everyday intergroup social interactions and feelings of safety and security.[14] Thus, as a measurement tool, the EPI differs markedly from those used by state officials and international organizations. Yet studies suggest that EPIs are often accurate and measure everyday interactions that have been shown to help prevent community violence.[15]

Building on the concept of EPIs makes it possible to focus this analysis on survivors' meanings and experiences of reconciliation. In fact, Charity's second definition of reconciliation—that her neighbor would take her to the hospital if she had an emergency—would qualify as an EPI that contributes to the peacebuilding processes. But rather than seeking to measure such processes, in this chapter I examine what they mean for survivors. This approach entails taking seriously survivors' stories: their (sometimes differing) narratives of reconciliation, their engagement with these narratives over time, and the varying impacts of these narratives on survivors' lives across different locations. In short, I focus on survivors' narratives of reconciliation because of the power stories hold for individuals and nation-states alike.[16]

After mass violence, nations create new national identities to foster citizen solidarity. Nations do this through stories that ultimately shape social policy, legal governance, and future peace and conflict. Benedict Anderson famously termed this process the creation of "imagined communities," referring to the social construction of a sense of community, imagined through nationalist projects.[17] The stories that are constructed after conflict are central to nation-building and, as illustrated in chapter 3, nation-building stories have the power to unify as well as divide. The government of Rwanda propagates an idealized narrative of the nation as a country that has accomplished the impossible—transitioned from genocide to stability—and in the process demonstrated it is a nation worth investing in, both financially and ideologically (see chapter 1).

But these stories also matter to the individuals who are struggling to reinvent themselves after extreme trauma.[18] Stories can constitute a "socially acceptable self."[19] Sociologists have argued that people often tell stories that fit some manner of cultural prototype.[20] Individuals narrate stories about their lives in ways that others can easily understand, often applying discernable formulas. Stories that become dominant and familiar are usually the ones that best mesh with a society's deeply held ideological values and norms. In many ways, formulas provide far more socially acceptable story lines than the everyday complexity and messiness of reconciliation, in which some can forgive and some cannot, especially during the mourning period, when emotions are raw.[21]

The reconciliation formula is compelling because we want to believe that people are capable of forgiveness and change, that those who killed can make things right, and that victims can live on in peaceful communities after war and mass atrocity. Genocide survivors may feel pressure to model and embrace decipherable aspects of restorative justice and forgiveness that are hailed by the government and others as pathways to reconciliation. The Rwandan gacaca courts, although their effectiveness is contested, were renowned for their truth-telling properties and restorative practices (e.g., having a perpetrator repair the home of a victim).[22] The promise of such practices, including finding out where loved ones' remains are buried, has deeply penetrated Rwandan society, and the vast majority of survivors I interviewed had attended a gacaca hearing in their community.[23]

The timing of a story also has power. Scholars of collective memory have demonstrated that the past is socially constructed, narrated through the lens of the present and representing contemporary interests and motivations.[24] At the time of my interviews, Rwanda was approaching the twentieth anniversary of the 1994 genocide against the Tutsi, and a central question of this moment was whether and how the country had fared at reconciling.[25] The success or failure of the reconciliation formula impacts Rwanda's image, affecting aid, development, and tourism. In telling this narrative—especially to a white foreigner such as myself—survivors emphasize a pathway to reconciliation, one that contributes to both national development and security.

I approach reconciliation as a dynamic process to be understood through narratives about lived experiences. This includes narratives that permeate the lived experience but never actually materialize as well as the micro-level mundane interactions of coexistence that may become concrete markers of social change. I begin now with the stories that center on the reconciliation formula, before turning to micro-experiences of reconciliation.

Macro Reconciliation: A Formulaic Ideal

Stories about the reconciliation formula in Rwanda—told by survivors, the Rwandan government, and Western reporters—powerfully infiltrate broader ideas about reconciliation among the survivors with whom I spoke. Survivors who have never seen this ideal come to fruition nevertheless describe its power to heal Rwanda's scars from the genocide. A small number of them, however, said that they did not believe that this idealized vision— even if it occurred—could achieve social harmony. Yet, even these individuals invoked the formula as they conceptualized the process of reconciliation. Elie, for example, initially laid out the reconciliation formula in much the same way Charity did, and like Charity and the others I interviewed, he had never actually experienced what he described. But unlike Charity, he expressed disappointment that the man who had killed his father had not confessed and asked for his forgiveness, even though later in the interview he said that he would not have forgiven the man anyway. In his words, forgiveness "wouldn't bring my father back . . . it wouldn't bring my childhood back." The formula was thus important to Elie not because it mirrored his reality, but because it gave him a sense of agency over the violence committed against his family. According to the formula, he could have pardoned the killer, but he would have refused. Yet, as time passed, the distance between the formulaic ideal and Elie's reality left him feeling increasingly frustrated: his sense of agency was slowly being replaced with disillusionment.

Despite the rarity of survivors such as Elie and Charity experiencing reconciliation according to the formula, this utopian vision of reconciliation dominated survivors' descriptions across various memorial sites. For instance, Patrick, who lived down the road from the CFC, said, "The most important thing about memorials is that it makes perpetrators think about what they did, and then they can ask for forgiveness from victims, and then victims accept forgiveness and then they can reunite again, and they live together." Robert, who worked at the CMSR, similarly stated, "When perpetrators visit these memorials, that's where they can see what happened and what they did. That's how heavy it was or how difficult it was, and they can come over and they ask for forgiveness from victims. And if they're forgiven, then they can live together with the victims, which is a sign of reconciliation and unity in Rwanda." Nadege, a guide at the CGPE, explains, "On the side of the perpetrator . . . a memorial is one sign to show of what he did. The perpetrators accept of what they did, and even the victims accept and forgive, feels what those people did to them. So, memorials play a very good role in unity and reconciliation." Like Patrick, Robert, and Nadege, survivors who described the reconciliation formula stated that they had not experienced or witnessed this process, nor did they know of someone who had. What, then, is so compelling about this story? Why is it shared by survivors across social locations and physical sites?

One central reason is that this narrative has been supported by the Rwandan government and the global community. From the Rwandan government's perspective, the formula offers closure for perpetrators and victims alike, along with the prospect of social harmony. From the global community's perspective, the formula represents a means of resolving some of the guilt over international inaction.[26] Beyond the West's investment in the formula, the appeal of this tale of triumph after mass human rights violations is not lost on the government of Rwanda. Reconciliation formulas tied to state-led liberation movements can be found in a range of political projects after conflicts and often serve as mechanisms to reproduce and consolidate present-day state power.[27] In her work on South Africa's Truth and Reconciliation Commission, Claire Moon explains that reconciliation, as a narrative of forgiveness and national healing, legitimizes "certain political decisions (amnesty) and proscribes others (such as punishment), and brings into being particular protagonists (or subjects and agents, namely victims and perpetrators) as central to that story."[28] In Rwanda, too, the reconciliation formula offers a government-supported pathway to social harmony, securing the legitimacy of the present-day regime.

The forgiveness piece in particular reifies two distinct subjects, victim and perpetrator, reducing social actors to one of two labels and anticipating a single ending: social harmony.[29]

But individuals also find meaning in this formula and see it as more than just state propaganda. Embracing this utopian ideal—which unlike the everyday complexities of micro reconciliation offers hope and simplicity—gives some survivors a sense of agency. This vision of reconciliation is so omnipresent in survivors' lives that it informs their feelings about the past and their expectations of the future. As the quotes below about the formula's ingredients suggest, even though the reconciliation formula may give survivors hope for the future, it could also do damage if reconciliation fails.

Step One: Perpetrator Admits Guilt and Tells the Truth

The first ingredient of the reconciliation formula is the act of truth-telling on the part of perpetrators, which usually means telling survivors how their loved ones died, what their last words were, and where their remains are located. In Charity's case, for example, such truth-telling would mean an apology from the man who killed her husband and knowledge of where her husband's remains were left. Theo, a young man who survived the genocide when he was five years old, also holds out hope that one day he will learn where his mother's and father's remains are located: "I still have hope that one day I will know what happened to them and where they are." As Theo explained, "The foundation for reconciliation is understanding what happened."

Survivors find themselves especially frustrated and unable to move on when they haven't learned the truth about what happened to their loved ones. Keza, an older woman at the CFC, explains, "Reconciliation is important, but I never saw anyone come out and say, 'Please forgive me, I did this.' It would be more helpful if someone comes and says, 'Please forgive me,' and at least he or she shows you where the remains of the one he killed are, so that you can collect them and bury them. But no one did that, so people are still looking for those remains and waiting for them." Bisangwa said that if the formula occurs, victims are allowed to ask, as part of the forgiveness process, for facts about their loved ones' deaths, such as "their last words, where they are buried, or how they died." These details are thought to mitigate the survivors' pain.

Step Two: The Perpetrator Seeks Forgiveness

The promise of forgiveness, deeply intertwined with truth-telling, means that the pain survivors endure is publicly recognized when perpetrators seek their pardon. The choice to forgive is a unique opportunity for power and agency because the survivor can decide whether or not to pardon the perpetrator. In this imagined scenario, survivors have control over a situation in which until now they have had very little; if they do forgive, they are lauded by the government and fellow citizens as heroes who have made great sacrifices for their country by helping to rebuild a harmonious society.

Those survivors who have not been asked for forgiveness often feel deep disappointment and rage at having had no one come forward after all they have endured. These feelings are predominately expressed among young survivors, female survivors, and victims of significant loss. Many of them experienced the death of a spouse, parent, child, or multiple extended family members and/or rape or extreme physical injury (such as the loss of a limb). Carene cried as she explained, "No one has asked for my forgiveness." As Audrey put it, "How then can you forgive someone who didn't come to ask for forgiveness?"

The devastation experienced by female survivors is particularly acute, exacerbated by high levels of poverty and trauma. Younger survivors are also hit especially hard and express anger that they were "robbed of their childhood." These survivors belong to the same demographic groups that are marginalized in collective memory practices (see chapter 4) and neglected as a result of stratification of collective memory. The reconciliation formula replicates this stratification, leaving survivors on the lowest end of the social order to suffer the most when hopes of truth and reconciliation fail to materialize.

Step Three: Pardoning Perpetrators

The reconciliation formula situates social harmony as the end product of a linear progression in which pardoning perpetrators is the final step. And survivors who believe they may be given the option of forgiving can hope that they will gain much needed narrative closure.[30] Yet such closure remains elusive for the vast majority of them. Martha Minow argues that closure isn't always possible for victims of severe human rights abuses, and "even if it were, any closure would insult those whose lives are forever ruptured. Even to speak, to grope for words to describe horrific events, is to pretend to negate their unspeakable qualities and effects. Yet silence is also an unacceptable offense, a shocking implication that the perpetrators in fact succeeded."[31] The complexity and difficulty of moving forward, captured by Minow, is theoretically obscured in this simplified three-step formula, which offers a seemingly clear path out of the apocalyptic grief that was precipitated by the 1994 genocide against the Tutsi.

While many survivors imagine the good that might come from apologies, information, and forgiveness, women at all three sites struggle to even imagine pardoning perpetrators, even if they were to tell the truth, admit guilt, and ask for forgiveness. Amahoro, a woman in her forties, explained, "Forgiveness wouldn't change anything," for "it wouldn't bring back my husband or children or fix my house or life." Ava, a young woman at the CFC, echoed this sentiment, stating that forgiveness "had no point," and people only forgive "because of the government." Neza, at the CGPE, also characterized forgiveness as a government policy. She said, "No one came to me to say, 'Hey, I'm so sorry that you haven't been able to find this—or this person from your family. Let me show you where he is or she is.' And you ask me to reconcile with who? Why should I? Why should I—why? Is there any reason that I have? So, for me that's a government policy." Many of these survivors work at government-supported memorials and yet do not echo the government's investment in forgiveness. They often departed from the formula in their description that some crimes were too devastating to pardon. They found that this portion of the formula, almost two decades after the genocide, was something that benefited the government, not their own lives.

For some women, the idea of forgiving the brutal violence against women and children seemed ludicrous; nonetheless, they still placed importance on having the choice to forgive. Rebecca explained, "Women who were pregnant . . . they had their stomach cut and they [perpetrators] removed their babies . . . and they could get the babies and beat them on the walls. And then the girls and women by that time . . . have sex with people they don't know at all and they were forced . . . in those cases, forgiveness is not possible." Interviewees held up examples of sexual and gender-based violence, and violence toward mothers in particular, as instances in which forgiveness would likely not be granted. As Marie poignantly explained, "I waited to hear someone ask for forgiveness for what they did to women and children, but then I knew, so if they feel guilty, good for them but I cannot wait for their forgiveness. How can you forgive someone for something like that? Maybe the government can, but I can't."

Those who felt that forgiveness was not possible for certain crimes were also the ones who rarely had their stories, or ones like theirs, presented at memorials (see chapter 5). Women, especially poor women and those who survived sexual violence, were generally not represented in two of the three memorial sites chosen for this book (see chapter 5) and rarely represented in public commemorative gatherings (see chapter 4). In many ways, these survivors did not see themselves in the stories told about the 1994 genocide against the Tutsi, its aftermath, and the eventual success of some. These same marginalized survivors failed to see how they would be able to forgive, even if given the opportunity. As they saw it, the reconciliation formula had failed them.

Despite the idyllic nature of the formula and the rarity with which it is realized, it still affects people's lives in concrete ways. For some, it provides or has provided glimmers of hope for social harmony and learning the truth. Knowing that an explicit course was possible for attaining social harmony brought these individuals moments of assurance that life could indeed improve. But while the formula was promising on the surface, with bright prospects of truth-telling, forgiveness, and pardon, those marginalized in other postgenocide processes found it difficult to even imagine how such scenarios could possibly play out in material ways. When almost two decades later the formula had still almost never been realized in practice, these survivors experienced devastating disillusionment. For some, the knowledge that they had endured unpardonable brutality only increased their internal struggles.

Micro Reconciliation in Everyday Experiences

While the stories people told did not vary significantly in their depictions of the ideal reconciliation formula, their descriptions of local, everyday reconciliation varied much more widely. The variations occurred across governmental levels (e.g., state or communal) and across social factors (e.g., gender or generational). Survivors share an array of indicators that demonstrate significant social change since the time period immediately following the genocide. These everyday indictors of coexistence are often found in the mundane aspects of daily life: in school classrooms, on public transportation, and in the feeling of physical safety in one's own home.

I analyze these experiences along two dimensions: state and communal indicators. Reconciliation occurs on a state level through laws, policies, and institutional support for memorials and survivors. The interethnic shared use of public facilities and school classrooms was evidence of communal-level reconciliation. Understanding how everyday indicators of coexistence function on these two levels demonstrates to peacebuilding actors and scholars a range of settings and spaces in which everyday reconciliation is possible.

Among state-level indicators, survivors described three main markers of support that facilitate micro-level reconciliation: the presence of memorials, equal access to education, and services for survivors. The most widespread perceived marker of change that survivors mentioned in interviews was the presence of memorials; this should not be surprising as this sample of survivors was particularly dedicated to memory work. Audrey shared that memorials validate survivors' experiences and indicate that the government is serious about "honoring the victims of genocide" and "preventing genocide from occurring again." Preventing future crimes is essential to reconciliation because survivors believe that violence begets more violence. In Hope's words, "[if] we had revenge killings and then killings for those killings and then those it could go on forever." These survivors saw memorials as a necessary step for moving forward and beginning the process of reconciliation.

Memorials significantly mark a governmental effort, meaning they are supported on the state level, not just through funding but also through policy and employment. The government has a specific division dedicated to the upkeep of memorials, and survivors were keenly aware of its existence. The state effort toward investing in memorials stands in stark contrast to the genocidal government in power during 1994, according to survivors. As Fidèle explained, "There was very bad government, and now we have a government that supports us and does this with memorials and commissions so that violence won't happen like it did in the past."

While memorials are state markers of lived reconciliation, they are also spaces in which the lived practices intersect with the abstract, as they are believed to be a starting place for the reconciliation formula. Even though the vast majority of people with whom I spoke had not yet experienced this formula, memorials were thought to provide the context that would allow such actions to occur in the future. Memorials were described as being designed to, as Javier put it, "get everyone on the same page." According to Javier, a memorial "lets everyone know and believe the same thing about genocide, so then the perpetrators feel bad and want to ask for forgiveness." Those who held out hope that the formula's three-step process would eventually occur saw this as only possible with continued government investment in memorials. As Shema stated, memorials are where "perpetrators see what they have done to not just the victim but society and feel so sad in what they did and want to make it right." Memorials are linked to the reconciliation formula because they provide aspects of both truth and justice; by illuminating the truth of what happened, they intend to elicit a response from both survivors and perpetrators, making perpetrators regret the violence they enacted on victims.

Equal access to education was regarded as a state effort that facilitated micro-level coexistence. This indicator references the dismantling of the quota system that was in place prior to the 1994 genocide against the Tutsi. Afterward, the government established an anti-ethnicity approach, in which discussions and references to ethnicity were banned and citizens' identity cards no longer stated an ethnic identity. This effort was intended by the government to promote an ideology that "we are all Rwandans." Survivors echoed this ideology and drew on past reference points, such as when "Tutsis had to take extra tests in order to participate in school and got unfair treatment in the classroom," as Valentine noted.

Not surprisingly, survivors who had received an education were twice as likely to mention this as a sign of progress. Survivors with the lowest socioeconomic status (SES) were least likely to mention education as a state marker of reconciliation and change. This was undoubtedly due to the challenge of accessing education in poor and rural communities. Higher education in Rwanda is no longer ethnically stratified in the ways it once was but is still significantly unequal in terms of access and quality for the poor, especially the rural poor. Additionally, young people mentioned educational access more often than those over the age of thirty-six. This is likely due to the fact that young people have benefited from the change in education policy and are reportedly reminded of this difference by their elders. As Marie recalled, "My mother remembers when Tutsi in her village couldn't go to the school they wanted without being humiliated and here I am. I finished college and I have a respectable job."

The availability of services aimed at supporting survivors' resiliency was another marker of the state's promotion of social change in the direction of reconciliation. These services include counseling, support groups, financial support, educational assistance, and legal advice. Services are thought to, as Clause explained, "bring up survivors" so they can be more civically engaged in their communities. As Rebecca explained, "You can't discuss reconciliation unless you discuss hunger, and poverty." This comment is directed at the high prevalence of poverty among survivors and speaks to the privilege that one must have in order to participate in official reconciliation programs. Rebecca underscores how reconciliation can only begin to occur after physical needs are met, for how can you discuss "forgiveness with someone who is hungry or doesn't have a home?"

While survivors at all sites and social locations commented on the prevalence of services for survivors as a marker of reconciliatory progress on the state level, women over the age of thirty-five at all three sites remarked on this measure of progress more frequently because of the high incidence of sexual assault among this particular population. Several of the women I interviewed who are in this age group are survivors of sexual assault or counselors (themselves genocide survivors) who assist sexual assault survivors. This group overwhelmingly cited counseling, financial aid, and healthcare as essential to functioning in everyday life.

At the community level, survivors found evidence of reconciliation in the daily nonviolent interactions between ethnic groups. This included people of different ethnic backgrounds using the same buses for transit, shopping at the same markets, and sharing food and water without fear of being poisoned. Claudine, a friend of Charity's, explained, "When I take the bus, there is everybody on it. This would not have happened fifteen years ago, not just because we didn't have as many buses but because people were not able to go places and be in the same place." Fidèle, who lives thirty miles from Claudine, echoed a similar sentiment: "At the market everyone is there, and no one asks are you a Hutu or a Tutsi. This is progress."

Survivors from diverse backgrounds commented that the local experiences of coexistence were marked by shared uses of public services and facilities. People remarked on this experience of coexistence at the CFC more than at any other site. In this community, perpetrators and victims live side by side, as they did prior to 1994, in a rural area. Sharing space, and even food and water, marked a significant change from experiences immediately following the genocide, when perpetrators were either in jail or in hiding. In 2005, when several perpetrators were released from prison, some victims shared that they feared for their personal safety. The fact that they currently use the same public spaces and utilities without fearing for their life marks a transformation in communal social dynamics and quality of life.

The survivors at the CFC also commented on another marker of coexistence. As Charity explained, "Someone would take me to the hospital if I was sick," even if that someone was of a different ethnicity. This particular scenario is repeated by several survivors. Women and older men at all three sites indicated that an additional marker of coexistence is feeling physically safe in one's home or community. Frank, age sixty-five, commented, "I am not scared someone will come in here and try to hurt me. I can go outside my home here and feel safe." The frequency with which older men and women verbalized this marker relates to their generation. They were young adults during the time of uncertainty and fear before the civil war and the time of violence during the civil war and genocide. Feeling safe in their homes and communities marks a stark contrast to what they had experienced twenty years earlier. Additionally, women were particularly vulnerable to sexual violence prior to and during the genocide. Even the women with whom I spoke who were not sexual assault survivors related that they were keenly aware of and terrified of the threat of sexualized violence.

The complexity of survivors' narratives of reconciliation limits the conclusions one can draw from large data-driven measures. In the following section, I suggest six implications for researchers and scholars to consider when examining reconciliation.

Implications for Research and Practice

The disjuncture between the macro formulaic ideal and the micro everyday practices of reconciliation offer important insight into how we might conceptualize, measure, and analyze peacebuilding after mass violence. First, the abstract formulaic process and the range of micro indicators of co-existence teach us how different versions of reconciliation can simultaneously operate in the everyday lived experiences of reconciliation and are accessible through repeated in-depth interviews over time. Survivors detail their hopes for a future of social harmony; however, when pressed about their lived everyday experiences, instead of relating tales of apologies and forgiveness, they describe mundane interethnic interactions, resources for healing, and state policies that promote equality. This means that I am called upon as a researcher to ask several follow-up questions at different points in time and inquire beyond initial responses. What reconciliation looks and feels like for survivors changes according to temporal cycles since narratives of reconciliation are shaped by the time of year. When survivors were interviewed in the spring, during the mourning months, they seemed to consider forgiveness and social harmony significantly less of a possibility than when interviewed in the fall. What this means for researchers is that there are temporal patterns associated with and dictated by institutional practices, making narratives of reconciliation and forgiveness fluctuate. These fluctuations could have implications for practitioners who are conducting research or designing coexistence programs and peacebuilding initiatives. Furthermore, for Rwanda this means that the mourning period affects survivors' perceptions of reconciliation, making them feel validated in their experiences yet less inclined to believe that social harmony is a future possibility.

Second, the two different reconciliation processes, the macro and the micro, interact with one another in the lived experiences of survivors. At times survivors discount the significance of their everyday experiences of coexistence when discussing the reconciliation formula because the everyday interactions are filtered through the expectation of what reconciliation should be. During moments of disappointment and despair, micro indicators of social change rarely inspired feelings of empowerment because in comparison to social harmony, a shared bus ride felt insignificant, even when it brought hope in other contexts. As Siboyintore explained during the mourning month, "Yes, I feel safe in my home and I guess that is progress. But do I know the truth about what happened to my brother? No, and that still haunts me." The long-term ramifications of trying to heal a country with simplistic reconciliation formulas, which as we have seen, can cause survivors to feel disappointed and frustrated, is a topic that deserves further study. The allure of the formula highlights what is lacking in everyday, micro indicators of coexistence, which fall significantly short of satisfying the need for social harmony, narrative closure, and truth-telling.

Third, the persistence of the reconciliation formula says much about what is at stake for different social actors who tell their versions of this story. The reconciliation formula's power and clarity enable survivors across social locations and home sites to repeat the formula without straying from its key ingredients. As the literature on narratives argues, stories that are told and retold are shared for a reason. For survivors, the reconciliation formula offers glimmers of hope that social harmony can be achieved in the future if the formula is followed. It also assures survivors that there is indeed a formula, a one-size-fits-all model that works for every situation of violence and brutality, even the unforgiveable ones. This model, if achieved, results in lasting social harmony, trust, and, most important, a future that promises to be easier, brighter, and more secure than the present. These promises likely allowed survivors to maintain hope in the future during the first decade after the genocide; by the time of my interviews, such hope was waning. From the government's perspective, the reconciliation formula continues to hold up the impossible as a possibility for the future.

Fourth, the pitfalls of the idyllic formulaic narrative of reconciliation are steep, creating deep disappointment and, for some, despair. The formula creates expectations that are rarely satisfied and, in most instances, entirely unrealistic. Unfulfilled expectations have ramifications for survivors who once might have had hope and now feel disappointment over macro-level progress that never transpired. This disillusionment threatens progress that had been made through everyday reconciliation: during the mourning months especially, when survivors feel the distress most deeply, disappointment over unfulfilled promises of macro-level progress casts a dark, wide-reaching shadow over micro-level progress.

Fifth, the elements of everyday life that contribute to social change could be incorporated into reconciliation measurement instruments in ways that would illuminate how reconciliation is profoundly shaped by social location (gender, age, socioeconomic status, etc.). Analyzing the stories of the lived experiences of reconciliation could accompany large-scale data from the HDI or GPI, or from a national reconciliation barometer, to provide a fuller picture of reconciliation in postconflict societies. It could also complement measures such as Everyday Peace Indicators (EPI) by disaggregating the levels (state and communal) of these indicators. Such qualitative data provides researchers with rich insight into how reconciliation is shaped by gender, generation, and geographic location, revealing how social location shifts perceptions concerning which interactions constitute indicators of coexistence. For example, the varied conceptions of possibilities for forgiveness and markers of communal change highlight the strongly gendered experience of genocide and its aftermath. Gender is the strongest predictor of whether a person feels forgiveness is possible, with women across diverse SES and generations feeling less inclined to forgive or doubting that forgiveness could lead to social harmony. This is an important finding for a couple of reasons. In previous scholarship, women have been found to be the more forgiving gender and, in my personal communications while presenting at conferences, I have often heard scholars argue that Rwanda has not experienced widespread revenge killings because women make up the majority of its population.[32] While this could be true, the reason does not appear to be that women feel a particular inclination to forgive. The finding uncovered in this chapter, that women feel less inclined to forgive, significantly contrasts with the perceptions of survivors themselves, as many explained to me on multiple occasions that it was the older generation that presented the biggest obstacle to reconciliation since they are believed to be the ones least likely to forgive.[33] Furthermore, this finding contrasts with societal gender norms that assume women are more emotional and thus ready to forgive.

Finally, scholars and practitioners must take seriously the importance of both locating bodies and providing basic needs to survivors as central mechanisms of peacebuilding and transitional justice. One of the main allures of the reconciliation formula is its promise of information about loved ones' remains, a theme that emerged throughout several chapters in this book. Survivors who described the state markers of everyday reconciliation noted the importance of services that contribute to the resiliency of survivors, including counseling and providing for basic needs such as food, housing, and physical security. Such efforts are essential for coexistence. As Neza explained, "I could not think about reconciliation when I did not know where I was going to live or how I was going to eat. I had to solve those problems before I could even begin reconciliation." This means that investing in forensic technology and partnerships—as well as programs that provide immediate food, shelter, and physical security—should be top priorities for serious transformative peacebuilding agendas.[34]

For policy makers and researchers, it is vital to access the complexities in the lived experience of reconciliation outlined here in order to support measures that cultivate a meaningful and healthy society after violent conflict.

Conclusion

> If ethnic cleansing is successful, it removes victims and leaves the victor in possession of a terrain of undisputed truth. Who, after all, is left to remind the winners that someone else once owned these houses, worshipped here, buried their dead in this ground? Ethnic cleansing eradicates the accusing truth of the past. In its wake, the past may be rewritten so that no record of the victim's presence is allowed to remain.
>
> Michael Ignatieff, *The Warrior's Horror*

What distinguishes genocide from war, massacres, and interpersonal violence is its intent to destroy, or rather to eliminate, an entire population. Genocide is not just about obliterating a people from the current landscape to get them out of the way. It is about trying to ensure that they are forgotten in time, place, and historical memory. Genocide memorials, through their physical existence, resist collective forgetting and refuse to allow the victors "possession" of their own "undisputed truth." Memorials remind not just the "winners" but also those who will bear witness and those who will listen that "someone else once owned these houses," attended the schools, and raised their children in that community. Memorial spaces are deliberately designed to preserve the memory of what once was and to pay tribute to the dead as well as survivors and their descendants.[1]

The tremendous social disruption caused by brutal acts of mass violence can make a coherent narrative impossible. Trauma disrupts social and philosophical orders. Like cases of collective violence across the globe, the 1994 genocide against the Tutsi in Rwanda was one such instance of disruption. Trauma is not restricted to individual memories of violence. It also manifests in damage to communal concepts of moral order, ethical duty, and humanity.

The survivors in this book identify how memorials help order their trauma by telling a coherent story about their past. A story with a beginning, middle, and end lends a sense of stability to lives that have been upended by the havoc and brutal violence of spring 1994. In the aftermath of the genocidal violence, communities and state entities throughout the country argued that rebuilding a collective future required physical spaces for commemorating all that was lost in the genocide: lives, childhoods, hopes, family lineages, religious beliefs, sacred spaces, confidence in the international community, and more. In present-day Rwanda, these efforts occupy a prominent physical space throughout the country.

In theory, memorials in Rwanda represent an effort to showcase the truth of what happened and thereby resist attempts to erase history on the part of the genocide's perpetrators. But memory projects, including those in Rwanda, do not solely communicate the truth. As scholars have noted time and again, truth is rarely singular. This book, of particular interest to memory studies scholars, underlines the ways in which memorials and their corresponding narratives represent a series of choices about what aspects of the past are worth remembering. These choices are evident in the micro interactions of memory work. In creating an orderly narrative, memorials elevate certain events and experiences while marginalizing, altering, or even erasing others so that the story remains hopeful and bearable in the face of unimaginable destruction and pain. Social memory studies have noted that "memory is a field of cultural negotiation through which different stories vie for a place in history," resulting in the control of some narrative elements by those with the most social and political power.[2]

The choices made by those in power impact their respective communities because, as seen in this book, a memorial's orientation—its central narrative—shapes the stories people tell about the past and, more importantly, how people frame the future. The narratives disseminated at memorials affect how survivors see themselves, their future expectations, and the possibilities for reconciliation. However, survivors also exercise agency in creating their own narratives. Despite their discernable orientations, memorials do not have the power to control the stories survivors and nations tell themselves, but they can construct narratives that help shape those stories and provide a lens through which a society can order its shared trauma and experiences.

Ritual, Order, and Stratification

Making sense of the senseless partly entails the creation of new rituals, routines, and customs. For some survivors, memorials are the canvas upon which to create new rituals. Émile Durkheim asserts that ritual, organized around sacred objects, facilitates identification by individuals within a collective—an essential ingredient for social life.[3] Ritual and routine provide meaning and communal interaction that are fundamental to the fabric of society. Survivors in this book engaged in such rituals by meeting on weekdays in front of the CFC to walk together to school. These women all had family buried at the memorial. Some said a prayer in front of the church-turned-memorial before school, and a few returned in the late afternoon after classes to work at the memorial. The memorial became a centerpiece in the village—surely as a site for remembrance but also as one for the mundane patterns of everyday life.

Nicole, a survivor in her late forties, explained that she no longer attended church as she had prior to 1994. Her family was killed in a church by clergy members, and she can no longer commit to organized religious rituals. She sometimes prays in times of uncertainty, though not in churches. She explained that she was unsure whether she still believed in God as she once did, and she wondered aloud, "Maybe he was sleeping during the genocide? Maybe he tried to stop the genocide and couldn't? But I know the genocide was not part of God's plan." In losing religious rituals, she also lost the connections she had made at church—the exchanges of care and the resources offered by church members. However, what Nicole lost in religious rituals she regained through new rituals that revolved around memory and the memorials. She goes to the memorial every Friday to remember her parents and strives to embody the best parts of them in the following week. She volunteers at the memorial two times a month. Rituals order Nicole's loss; they don't erase her suffering, but they make it more bearable.

As sociologist Robin Wagner-Pacifici notes, "memories are never formless"; they materialize and are sustained through narrative, monument, ritual, or tradition.[4] In a sense, memorials are a mechanism for concretizing memories by arranging and transmitting them to publics through archived testimonies that are available for visitors to view, through guided tours and spaces that tell specific stories, and through commemorative events that bring communities together in shared rituals. Essential to the successful reception of these curated memories is the memorial's ability to "bring together public-event memories and private memories."[5] Communities come together through memorial attendance, new rituals, events, holidays, and education programs.

In Rwanda, the organization of memories occurs in ways that empower and stratify survivors, conforming to national hegemonic stories of the past while also challenging them. In chapter 2, we saw that memorials have an essential function in the rebuilding process because they house bodily remains and evidence that can form the basis of judicial proceedings that help civil society to move on. In chapter 3, we saw instances of empowerment and hope when participants who had suffered incredible loss described their belief in remembrance rituals and spaces as means of preventing future violence. This hope motivates people such as Anitha, Mihigo, and Honorine (see introduction), who dedicate a significant amount of time to memorials both in their professional and personal lives.

Anitha lost her mother and siblings in the early days of April 1994. Her belief that she can contribute to violence prevention by making the memorial a beautiful place to honor those who died gives Anitha the strength to go to work at the memorial each morning. Mihigo believes his participation in memorial programs helps pave the way to coexistence, preventing future violence. His belief that these efforts matter to his country's future motivates him to continue that work, despite difficulties traveling to the memorial because of the loss of his right leg. Honorine provides tours and support to the youth educational program because she believes that it is possible to prevent future violence through education about rights and the preconditions that lead to violence. Honorine's mother, who witnessed her husband being killed in the middle of the night, takes great pride in her daughter's work.

National memorials in Rwanda serve as tools the state can use to cultivate nationalism and a sense of shared community, and the survivors cited in chapter 3 largely adopted the official national narrative about the 1994 genocide against the Tutsi and the role of memorials, locating blame for violence in Rwanda's colonial and recent history (a focus on guilt) and paying tribute to those who died (a focus on innocence). The survivors argued that memorial sites organize memories in diverse ways that lead to a unified goal: investing in a future without a recurrence of mass violence. Correlating remembrance with the possibility of future coexistence is the central feature of narratives about the genocide in Rwandan government discourse, the state curriculum, and national speeches by political leaders and international actors around the world.

While survivors tended to agree with the nationalist narrative's position that remembrance holds great power to prevent future violence, their practices in relation to the past are more complicated than simply trying to realize the state narrative in their lives. The survivors with whom I spoke embrace the state narrative yet also contest it and personalize it through their own ideological processes of organizing memories of the genocide to create meaning in their lives. Still, framing memory work as a means to prevent future violence validates survivors' dedication to memorial spaces and helps survivors order their trauma. While national memorials in Rwanda, like those across the world, are a tool of the state—an efficacious device in the cultivation of nationalism and imagination of shared community—survivors use nationalist narratives for their own healing in ways that make their suffering slightly more bearable.

As we saw in chapter 4, the issue of who is invited to speak at public memorials and commemorations, which in Rwanda can draw crowds of five thousand or more, is a point of contention. Commemoration staff decisions about testimonials adhere to specific notions of trauma and its relation to public health. Officially, trauma tends to be viewed as detrimental, and on that basis, testimonies that might cause collective trauma are often excluded at official commemorations, creating a hierarchy of narratives of survival. At the top of this hierarchy are narratives that avoid upsetting the audience: stories of surviving physical injury, completing education, and succeeding in respected careers are singled out for celebration. At the bottom of this hierarchy are stories of poverty, sexual and gender-based violence (SGBV) violence, and mental health challenges. The resulting official stratification of memory and survivors' stories mirrors the already stratified social order, with women and poor survivors at the bottom. These survivors' exclusion results in commemoration testimony that is highly gendered and classed. At large-scale commemorations, including those held at the three sites featured in this book, stories of triumph and healed physical injuries are the most visible and typically told by professional men. Stories of sexual violence and persistent poverty are rendered invisible. As a result, those marginalized by their traumatic experiences, particularly sexual violence, are held back further and watch their needs go unmet as resources and public understanding focus elsewhere. Advancing a singular narrative of hope comes at the expense of silencing marginalized survivors and sacrificing the diversity of survival narratives.

The narratives presented at memorial sites are inextricably linked to the orientation and internal organization of each particular memorial. Chapter 5 illuminates how the disclosure of SGBV memories depended on the site's orientation. The CFC's orientation toward commemoration and availability of evidence used to torture and rape women lends itself to discussions with visitors about the SGBV that occurred during the genocide and its aftermath. The CGPE, which emphasizes education, has used its social program for women with HIV/AIDS as a launching point to render visible women who contracted HIV from genocidal rape. Guides here crafted situations in which visitors might ask questions about the site's social program, freeing them from proactively introducing the difficult topic of SGBV and allowing them to address these issues in their role as educators answering visitors' questions.

While the CFC and the CGPE do not shy away from mentioning SGBV, the CMSR's orientation toward reconciliation prevents an examination of how SGBV was used as a weapon of genocide that affected women's lives decades after the violence ended. The site focuses on Rwanda's abandonment by the UN and the international community and also on the reconciliation programs housed at this site. Because the brutal gendered crimes and crimes against children that occurred are so unfathomable, silences about SGBV and the "most unforgiveable crimes" function to avoid casting doubt on the validity of reconciliatory programs. To advance its narrative about reconciliation, the CMSR privileges information about the UN's withdrawal of troops and the burgeoning reconciliation program, along with the testimonies of survivors who feel able to reconcile. Narratives that potentially disrupt this agenda are effectively silenced.

Chapter 6 similarly complicates memorials' ability to organize memory by demonstrating the disjuncture between what survivors believe must occur for reconciliation to materialize and what actually occurs on the everyday local level. Those who interact with memorials imagine their overarching goal of reconciliation to follow a certain formula, which includes perpetrators admitting wrongdoing and apologizing to victims, followed by victims forgiving them. To survivors' dismay, this formula not only rarely follows this sequence, it rarely occurs at all. When asked what reconciliation looks like today, survivors emphasized the lived everyday micro indicators of coexistence—sharing public spaces, feeling safe in their homes, seeing the end of education quotas, and remembering the violence at official commemorations.

Survivors understand that memorials represent reconciliation and progress, especially from the perspective of the government that supports their efforts. Memorials are also ultimately a reminder of the palpable failure to facilitate reconciliation through the apology-and-forgiveness formula. This failure is felt most devastatingly by those at the lower end of the social order, particularly poor women who have lost the most economically, emotionally, and physically, and whose experiences tend to be least represented in public narratives. In this sense, the unequal ramifications of genocide go beyond narratives that elevate or exclude particular experiences: they extend to direct health and economic consequences that themselves are experienced in similarly stratifying ways. Poor women in particular expressed disappointment over not being considered worthy of an apology from perpetrators and still not knowing the truth about where their loved ones were buried. Their disillusionment was also directed at the government for not doing a better job of facilitating apologies and for expecting forgiveness on the part of survivors. Memorials thus serve as venues for experiencing the incongruity between survivors' lived practices of coexistence—such as going to the same market as perpetrators—and their beliefs about how memorials should actually cultivate the reconciliation formula. However, even amid such disappointment around memorials' inability to make reconciliation occur as they imagine it should, survivors still remain largely dedicated to everyday interethnic interactions and to memorials as important communal spaces and markers of social change.

Memory and Transitional Justice

After the 1994 genocide against the Tutsi, Rwanda implemented several judicial and truth-seeking efforts besides memorials, including various types of courts, a National Unity and Reconciliation Commission, and survivor compensation programs.[6] Rwanda is unique in its development of numerous memorials in a relatively short time period. These memorials shape survivors' lives not only in the realm of memories and the retelling of history but also by offering spaces to honor loved ones, connect with other survivors, and imagine a better future. Even as they envision a future free from violence, survivors continue to struggle, almost two decades later, with how to commemorate the past, how to move on, and what reconciliation means in the present and for the future. These questions are central to working out how various truth-seeking projects may work in tandem. Scholars have emphasized in recent years the importance of truth-seeking projects in order to prevent future violence.[7] Truth commissions, along with tribunals, are thought to serve psychological and judicial purposes through their rigorous fact-finding and the creation of a public record of atrocities, requiring people to bear witness to past injustices.[8]

In many ways, the claims survivors make in this book about the significance of memorials mirror those made about truth commissions: their ability to strengthen democratic institutions by creating a consensus about the past, educating the nation about violence to prevent future aggression, and deterring future perpetrators from committing crimes against humanity.[9] Memorials grapple with challenges similar to those addressed by truth commissions and international tribunals (minus the obvious amnesty feature), including the marginalization of women's testimony and the risks of retraumatizing survivors by having them retell their stories.[10] However, unlike tribunals and truth commissions, memorials have permanence because of their physical structure. Memorials do not end when the trials conclude or the final report is published; rather, they live on in communities for decades to come. This permanence can enable fluidity, allowing spaces to change and morph into different entities over time. The nature and scope of these possibilities are potential areas for future research. The multitude of memorial spaces allows for a diversity of mechanisms (including, for example, evidence, testimony, survivor services, and architecture) for remembering the past. This variance could be used to leverage the multiple modes of survivor participation that we saw in this book—survivors seeking services, mourning, gardening, leading tours, educating youth, participating in reconciliation programs, and so on. These multivalent modes of survivor participation transform into rituals—new daily practices that bring about order and stability.

Identifying these modes complicates our understanding of memorials in postconflict zones by demonstrating their diversity in terms of locality, orientation, and impact on the stories people tell. While we know from previous research that the stories told in memory projects reflect certain choices, until now, we knew much less about how those decisions are made.[11] The majority of previous studies deploy memorials as the units of analysis rather than focusing on the individuals who interact with those memorials. Analyzing how people interact with memorials answers important calls for more research centered around micro interactions since it allows us to see what these interactions look like, how decisions are made, and what justifications are used for the choices made about organizing memories.[12] Justifications may be based on assumptions about what is healthy for the public, the memorial's physical and internal structure, and beliefs about what reconciliation should look like. This shift in the unit of analysis, from memorials to individuals, gives us a snapshot of how survivors use memorial spaces—both in intended ways, such as commemorating and sharing testimony, and in unintended ways, including social networking, accessing resources, and securing employment. We learn that certain types of memorialization lend themselves to particular stories about the past in ways that both empower and stratify survivors—the very population they aim to honor and commemorate. Finally, we learn how memorials matter to survivors themselves, in their own words.

Survivors in this book also show us that "memory practices are an integral part of modern life," and they illustrate the importance of "how, when, and why individuals and groups turn toward their pasts."[13] Survivors not only use spaces of memory on a regular basis; they also turn toward their pasts as a means to pay tribute and move forward. In some instances, my interviewees saw memorials as their only option for survival, even when they were left out of the central stories told at those memorials. In Rwanda and across the globe, institutional power controls which stories become public and part of the collective memory.[14] As historian David Thelen notes, "The struggle for possession and interpretation of memory is rooted in the conflict and interplay among social, political, and cultural interests."[15] Variously situated stakeholders struggle for control over memory because of its power and significance, "since memory is actually a very important factor in struggle . . . if one controls people's memory, one controls their dynamism."[16] However, we also see paths of resistance to institutional power. These forms of resistance are evident in the guides that discuss SGBV; in angry women telling commemoration staff they should not shy away from strong images; and in survivors networking with other survivors to share resources, study, or provide support to one another. Resistance also takes the form of stories told about how memory prevents future violence—not because that is the narrative of the Rwandan government but because it enables survivors to gain meaning and solace from their work at memorials. These power-laden processes of remembrance are evident in choices about which memories to elevate and which to disregard; they can also be seen in resistance among those whose experiences are being marginalized. The narratives in this book assert that such stories matter, even when fictional or imaginative, as a basis for hope—a sentiment that, in turn, can translate into real possibilities for coexistence. But, as we have seen, these stories also come with challenges and disappointments when they do not materialize. Memorials in postgenocide Rwanda illuminate how stratification plays out in less obvious ways after violent conflict. Collective memories, as a dynamic essential to reconciliation, continue to privilege those in power.

Focus on the Banality of Everyday Memory and Coexistence

This book concentrates on the banality of everyday memory work and coexistence after mass atrocity.[17] The focus on the local, micro experience was in part a response to the call from scholars in sociology, peace studies, African studies, and memory studies for more local-level research.[18] At the same time, the focus came out of a desire to understand how memory and coexistence functioned after mass atrocity by asking the people who were living through the aftermath of genocide. I describe this in depth in the methodology section in the appendix, along with ethical and research conundrums, all of which I hope address honestly what it is like to do qualitative international research in postconflict societies.

My emphasis on everyday micro interactions and how these experiences interact with national-level dynamics yields several important findings for a range of disciplines (e.g., sociology, peace studies, and social memory studies) with an interest in transitional justice, stratification, and the creation of national collective memory. Beyond demonstrating how memorials are an important mechanism of transitional justice, survivors' narratives about the importance of locating the bodily remains of their loved ones emerged as a theme throughout. Survivors in Rwanda are not unique in their desire to know the details of their loved ones' deaths and the locations of the bodies.[19] This desire motivates many to believe in the reconciliation formula discussed in chapter 6; for if someone were to admit to killing their families, these individuals could theoretically find out where the bodies are and recover them for proper burial.

However, the formula did not materialize for the vast majority of survivors with whom I spoke, and their loved ones, assumed dead, were still missing. They were not simply missing persons but also people who were missed by the ones left behind, who needed the closure of seeing their beloveds' bodies and knowing there was no longer any hope that they were still alive. Without this closure, families are unable to move on and accept coexistence. They are often haunted in their sleep and waking moments. This book argues that peacebuilding and transitional justice initiatives must take seriously the impact that missing persons have on survivors' goals, prioritizing the forensic technologies and partnerships needed to identify bodies and discover those that have yet to be located.

Like the work of the Everyday Peace Indicators, the focus on daily and sometimes mundane occurrences in this book led to a greater understanding of coexistence on the micro level.[20] Scholars have argued that the micro level impacts macro-level peace.[21] This means that, for survivors, macro-level stability is helped by micro-level interactions, such as sharing a communal space or having neighbors they know would take them to the hospital in an emergency. Like other scholars, I found that mundane interethnic interaction is significant for reducing large-scale violence.[22] Everyday markers of coexistence, whether at the national, communal, or individual level, starkly contrasted with the uncertainty and eminent danger felt immediately after the genocide. Peacebuilding initiatives should therefore ask survivors to rate progress toward coexistence at all three levels. A broader top-down reconciliation agenda would need to consider not only macro-level indicators but also survivors' basic needs, such as food, housing, and physical security. As some interviewees asserted, it is impossible to discuss reconciliation when one is starving.[23]

Finally, for those interested in the stratification of collective memory in the aftermath of mass atrocity, this book has several important lessons. First, narratives that become part of a nation's collective memory are built upon a series of micro-level choices and interactions that accumulate into a larger national story arc. These micro-level interactions regarding memorials and commemorations after atrocity are documented for the first time here—among guides who either discuss or avoid discussing SGBV, in the assertions that certain stories are better than others for public health, and in the dialectic relationship between individual meaning-making and government-supported historical accounts. To understand how macro narratives come to fruition and are further disseminated, we must also analyze the micro and often seemingly mundane everyday interactions and experiences of memory work.

Second, social and political conflict stratifies populations because the vulnerable are disproportionally killed and harmed, so it is not surprising that the aftermath of conflict similarly disenfranchises those at the lowest end of the social order. Because this stratification is felt and narrated, and ultimately plays itself out, in micro-level decisions survivors make about what to say, or whether to participate in reconciliation programs, these decisions should be studied through local-level analysis.

Finally, as in other postconflict zones, those without resources and capital have few opportunities to contribute to narratives of nation-building precisely because those with power silence those at the margins. The absence of marginalized narratives not only silences individuals and their experiences; it also makes those groups of individuals less likely to participate in civic engagement and reconciliation programs that are critical to everyday acts of nation-building. Sexual assault survivors and the poor may not have idealized narratives to share, but they nonetheless believe that their stories of survival are also important for the nation to hear. These survivors want to do right by those who died by participating in reconciliation and rebuilding, which they only do when they feel valued as citizens.

After Genocide is a story about communities whose stories are relegated to the margins of memory projects and reconciliatory efforts. They desire peaceful coexistence as much as those with power. These communities include survivors whose losses in the genocide were unimaginable. Agathe, who breastfed orphaned babies during the genocidal violence, witnessed her husband and older daughter being killed and finally crossed the border with two babies on her back, two children in her arms, and four by her side. She is still fighting for coexistence. Agathe ultimately became a leader in an organization dedicated to serving widows and women with HIV/AIDS. She went on to adopt eight orphans, all of whom suffer from significant challenges, ranging from HIV/AIDS to severe trauma disorders. With fourteen children in total, eight of them still at home, she said this about adopting children: "It was my commitment, seeing that many mothers died and I had a chance to survive. It is not that I have enough to feed them, but I have love." Memorials matter to people like Agathe, and remembering those who died gives her the courage to go to work every day bearing witness to the hardships of other survivors. She said that commemorations are important to her because "what you find here is that there are other people who experienced a worse situation than you. I remember in the beginning, I was thinking that it was me who suffered so much, but after I realized it was easy for me compared to others . . . and it is in this way that encourages you in a better way." Memorials can be spaces that aid in moving forward, imagining a brighter future, and being part of a collective. In Agathe's case, this meant going to the memorial to feel less alone and more hopeful, and when she felt less alone, she found the strength to advocate for others.

Ultimately, I believe Rwanda is unique in its particularities though not in its contours. As I write this conclusion, I am in Montgomery, Alabama, to attend the official opening of the Legacy Memorial, America's "first memorial dedicated to the legacy of enslaved black people, people terrorized by lynching, African Americans humiliated by racial segregation and Jim Crow, and people of color burdened with contemporary presumptions of guilt and police violence."[24] Visitors to this memorial are invited to remember and honor the lives lost to lynching and to reflect upon how acts of past racial violence have shaped contemporary racial injustice. At the same time, I have just learned that a previously unknown mass grave was uncovered outside the capital city in Rwanda.[25] In the coming days, Rwandans will have to decide how to proceed with the recovered remains while assisting the community in which they were uncovered.

As countries discover mass graves and seek to remember past atrocities or begin anew after war and human rights abuses, communities across the globe look to memorials to discuss the enduring legacies of injustice, bring hope to the hopeless, and honor the lives stolen by violence. In remembrance, we must listen hard for silences, notice who is not represented, and ask who is not at the table. For remembering has serious responsibility and great power: the power to marginalize, the power to heal, and the power to make our world a more just one.

Appendix

Data, Methods, and Stories from the Field

This appendix seeks to highlight the pieces of research most scholars attempt to conceal: the messiness of qualitative data, situations wrought with complexities, and emotional moments in the field. The stories I tell here reflect the precariousness of using qualitative methods in postconflict zones, an uncertainty that I embrace. Unfortunately, there is no instructional roadmap for plunging into a qualitative research project in a postconflict zone with multiple barriers, including linguistic and cultural differences. This appendix represents an attempt to lay out only some of the questions and problems I had to address when undertaking this research. The approach I lay out in this appendix is twofold. In the first section, I detail my definitions and terms, methodology, and research design for the book. The beginning of this section clarifies the book's working definition of survivor, my reason for calling the genocidal violence "the 1994 genocide against the Tutsi," and the political backdrop for this label. This section continues with an explanation of how I analyzed the data—which included my informants' silences as well as their words—and how I adjusted my interview questions over time to accommodate specific circumstances and limitations. I hope that this section will be of use to those who embark on their own qualitative research journeys.

The second section contributes to the ongoing dialogue about feminist qualitative research ethics, pulling back the curtain on the convolutions of fieldwork by sharing a few raw behind-the-scenes moments. This section responds to the push-back against open public dialogue about the emotional dimensions of research, especially those of the researcher. Resistance to acknowledging the humanness and emotionality of the researcher is motivated by the absurd assertion that emotional involvement disrupts objectivity.[1] I would argue that it is ethically imperative to reflect on and acknowledge the emotional dynamics of research, especially scholarly inquiries that center on violence, inequality, or mass atrocity. As anthropologist Renato Rosaldo explains when reflecting on how scholars might perceive his writings that connect his own experience with grief to the pain felt by his participants, "By invoking personal experience as an analytical category, one risks easy dismissal. Unsympathetic readers could reduce this introduction [about my own grief] to an act of mourning or a mere report on my discovery of the anger possible in bereavement."[2] However, Rosaldo concludes that "the truth of objectivism—absolute, universal, and timeless—has lost its monopoly status."[3] It is in this vein that I share in section two the ethical conundrums I faced, the moments when I tried to give back to participants, the dynamics of my own positionality, my experiences of secondary trauma, and a few funny and challenging stories from the field. My aim here is to provide an honest assessment of what can transpire in the field. What happens if you get your host family's car stuck in a ditch? Is it okay to cry when a participant tells you how her family was murdered? How should you take care of yourself when you witness mass trauma? How do foreign languages and translation impact the research process? These are a few of the questions I grapple with in the following pages, beginning with a note on constituencies and naming.

Definitions and Naming, Data Collection, Silences, and Life in Rwanda

Constituencies and Naming

I define genocide survivors in this book as individuals who feared for their own or their families' personal safety during the period of genocidal violence in April–July 1994 in Rwanda. This includes Tutsi, Hutu, and Twa who, during those horrific three months, were in danger because of perceived ethnic identity, appearance, or association with Tutsi (the direct target of the genocidal project). In this book, survivorship is represented by both Tutsi and Hutu (Hutu who saved Tutsi, and thus for the most part had close affiliation with Tutsi). The memory and voices in this book are from that specific constituency: Tutsi genocide survivors and Hutu survivors who rescued others.

The two groups, while central, are not representative of the vast range of other social actors who also suffered during and after the genocidal violence. These other survivors include the descendants of those who survived the 1994 genocide against the Tutsi; survivors of the civil war violence that occurred prior to and during the 1994 genocidal violence; returned refugees who were targeted in earlier episodes of ethnic violence and lost loved ones in 1994; Rwandans in the diaspora whose family members, friends, and homes were brutally taken; UN and aid workers who arrived late to the genocidal scene to find corpses, destruction, and chaos, and who left with a lasting trauma that shaped the rest of their lives; and those who lost loved ones after 1994 in refugee camps, in revenge killings, or in jail awaiting a trial.

These diverse social actors who suffered great personal loss, including their livelihoods, are often not the ones represented in memorial projects in present-day Rwanda or considered worthy of memorialization and visibility. Memorialization is inherently political and subject to state or political interference on the matter of which stories are elevated in public forums. As we saw in chapters 4, 5, and 6, commemorative narratives of the genocidal violence leave out specific social actors' experiences. The same politics occur around the name used to denote the genocide and are reflected in the deep cleavages among scholars of Rwanda.

I was once at a dinner with a large group of scholars of Africa, and someone joked that if the president of the African Scholars Association wanted to divide the members, all they would need to do is say something about the Rwandan government because everyone has a strong opinion on Kagame and his leadership. Academic scholars' research, experiences, and feelings about the government range from praise for the miraculous recovery after the genocide to unwavering critique of the country's authoritarian rule. The polarity of feelings is reflected in research questions, scholarship, and, more recently, in the naming of the genocide. The government of Rwanda, along with others, in 2007 began insisting that the genocide be called "the 1994 genocide against the Tutsi" in order to highlight that Tutsi were the targeted population. Some felt that this left out Hutu and Twa survivors. Western scholars for the most part tended to call the genocide the Rwandan genocide.

In January 2018 the UN General Assembly amended the title of the annual observance (resolution 58/234) by declaring April 7 to be the International Day of Reflection on the 1994 Rwandan Genocide against the Tutsi. A representative of Rwanda said the change "sought to correct inaccuracies in the Assembly's 2003 resolution establishing the International Day of Reflection on the 1994 Genocide in Rwanda . . . captured the historical facts of what happened in 1994—genocide against the Tutsi in Rwanda—and left no room for ambiguity. The tactics of genocide denial and revisionism were well known and documented. Some people promoted the theory of double genocide."[4]

The change in the UN's nomenclature was felt by some stakeholders as a move against denialism or attempts to forward a theory of "double genocide" between the Hutu and Tutsi. The name change is in no way inaccurate, as the violence in 1994 undoubtedly comprised genocidal killings and harm inflicted on Tutsis and those associated with them in an effort to destroy and eliminate the Tutsi population. However, critics expressed concern that this designation would marginalize non-Tutsi survivors and create tension and stratification in a country that was recovering from near annihilation. The words used to denote the genocide are highly politicized and matter deeply to scholars of Rwanda and also, most importantly, to those living in Rwanda. The term I use in this book comes after much reflection and research.

As a Western academic, I felt hesitant to use "the 1994 genocide against the Tutsi" because it seemed redundant and inconsistent with the naming of past genocides. When discussing the Holocaust, even as someone who lost distant Jewish relatives at Treblinka, I would never call the Holocaust "the Holocaust against the Jews." This would leave out the six million others who were also deemed undesirable and killed. It also seems unnecessary to reiterate that Jews were killed in the Holocaust as that has been well-established in the literature and popular culture. I do not find it ethical to call the Cambodian genocide the "Cambodian genocide against the intellectuals," because that would negate all the other victims who were targeted. Since genocide is one-sided killing with the intent to kill a specific group in part or altogether, it was already clear from the name "Rwandan genocide" that specific individuals and others like them were targeted for elimination and that using this title already pointed to the undebated fact that genocide occurred in Rwanda against the Tutsi. I have yet to encounter any respected researcher who has claimed that anything but genocide occurred in Rwanda against the Tutsi population. This is not to say such scholars are not out there, but they are certainly not at the center of the most prominent, rigorous, and widely read scholarship on Rwanda.

The change of nomenclature for the 1994 genocide against the Tutsi was championed by the Rwandan state and ultimately accommodated by the UN. For democracy to prosper, I believe it is vital for scholars, journalists, civil servants, and ordinary citizens to freely and respectfully distance themselves from governmental positions. Over the last decade, I have seen some scholars (whose research I respect) depart from the language the government uses by referring to "the Rwandan genocide." These scholars have then faced accusations of denial or divisionism. One concern I had with adopting the designation used by the UN and Rwandan government was that I would be aligning myself with those who were silencing independent voices, experiences, and perspectives.

A further complication that undermines the official name forwarded by the Rwandan government and the UN is the targeted killing of Hutu that the genocidal regime supported but was distinct from the genocidal motivations aimed at exterminating the Tutsi. While the Hutus in my interview sample were targeted for their association with Tutsis, some Hutus were targeted for a different reason: as a tactic to consolidate power by the *génocidaires*. In the early days of genocidal violence, Prime Minister Agathe Uwilingiyimana and other Hutu moderates and opposition leaders were deliberately and intentionally murdered to destroy the existing governmental structure in hopes that no one in power would be left to halt the genocidal project. Such a tactic is powerful and effective in gaining control of the masses in order to execute the genocidal plan of destruction.

While this reasoning inclined me against adopting the designation used by the UN and the Rwandan government, I experienced pushback from Rwandan colleagues, participants I interviewed for this book, and even Rwandan friends. After multiple heated arguments during trips to Rwanda in 2017 and 2018, I reflected on these discussions and noticed that I had been talking more than listening. In April and June 2019, during trips to Rwanda for another project, I met up with some of the survivors I had interviewed for this book. I have stayed in touch with them and see them regularly, and I explained my conundrum regarding the name used for the genocide and sought their input. Those with whom I spoke were insistent that they would like it to be called the 1994 genocide against the Tutsi. Their rationale was that Hutu were targeted because of their relations with Tutsi or because they were mistaken for Tutsi, but they were not killed for being identified as Hutu. Hutu most definitely were killed and murdered for not killing when instructed to do so—but again, the killers' intent was to destroy not all Hutus but all Tutsi, and genocide's defining feature is intent. They also said they would like my book to be available in Rwanda, and if I did not call the genocide by its proper name according to the government, the book would not be sold or read in Rwanda, and their stories would not be heard by those in power.

While in Rwanda from 2018 to 2019, I also talked to several Hutu rescuers who were demographically similar to the individuals I had interviewed earlier as I had lost touch with several of my Hutu interviewees. These rescuers also insisted that I should use the UN designation. One woman explained that while she suffered significant trauma and grief after her husband was murdered for not killing her Tutsi neighbors, she was spared when the militia came to her house because she was Hutu. The militia did not know she was a rescuer. She pointed out that if she had been Tutsi, she would have been killed at that very moment, and her husband had been killed for not killing Tutsi, not because he was Hutu. Another Hutu rescuer agreed with this reasoning, explaining that he had been targeted for his friendships with Tutsi, but not because he was Tutsi.

Rather, the motivation for this killing was his relationships but not something the killers found innately intolerable about his existence.[5]

Therefore, in deference to those who lived through the genocide and in acknowledgment of the accuracy with which the title identifies the intent of the violence, even though Hutu and Twa were also killed in the process of carrying out those intentions and a range of violent episodes continued long after July 1994, I adopt the name put forward by the Rwandan government and the UN. While it may seem redundant to me, I did not live through what they did. I believe the title is accurate and that leading scholars of both Rwanda and genocide studies in general would agree that the events in 1994 were a concerted and organized effort by militias who had intentions to annihilate the entire Tutsi population. My aim is not to marginalize non-Tutsi survivors or acquiesce to the Rwandan government's demands but to honor the requests of the people who graciously gave me hours upon hours of their time, who invited me into their homes and lives to show me how memorialization mattered to them, and, most importantly, who suffered the most horrendous atrocities and continue to survive in spite of that.

Data Collection and Research Design

The data collected for this project spans nine years. I first went to Rwanda in 2009, traveling with an organization that introduced me to a CHH village where I volunteered for two weeks, facilitating a photography project. Afterward, I stayed with friends and traveled to memorials in the central region of the country. There, I began to observe some of what survivors had told me during a preliminary project on Rwandan refugees living in the US.[6] On this trip, I observed memorials and went on memorial tours, but I did not interview any survivors until 2011, when I received my research permit from the government of Rwanda.[7]

While waiting for government approval in early fall 2011, I traveled the country, visiting both national and communal memorials and finalizing the sites of focus for this book. I chose the three sites described and analyzed throughout because they were all within forty miles of one another, meaning that the onset of the violence in 1994 unfolded in a similar way (and occurred at the early stages). At the time, all three were deemed national sites by the Rwandan government, which meant that they were all funded and maintained by the same governmental entity (detailed below). The sites' different orientations (see introduction) made them suitable for a study based on interviews with survivors who had regular contact with the country's genocide memorials.

Once I had chosen the sites, with my research permit in hand (and Institutional Review Board [IRB] approval from my home institution), I began interviewing survivors who worked at, lived near, or regularly engaged with the memorials. Per my IRB application, I obtained informed consent orally and provided participants with an informed consent information form, translated into Kinyarwanda, that included my information and a list of social services in their area. I returned to Rwanda to conduct additional interviews with the same participants in 2012 and returned again in 2017 and 2018 to revisit the memorials, observing how they had changed and where survivors were in their lives five years later. Visiting Rwanda in this way—on multiple occasions over relatively long periods of time—is part of what Bert Ingelaere terms "iteration." Iteration "not only refers to the physical movement of continuous return and rotations within the field, it also evokes the reflective and adaptive nature of the research process. . . . In the aftermath of mass violence and in times of transitional justice, the field is riddled with a range of obstacles that demand a practical understanding of navigating the terrain."[8]

For me to understand the complexities of the region, including the surrounding countries, I had to visit on multiple prolonged trips (including visits to neighboring countries such as the Democratic Republic of Congo, Burundi, and Kenya). Repeated visits allowed me to grasp the pace at which Rwanda was changing: every time I returned, even after only a few months, new buildings, shops, and roads had sprung up. Iteration permitted the development of working relationships with participants through multiple interviews over an extended period of time. Indeed, multiple interviews over time facilitated trust, enhanced the depth of interviews, and illuminated how emotions or perspectives vary during different temporal periods, especially during the months of mourning. The late Lee Anne Fujii explains that conducting numerous interviews over time can help combat the anxiety or apprehension that is widespread in post-atrocity communities.[9]

In 2011 I spent most days over the course of three months interviewing different participants, none of whom I had known prior to 2011. On days when I did not conduct interviews, I spent time at the sites, taking notes on daily life and the tour groups that came and went. On interview days, I would try to listen to the audio recordings the same evening, taking notes or beginning transcription. I uploaded some of the interviews overnight to a transcription company site where they would transcribe the audio recordings and email them back to me. On this trip, I interviewed multiple participants twice and then a third time during the mourning months. This allowed me to gain my interviewees' trust and to see if I could discern temporal patterns in their narratives of reconciliation and forgiveness in particular (described in chapter 6).

Analyzing data while still conducting interviews is a purposeful tool used in grounded theory.[10] Using this approach, I could give participants the opportunity to share candid stories or expand on a question, after which I could evaluate where my interview guide was working and where it fell flat. For example, in early interviews, I asked participants general questions about reconciliation with the intention of ensuring that I was not injecting any preconceived ideas about reconciliation into the conversation. I hoped the question would elicit explanations of any aspect the participants considered important. However, in reality, what materialized were general answers of "yes, reconciliation is happening," with a hint of annoyance and little in the way of explanation or further detail. I soon realized my question was at fault because it was too vague and not situated in the guide in a way that made sense. These initial coding sessions allowed me to theorize about what may have gone wrong and adjust my interview guide to ask more specific questions and preface them with an introduction connected to previous sections in the guide about memory:

- Do you feel memory and reconciliation are connected in any way? How?
- In an ideal world, what would reconciliation look like to you?
- Do you feel moments or interactions of reconciliation are happening today, even if they differ from the ideal?
  - What does that look like?
  - How does it feel?
  - How do you know it is happening?
- Could you give me examples of what reconciliation would/does look like today?
  - Who does this happen to? Why?
- What are your hopes for reconciliation in the future? How would that look?
  - How would it change your life as it is today?
  - Whose life would be most impacted?
- How would you measure reconciliation if you were trying to understand it?

These questions yielded the rich data on reconciliation in chapter 6; I asked these revised questions in follow-up interviews and integrated them into the interviews I had not yet conducted.

After my first three-month research trip, I returned to the US and began my line-by-line coding with the assistance of ATLAS.ti, a computer software program for qualitative data.[11] During the months between research trips, I applied for grants to fund my second research trip to Rwanda. Generous grants were awarded from the National Science Foundation, the Research Circle on Democracy and Cultural Pluralism, the TAG Institute for Jewish Values, the Andrew W. Mellon Foundation, the Society for the Scientific Study of Religion, and the Maurice J. and Fay B. Karpf & Ari Hahn Peace Endowment.

In 2012 I returned to Rwanda, conducting interviews with the same participants and new ones from the CGPE. I interviewed all participants two or more times at different points of the year, comparing answers that participants gave in the fall or winter to those they gave during the mourning months. Interviews during these different temporal periods demonstrated how some perspectives remained stable throughout the year while answers on topics such as possibilities for forgiveness varied during the mourning months. Such information is essential for those involved in developing truth, forgiveness, or reconciliation projects since the time of year when implementation and evaluation take place may shape the information received. During the mourning period, I attended commemorations, meetings, burials, and preparation events at all three sites and throughout the country. I was also honored to attend smaller-scale commemoration events, burials, and masses upon invitation by participants.

The three memorials I chose for this project were ideal for a comparative research design because they allowed me to isolate factors that contribute to specific dimensions of narratives about memory (e.g., rural vs. urban; whether they focus on reconciliation, memorialization, or education; availability of social services). Because of their physical proximity to one another, I was able to keep constant the spatial variations of violence as violence spiked in all three sites within two weeks of one another. Of the seventy-two survivors I interviewed, thirty participants spoke solely in Kinyarwanda, and forty-two spoke in English and Kinyarwanda. When the participant preferred English, I usually conducted the interview alone. However, if the participant preferred Kinyarwanda, I had a translator with me for the interview. In these instances, I would greet the participant and explain the purpose of the research, ask about the individual's family and community, and ask a few of the research questions in Kinyarwanda. However, for most of the interview, a translator would be used for translating both my questions and participants' answers.

Observing and Listening to Silences

When I attended commemorations, I felt uneasy and pulled in different directions. On the one hand, I was told by survivors that it was important for visitors from Western countries to see their pain and report on it back home. On the other hand, I felt ambivalent about witnessing sadness and pain for the sake of research that felt like a violation of the privacy of grieving people. Feminist ethnographer Janet Jacobs describes this pull in opposite directions as a form of "double vision," in which the researcher is both a witness to the aftermath of crimes against humanity and an ethnographic observer in search of qualitative data.[12]

The ethnographic data I gathered in both observations and interviews included silences—untold stories; incomplete sentences; and heavy, long pauses. Lee Ann Fujii has called these "meta-data": "[Meta-data are] the spoken and unspoken expressions about people's interior thoughts and feelings, which they do not always articulate in their stories or responses to interview questions. Meta-data can take both spoken and unspoken forms. They include rumors, silences, and invented stories. Meta-data are as valuable as the testimonies themselves because they indicate how the current social and political landscape is shaping what people might say to a researcher."[13] Especially in postconflict zones, it is important to focus on the memories that are not (yet) part of a testimony: memories in which the limits of language are too great to do justice to the event in recollection.[14] While debriefing trauma can be a vital tool in recovery, narration might be insufficient for "devastating experiences of atrocity [that] actually deprive language of its capacity to construct meaning and coherence."[15] Such silences reflect the inadequacy of narratives to capture some meanings.

During the interviews, survivors described how living through genocide had made them feel disorientated because of how difficult it was to come to grips with what they had lived through. Imposing the order of storytelling on the profoundly traumatic experiences they had to relate at times seemed impossible. In research on refugees, some scholars have found that "when participants' experiences essentially revolve around the lack of meaning, accepting absurdity and meaninglessness might be as supportive as reconstructing narrative continuity."[16] Silences may be the best way to express the disorder of trauma and the lack of meaning in its aftermath.

Silences during interviews, or in midstory, sometimes manifested as pregnant pauses that felt as if they would last an eternity. In those moments, I anxiously allowed the silences to offer a space for not telling. If a silence felt excruciating or appeared to compel the interviewee to narrate further even though they were uncomfortable, I interrupted; said how sorry I was for the pain; and offered to sit together in silence, stop the interview, or talk about something else. All three of these options were taken up by participants at different moments in time. Sitting with the silence was the most difficult for me, yet it was a powerful way for some respondents to express the horrors they had survived. Elaine Scarry, who has studied the physical and mental pain of torture, has remarked that pain lacks a sufficient language because it is inextricably bound up with power.[17] The burden of describing the indescribable falls on those who embody the pain, the ones who suffer. If they are unable to describe the pain, the ones left to describe it are those who did not experience it.

In this project, the indescribable pain of living with memories of sexual violence led to heavily burdened silences. Sometimes narration could capture the events or moments prior to the outbreak of sexual violence, which was used as a threat or weapon to destroy, but once memories had flooded into the mind, it seemed that narrative order was no longer possible. Survivors sometimes took a deep breath, at times followed by tears, and then the conversation moved on or ended, replaced with sips of water or Fanta. Sometimes the silences implied what was left unsaid, as when the disclosure of a child's age indicated that the interviewee had become pregnant through rape during the genocide. Often it wasn't until the second or third interview that silences became noise—cries, disclosure, or matter-of-fact descriptions that fell short of capturing their agony. Scarry asserts that "[physical pain] is language-destroying. Torture inflicts bodily pain that is itself language-destroying . . . it visibly destroys the prisoner's voice." The violence that occurs during atrocity also destroys language. Survivors may not regain words and descriptions, but powerful silences may allow them to regain their voices, and the researcher has the responsibility to care for and listen to those silences.

Translations of Culture and Language

My research assistant and translator for this project, Ntwari, is a former village leader of a CHH community whom I met during my first trip to Rwanda.[18] He is fluent in English, Kinyarwanda, and Swahili and has lived in Rwanda his whole life. This was important as participants recognized his dialect of Kinyarwanda as that of someone who had lived in Rwanda all his life; it was similar to those with whom he was speaking during the interviews. Additionally, he is a survivor who also collected testimonies for other projects and has a professional yet caring demeanor when asking sensitive questions. A second native Kinyarwanda speaker checked his initial interviews to ensure the accuracy of his translations.

Ntwari also served as a cultural translator, helping me understand and acquire new lexicons, social norms, and mannerisms.[19] He would often translate moments of awkwardness and assist me by translating cultural cues. For example, when I was first scheduling meetings with survivors, I attempted to do so one or two weeks out in order to give interviewees enough time to plan. This turned out to be disastrous as I would regularly show up for interviews only to be stood up because the interviewees didn't recall our conversation two weeks prior. Only after my research assistant informed me that it would be better to schedule only one or two days in advance, going in person to schedule the appointment when possible, did the interviews begin to run more smoothly.

Ntwari was especially helpful to me when I encountered unfamiliar situations. For example, we were once traveling to a commemoration in the eastern province when our bus suddenly pulled over to the side of the road. All passengers were required to get off the bus and form a line. Army officials were waiting outside to pat us down and took our passports for inspection. In other situations, Ntwari and I would have an ongoing question-and-answer banter in which I would ask, "Ntwari—is this normal?" and he would grin most times and say, "Yes, Nicky, it's normal." On the occasion when our bus was pulled over, I looked over at him as I handed over my passport to army officials and whispered, "Is this normal?" to which he responded, "No, this is definitely not normal." I was nervous, but not outright scared, until the men and women were separated into two lines for pat-downs. A woman three people behind me began traumatizing, screaming and yelling. Likely this woman was a survivor experiencing flashbacks of a road blockade in 1994. She was comforted by soldiers and taken to a vehicle on the side of the road behind the bus and given water. Shortly after our pat-downs, we were loaded back onto the bus on our way to our destination. I later found out that there had been a grenade attack somewhere near town and they were inspecting all buses for the culprit. I was grateful to have Ntwari on the bus with me as a linguistic and cultural translator.

During my time in Rwanda, I took Kinyarwanda language lessons from a tutor once a week and attended a weekly two-hour language class for foreigners. In addition to these lessons, the matriarch with whom I lived was a former teacher who studied with me nightly. She often had me share what I had learned that day in front of family, neighbors, or visitors to further my skills. This proved to be both embarrassing and fruitful in advancing my ability to communicate in Kinyarwanda. With these lessons, I was able to introduce myself and my study to participants, speak about my favorite foods, bargain, ask and (sometimes) receive directions, and pose some interview questions to participants. My efforts to speak Kinyarwanda were generally well received by both participants and people in the community.

During each of my trips to Rwanda, I stayed with a family that soon became my own. I had known several of the family members from the US prior to living with them, and I became part of the family during my stays in Rwanda. Living with them gave me rich insight into Rwandan life, from the kinds of food people eat to cultural norms of hospitality, gender, and family. Beyond being a deeply enriching experience on a personal level, living with such a generous, smart, and lively family was beneficial to my research in several ways. Because I lived with Rwandans with whom I was comfortable, I was able to ask questions about cultural norms, as I did with Ntwari. For example, on several occasions, participants were late for an interview appointment and I was concerned that these participants felt obligated to be interviewed and did not want to talk about their experiences. One of the women with whom I lived explained, "Rwandans are not like Americans, we don't think 'time time time.' We are on African time, not muzunga [white people] time. We don't have the belief that time is money, because if we did we would be much richer! [*laughs*] The social is the priority." As I began to understand Rwandan notions of time, I built waiting into my schedule.

Positionality, Trauma, and Stories from the Field

Scholars are expected to advance theories, talk authoritatively about facts, and develop precise methodological practices that produce answers. Scholars are not supposed to analyze themselves or appear self-indulgent. Those who agonize over the ethics of their positionality or the emotional labor of fieldwork risk appearing "sloppy."[20] For some, "sloppy sociology" might include thoughts about one's own whiteness or Jewishness, or confessions about vomiting on the side of the road after hearing a particularly harrowing story of survival or lying to a group of priests over a beer about liking the taste of goat meat. The assertion that reflection and emotions are the inverse of rigorous research makes scholars complicit in a gendered historical pattern of marginalizing women's scholarship, or work that appears feminine, as well as the role of emotions in processes of knowledge production.[21]

Thoughtful qualitative research *is* emotional labor, and developing an ethical sensibility as a researcher is an exhausting and nearly boundless task.[22] Studying people's lives comes with grave responsibility, and inserting one's self into a postconflict community entails an additional level of ethical and emotional work to assess whether witnessing and potentially inflicting pain through interviews yields potential benefits to respondents who have already suffered so much. The means are not simply justified by the ends in postconflict research—the means matter, and not just for the researcher. As Rebecca Campbell writes of qualitative research on rape, we must "do no harm" because "plenty of harm has already been done."[23] Aligned and in solidarity with past feminist social scientists and researchers, I begin this final section by reflecting on my own positionality in conducting this research.

Positionality

Gender and power are the cornerstones of feminist methodologies, and reflexivity and analysis of positionality are key tools in addressing the inequality at the center of all fieldwork.[24] As Steve Smith explains, "There is no view from nowhere . . . and there is no 'purely' academic perspective, secured, isolated and protected from ethics and power."[25] While I was in Rwanda, and also as I was writing about Rwanda, I never forgot I was white and Jewish. In Rwanda, my whiteness drew attention, turned heads at times, and once caused a ruckus at a rural soccer game when a community leader caught children plucking out strands of my hair when their curiosity got the best of them because they were seeing a white person's hair for the first time. Like Bert Ingelaere, I was keenly aware of my status as an American, equipped with a credit card in my wallet and an American passport, while I sipped bottled water and interviewed people who had lost everything. As other scholars of Rwanda can attest, one can try to learn "to be Kinyarwandan," but clearly, no number of language lessons or trips to Rwanda will make that happen.[26] I ate Rwandan food, got excited when my bucket shower was filled with warm water, drank African tea, and even picked up some Rwandan mannerisms. As comfortable and accepted as I might have felt at times, my whiteness and privilege were undeniable and continually present.

At times, my whiteness played out in unexpected ways. After getting to know a few women quite well, I had a group from a CHH ask me to write a formal letter to the mayor of their district requesting safe and functioning toilets for their village. I showed up with my computer the next day to do so, imagining that they would dictate the letter and I would print it for them to sign and deliver. However, what they wanted was for me to assist in writing the letter in a formal style, print it, and deliver it myself. I was nervous and cautious about taking over their efforts to improve their own community and expressed the desire to assist them in whatever way they wanted me to. They responded that because I was white and American, if I delivered the formal typed letter, the sector leader would know that the "white world is paying attention." My privilege was thus leveraged to do a little good for the people I interviewed. When I came back months later, their requests had been answered and construction had started on new toilets for the community.

I was nervous about asking people to spend their time with me, missing out on work or family time to talk about memory and violence. I never asked people about their survival stories but instead inquired about the role memorials played in their lives and how they imagined or experienced reconciliation. However, after my first couple of interviews, I found that these conversations often resulted in survivors disclosing their experiences during the genocide, even when I did not ask them to. I felt guilty for asking so much of them given my own material comfort and the distressing nature of their experiences. To my surprise, many of them thanked me for interviewing them, especially on return visits. I thought that these follow-up interviews might be a burden on them, but more often than not my interviewees welcomed me back with warmth. In 2019 I returned with photos of my children to one of the communities in which I had spent time. One woman I had interviewed saw me from the other side of the memorial, ran over and hugged me, and exclaimed, "I knew you'd come back!" She was thrilled that I was "finally" a mother.

I did not pay participants for their time, but I did provide every participant with a small gift of lotion, soap, cookies, or nuts from my hometown. Prior to my first trip, I also asked colleagues in Rwanda what they suggested I take with me to donate or give away. They recommended maxi pads, toiletries, and school supplies. I asked my synagogue and community members I knew for donations and received generous amounts. At first I felt awkward giving out maxi pads and didn't want to embarrass people or appear presumptuous of their needs prior to asking what they were, but the recipients were appreciative. After my first trip, I asked the communities where I was interviewing what they would like me to bring them from the US when I returned. The most common request was for sanitary napkins, school supplies, soap, shampoo, children's shoes, and clothing. I collected these items from friends and family and arrived with three (very large) full suitcases. During my second trip, my generosity with maxi pads earned me a nickname in one village— *kubu my mihango muzungu*, which I later found out meant "the menstruation white lady."

Second and third interviews were always smoother and, unsurprisingly, more revealing than the first ones. First interviews sometimes occasioned suspicion, especially if I did not have a gatekeeper to vouch for me. After asking me about marriage and children, some participants followed with questions about why I cared about genocide and what my connection was to the project. I began each interview with an opportunity for participants to ask me anything they liked, and I answered honestly. This is what I later termed a "reverse interview." Reverse interviews varied in their intensity, with a few lasting up to thirty minutes. Interviews were "relational" in the sense that they were a two-way dialogue and semistructured.[27] When asked why I study genocide, I explained that my grandparents had lost many of their loved ones in the Holocaust, and that I saw how that affected them and my mother throughout their lives. I explained that this personal experience made me curious about how violence affects communities in its aftermath and how people rebuild their lives.

After I revealed this personal information several days in a row, Ntwari noted that he perceived participants feeling more comfortable when I disclosed my Jewish identity earlier on in the interview than when it was not disclosed or was disclosed only at the end of the interview. He suggested that I convey information about my identity prior to the interview, making people more comfortable and less suspicious. From an ethical perspective, I was unsure what to do with this information. I naturally wanted participants to feel at ease when disclosing information to me, but leveraging my identity and my grandparents' suffering felt manipulative. I wrestled with questions such as: Should I share my grandparents' history and my own for the purpose of getting better data? Is that ethical? Or am I making interviewees feel less alone and easing their anguish by sharing the story of my own ancestors' suffering? I let these questions steep for a weekend and resolved that in my introduction I would continue with the Kinyarwanda opening I had been saying in all the previous interviews. Ntwari would then continue to explain, just as before, that participants could ask me anything prior to or after the interview. However, I asked him to include examples of questions, such as inquiries about my family or life, or how and why I became interested in Rwandan memorials and reconciliation. Most participants took me up on this question, but not all.

To my surprise, many participants were familiar with Judaism. Being Jewish in Rwanda was not a lonely experience. Many of the white people I met in Rwanda were Jewish, and it was in Rwanda that I attended the largest Rosh Hashanah dinner I have ever been to, equipped with tents, multiple tables, and a huge feast. I also hosted my own Rosh Hashanah and Passover dinners, which my Rwandan family and their friends enthusiastically attended. I lived with a brilliant seven-year-old who regularly translated for me in the home. When we were shopping in a grocery store located in town, a white nun wearing a religious habit walked past us speaking in an American accent to her colleague. The seven-year-old pulled me aside and whispered quite loudly, "Look at that Jew wearing a nun's outfit!" I explained that she was indeed a nun, just an American one. He vehemently disagreed, explaining to me that Jews were white and nuns were African, so she must be a Jew dressing as a nun. This amusing conversation points to the noticeable presence of Jews in Rwanda.

Trauma

Researching trauma is painful. Researchers bear witness to participants' suffering and institutions' failures yet lack the training or means to solve any of these problems. Researching trauma and violence often feels devoid of hope and meaning, and it can permanently change the researcher's world view. Scholars have found that those who study sexual violence in particular experience emotional responses including anger, guilt, fear, and sadness.[28] Rebecca Campbell discusses how researching rape through "repeated exposure to empathizing with victims" puts researchers at risk of experiencing strong emotional responses such as constant fear, shame, and depression.[29] Campbell writes: "We are studying something from which we have no immunity. There is no line that separates us, the researchers, from them, the survivors. We knew we could be or could have been on the other side of the interview—telling a story of surviving rape, not listening to one. It became more and more difficult to think about rape when the very things we were hearing and learning in our research project reminded us of our own vulnerabilities."[30] Likewise, when sexual violence occurs during war and genocide, researchers need "to pay close attention to painful human experiences and listen to stories of intense suffering and injustices which may personally affect them."[31]

Since I can remember, I have been preoccupied with understanding atrocity, especially the gendered dynamics of violence. This led me down a road of studying domestic violence, sexual assault, war, ethnic cleansing, and ultimately mass atrocity and genocidal rape. These intellectual pursuits may have taken root in mundane discussions during my childhood about Nazis and concentration camps, or from hearing stories of close friends surviving sexual assault. My dedication to the study of mass atrocity is fueled by a steadfast belief that one must understand violence in order to eradicate it. Earlier work of mine on the grandchildren of Holocaust survivors and interviews with Rwandan refugees somewhat prepared me for the pervasiveness of trauma in present-day Rwandan life.[32] However, it was impossible to fully prepare, as the paragraphs that follow can attest. (Some of these details are harrowing, so please skip to the next section if need be.)

One of the first commemorations of the 1994 genocide against the Tutsi I attended was in 2009 in the US. This commemoration marked only one of the two times that I felt physically ill after hearing a testimony of survival. The woman who was providing her testimony at this commemoration in 2009 told a detailed story of the deliberate drowning of her baby and her search for him in the river after the militia intentionally left her barely alive. She sobbed on stage with such agony that I, too, wept. Her story, of which I will spare the reader the details, was horrific. I couldn't believe she was standing on the stage—alive, poised, strong, eloquent—in front of me. After her speech, I (along with a few others) stepped out of the auditorium to catch my breath and try to manage my nausea. I crouched down and, after suppressing my urge to vomit, went back into the auditorium.

Such nausea didn't return until a conversation with a survivor in 2012. I of course experienced sadness during many interviews, but my emotions felt manageable and in control. Her story involved forced cannibalism, and the killing of children in front of their parents. As the story unfolded, I began to feel dizzy. I knew this person, and had interviewed her months before, but she had not previously shared these details. She cried and expressed her guilt for not being able to save her children. I also shed tears but for the most part kept it together, telling her how brave she was, how none of it was her fault, and how so very sorry I was for all she endured. While I knew this story was going to haunt me for the rest of my life, I felt I could not ask her to stop telling it to me, for she had lived it, and I was just bearing witness to her testimony. She deserved to have someone listen, and she explicitly said she wanted the Western world to know how horrible the genocide was. When her story was over, and she said she felt better, we hugged, and I walked back to my car.

That night was different from other evenings of difficult interviews. Something had changed. I drove back home in shock—my view of the world permanently altered. I knew people did awful things but was able to detach from them by theorizing about social situations, inequality, and the power of political institutions. This was something else—a tipping point. I felt physically ill, suffocated, and guilty for my reaction, as I had only heard the story, I hadn't lived through it. After dropping off Ntwari, I felt my thoughts begin to crowd out my ability to focus on the dirt road ahead of me, and I pulled over onto a rare flat shoulder off the road. I had to catch my breath. I walked over to the passenger side of the car to try to breathe deeply and be out of the way of oncoming traffic when my mind was flooded with images of the horrors just described. Uncontrollably, as I attempted to lean back on the passenger side door to look up at the stars and reorient myself, I was soon forced to hunch over, leaning on my knees for support as I violently vomited. My vomit hit the dirt road with such force that dust billowed up in my face as I wiped the saliva hanging from my mouth with my sleeve. I sat there and cried on the side of the road for a minute, swished water in my mouth, and got back in the car to go home.

After that night, I did not allow myself to remember that horrible story for the remainder of my trip—I couldn't. Compartmentalization was brilliantly successful for the remainder of my trip and dissertation writing, but not forever. I am still haunted by the story today, and after the birth of my first child, this story, along with others that I hadn't thought of for years, flooded my mind. When he was an infant and I was postpartum, people would in good faith jokingly tell me how cute he was and how they could just "eat him up." Such colloquial speech would remind me of this woman's story and sudden feelings of fear and disgust would overwhelm me, leaving me nauseous and unsteady. These stories came back again with the birth of my second child and haunt me throughout mundane moments of motherhood, intertwined with guilt, shame, confusion, and horror. Such emotions are likely a form of secondary trauma, a response that took a more typical form during the mourning period in 2012.

Attending commemorations during the mourning period in 2012 was agonizing and at times terrifying as I observed so many people in such profound grief. After attending ten commemorations in the first two weeks of the mourning period, I took a break one Sunday and took the children I lived with to a pool at a nearby hotel. While the children were swimming, I kept hearing survivors scream from flashbacks of the genocide and would turn around to look for survivors that might need assistance. As I looked around to see where the survivor was, I saw there were only children playing in the pool or sitting on the pool deck. It was so bizarre: I was sure that I had heard the sound of someone having a flashback, someone traumatizing like those discussed in chapter 4, but no one was there. My dreams that night were the same, featuring survivors screaming in agony and believing that their lives were at risk. I told one of my friends who was a priest and educator about this. He said it was a typical case of secondary trauma, and that it was time to take a few days off and rest. During this time, I began to get a small glimpse of what trauma counselors might experience, though the depth of what I observed paled in comparison to what they do on a regular basis.

To cope with some of the stories I was hearing and the trauma I was witnessing, I took breaks from research when possible on the weekends and spent time with the children at my host family's home. I also ran on a treadmill at a hotel in town after lengthy days, sometimes for long periods of time until my head cleared, or until I was too exhausted to think. Exercise is one of the coping strategies used by researchers who work on traumatized individuals, as is refraining from watching violent media.[33] It is for this reason that, to this day, I have not seen most documentaries about Rwanda or genocide.[34]

Stories from the Field:
Cars and Ditches

When I was in Rwanda in 2011, many roads and parking lots were unpaved, and several had numerous holes and ditches. One evening, after picking up bread for the family, I reversed, forgetting about a giant ditch that was not in my field of vision but that I had routinely seen and avoided. I heard the dreaded *crunch* as the side of the car hit the ditch when the passenger's side tire got stuck, leaving the car at an unnatural angle. When I got out of the car, I saw the SUV leaning sideways, and my heart sank as I imagined how I would tell the family that I had totaled their car. About twelve men who had been sitting on the sidewalk in front of the ditch gathered around to see what I had done; this was both embarrassing and moderately scary. I suggested we lift it out of the ditch together—and some of the men laughed at me.

Out of nowhere, an Australian man fluent in Kinyarwanda offered to help me get the car out. He got in the driver's seat and put it in 4-wheel drive, and the twelve men lifted the car out of the ditch. He drove it to the side of the road, making it easy for me to merge back onto the main road. This would have been fine, except the men who lifted the car out all wanted money from me, yelling words in Kinyarwanda that I didn't know, chasing after me, and grabbing my purse. I thought one man was going to steal my purse. For the first time, I felt fearful in Rwanda. I eventually got in the car and drove to the turnoff to my dirt road, where I strategized about what to do. There was no IRB protocol or manual for what you do when you crash your host family's car! Would I need to go home early? Would everyone be mad at me? How would I do my interviews without a car? What if it costs a fortune to repair?

I was scared and upset that I had damaged my friend's car and worried she would be angry with me. I called to tell her, but she didn't answer, so I called her sister, my best friend. She answered the phone, and that's when tears drizzled down my face. She assured me it would be fine and to just get home safely, and that her husband would meet me there to look at the car. When I got home, one of the young women I lived with had just returned home from high school, and I told her about the incident, clearly upset. She apparently called her uncle, who rushed home thinking I was hurt. Within an hour, one of the women I lived with came home with her other sister, her husband, his brother, and his friend. They went out and looked at the car, and I don't know how it was possible, but only one little scratch was present on the side fender, and most of the scratches were underneath the car. They assured me this was not something that needed fixing, for the family driver could easily repair the fender with a screw that he had out back. My friend's husband explained that people scratch their cars all the time, and everyone took turns telling me about the scratches on their own cars.

When my friend, the one who owned the car I was using, walked into the dining room around 9:00 p.m. that evening, I immediately apologized. Apparently, her sister had warned her that I had cried over this event, and she covered my mouth as I was trying to talk and said, "Shhh . . . baby, don't cry, are you safe? Yes. Are you hurt? No. There should be no tears, only joy." I asked her if I could show her the scratch. She said no, she was tired, her feet hurt from her heels, and she could see it later. She poured me a drink, two shots in a single glass, to be exact. She said I should have that drink to calm down and go to bed. I drank the two shots the way many Americans would put away a shot of strong liquor: in one gulp with a chaser, thumping the empty glass down on the table afterward. I looked over at her as I shook off the taste and noticed her expression and that of her seven-year-old: both had eyes wide open and mouths agape, looking quite shocked. He said, "Mama, is that how you are supposed to drink it?" She replied, "No, that is not how you are supposed to drink that, but remember you think she is African, but she has some

American left in her." In the days that followed, I learned how common it was to get a vehicle stuck in a ditch or in the mud, and how one should always keep change in the car in case young men offering assistance request their customary tip. And one should always sip from a shot glass.

Stories from the Field:
Costs of Not Returning

A group of Rwandan university students worked with me to cross-check interview translation accuracy. One of the young men, Sergio, was also a survivor of the 1994 genocide against the Tutsi.[35] In July 1994, Sergio had escaped with his mother and sister to a refugee camp, where his mother vowed to do whatever it took to never return to Rwanda. Sergio and his sister wanted to return, and in the years after the genocide, with their mother's declining mental health, they did. They received some government assistance, obtained orphan status, and relocated to a CHH village. Their mother married a man from Congo and moved there to be with him.

Upon walking into the café where we were meeting to go over translation checks, Sergio asked if he could speak with me alone. We stepped outside, where he explained his mother was in the hospital. She and her husband had been fighting often, and he was physically abusive. The previous night, the violence had escalated, and his mother's husband beat her so badly that she was in an intensive care unit with internal bleeding. He wanted to know if he could borrow money from me to visit his mother, pay her medical bills, and try to move her out. I readily agreed, even while knowing that Sergio was unlikely to be able to pay me back. At the time, I was a graduate student and had little money of my own, but I could certainly manage.

Over the course of the next several weeks, Sergio provided me with updates on his mother. She recovered and contemplated leaving her husband but would not consider moving to Rwanda with her children. Sergio explained that what she observed in Rwanda had taken everything out of her, and she could no longer be a mother or return to Rwanda. That is why she married the first person she could. Even if he was abusive, in her mind, at least she was not in Rwanda, and he supported her during her flashbacks and traumatic episodes. When I would see Sergio in the coming weeks, I made sure to ask about his mother until his answers became shorter and his eye contact ceased. I stopped asking and brought up only his sister, who was earning high marks at a Catholic school in the Western province; I followed his lead and avoided discussing his mother. I do not know what happened to her, but I do know that after the genocide, people, women in particular, had to make difficult choices and sacrifices to survive. For Sergio's mother, the costs were high.

Stories from the Field: Goats and Beer

One of my very best friends in Rwanda was a Catholic priest, who generously shared his group of friends (fellow priests) with me. We often went out for beers. Primus was the brand of choice to wash down goat brochettes, the national food of Rwanda, as I have been told. I am personally not a fan of goat meat, which I find too chewy, but I never wanted to offend anyone, so I ate it when we got together, and when my jaw got sore from chewing too much, I subtly spit it into my napkin after wiping my face. The group of priests I would hang out with were funny, smart, and caring. Originating from Uganda, they spoke English and offered a respite from occasional frustration over the language barrier.

One night, when celebrating my best friend's birthday, after several beers, a light-hearted conversation began with one of the priests, who said to me with a contagious, jovial smile:

> PRIEST 1: You are just like one of us!
> ME: Yeah, except I am not a priest.
> PRIEST 1: Well, yeah. There's that.
> ME: And I am a woman.
> PRIEST 1: Well, that too, but that's it!
> ME: And I am Jewish.
> PRIEST 1: Yeah, I guess there is that too.
> PRIEST 2, LAUGHING AND SLAPPING HIS KNEE: And she doesn't believe in our savior!
> PRIEST 1: Okay, yeah, there is that too, but our savior was Jewish.
> ME, SARCASTICALLY: Is that all our differences? Umm . . .
> PRIEST 3, JUMPING IN LOUDLY: And she doesn't like goat!
> ME: How did you know that? I keep trying to like it!
> PRIEST 3: That's why I never said anything, I liked watching how you try it each time!

We laughed about the goat, and I kept laughing about my kind friend who saw past our differences so earnestly through a Primus beer-induced lens.

Qualitative research requires consistent, rigorous, and methodical reflection on the questions asked, the research design, and the researcher's own positionality. Such reflexivity means adjusting interview questions, listening to the silences of participants, and reflecting on interactions or situations that could have been handled better. I learned that while I thought I was being respectful of people's time by jumping into the interview and research project right away, my haste was perceived as carelessness. It was more appropriate to talk with participants about our families and engage in small talk, in my limited Kinyarwanda, about the foods and places I loved in Rwanda. While my intentions were earnest in getting straight to the interview, they did not map onto Rwandan cultural norms.

In the research design for this book, I had to ensure that the methodologies I adopted would allow me to answer the questions I was trying to understand. One key to understanding memory culture in Rwanda after the genocide would undoubtedly be spending time attending memorial tours, commemorations, and memory rituals, but observations made in these settings would only give me part of the picture. To research the emotional landscape of remembrance after atrocity, I would need to conduct in-depth interviews, as conversations with survivors showed me "not just what they think and feel, but how it feels to feel that way . . . the emotional environment that they inhabit and the particular pressures that this cultural world puts on them."[36]

In the design for this project, reflexivity also meant planning ahead for situations that were unfamiliar to me as an American. For instance, I was once offered milk in the home of a participant; I was fairly certain it had not been boiled or refrigerated, and the likelihood of me falling ill from the bacteria was relatively high. I did not know what to do in this situation to avoid appearing rude or ungrateful. I drank some of the milk and was sick within eight hours. Later I discussed with Ntwari how I could have handled that situation better. He suggested telling them I had just eaten, which I later did in several situations, but that strategy did not work well with beverages. Ultimately, I decided that when I was invited to people's houses, I would arrive with Fanta and bottled water for everyone. This allowed me to thank participants for their time and avoid unsafe beverages.

Finally, reflexivity also meant questioning aspects of my own identity, both those that can be seen and those that can't. My identity as a young white American woman was discovered as soon as I was seen and spoke with an American accent. However, my Jewishness was not easily identified, and I had to evaluate how I wanted that piece of myself and my family's history to function in interviews.

Researching violence of all types is painful, but there are moments of hope, such as learning that individuals encountered during fieldwork have since received counseling or other resources that have helped them manage their pain; or experiencing participants' feelings of empowerment after being able to describe their experiences. There are moments when it becomes clear what real-life heroes are: those who perform superhuman acts of rescue, bravery, or compassion in a time of political chaos. In all honesty, these moments are few and far between, and the idea of striking a balance between hope and despair is in large part a masquerade. The hopeful moments are sometimes indeed truly hopeful, but often they feel hopeful only in comparison to the deeply unjust experiences that participants have endured.

This appendix stands in contrast to much of the book in the sense that the book is ordered and sequential. The research process itself lacks the same organizational control that the end-product displays. Qualitative research is precarious because of uncertainties. Conclusions and claims are unstable because such assertions change over time. Positionality raises questions: Should the researcher disclose or remain silent about her own identity? Circumstances may jeopardize one's ability to do fieldwork: What happens when the car gets stuck in a ditch? How does one access a participant who lives in a home with no road access? Interview narratives may leave the researcher in a precarious position: Will a story impact her so strongly that she finds herself vomiting at the side of the road? Will a participant she knows well unexpectedly disclose a story that will haunt the researcher for years to come?

Qualitative research involves a level of unpredictability that reflects the instability of the social world. The precariousness of research means the ifs are the one predictable part of the research, something not just to become comfortable with but to embrace. Researching the social world, especially the worst of it, means you can't shield yourself from your own reactions. However, the more human we admit we are, the more insightful our research can be. It is in moments of precariousness that meaningful theories of injustice are formed.

Notes

Introduction

1. Allan Thompson, ed., *The Media and the Rwandan Genocide* (Ann Arbor: Pluto Press, 2007). For example, see William E. Schmidt, "Deaths in Rwanda Said to Be 20,000 or More," *New York Times*, April 11, 1994.

2. Trauma can be described as an experience of "overstimulation of a person's psychic structures so that the individual needs to reinvent or repair basic ways of making meaning and bounding the self and others." Martha Minow, *Between Vengeance and Forgiveness: Facing History after Genocide and Mass Violence* (Boston: Beacon, 1998), 64.

3. Duncan S. Bell, "Mythscapes: Memory, Mythology, and National Identity," *British Journal of Sociology* 54 (2003); Nuala Johnson, "Cast in Stone: Monuments, Geography, and Nationalism," *Environment and Planning D: Society and Space* 13, no. 1 (1995); Brad West, "Collective Memory and Crisis: The 2002 Bali Bombing, National Heroic Archetypes and the Counter-narrative of Cosmopolitan Nationalism," *Journal of Sociology* 44, no. 4 (2008).

4. This project takes seriously scholars of Rwanda who call for local-level narrative analysis. Susanne Buckley-Zistel states, "It is paramount to ask why different groups draw on a particular narrative of the past; what form of belonging they seek to create in the process; and what function this serves in contemporary Rwanda." Susanne Buckley-Zistel, "Nation, Narration, Unification? The Politics of History Teaching after the Rwandan Genocide," *Journal of Genocide Research* 11, no. 1 (2009): 48. Bert Ingelaere writes, "Large-scale research projects of all sorts exist, but what is lacking is local-level research and analysis of the micro-level processes at work in smaller communities." Bert Ingelaere, "Do We Understand Life after Genocide? Center and Periphery in the Construction of Knowledge in Postgenocide Rwanda," *African Studies Review* 53, no. 1 (2010): 47.

5. Unfortunately, no Twa were interviewed for this book.

6. Hilary Appel, "Anti-Communist Justice and Founding the Post-Communist Order: Lustration and Restitution in Central Europe," *East European Politics and Societies* 19, no. 3 (2005); Judy Barsalou and Victoria Baxter, *The Urge to Remember: The*

Role of Memorials in Social Reconstruction and Transitional Justice, Stabilization and Reconstruction Series 5 (Washington, DC: United States Institute for Peace, 2007); Alexandra Barahona De Brito, Carmen Gonzaléz-Enríquez, and Paloma Aguilar, eds. *The Politics of Memory: Transitional Justice in Democratizing Societies* (Oxford: Oxford University Press, 2001); Alexander Laban Hinton, ed., *Transitional Justice: Global Mechanisms and Local Realities after Genocide and Mass Violence* (New Brunswick, NJ: Rutgers University Press, 2011).

7. Michael Wenzel et al., "Retributive and Restorative Justice," *Law and Human Behavior* 32, no. 5 (2008).

8. Howard Zehr, *The Little Book of Restorative Justice: Revised and Updated* (New York: Good Books, 2014).

9. Kathleen Daly, "Restorative Justice: The Real Story," *Punishment & Society* 4, no. 1 (2002).

10. Paul McCold, "Toward a Holistic Vision of Restorative Juvenile Justice: A Reply to the Maximalist Model," *Contemporary Justice Review* 3, no. 4 (2000).

11. Adama Dieng, "Capacity-Building Efforts of the ICTR: A Different Kind of Legacy," *Northwestern Journal of International Human Rights* 9, no. 3 (2011); ICTR, *Symposium on the Legacy of International Criminal Courts and Tribunals in Africa* (Waltham, MA: International Center for Ethics, Justice, and Public Life, Brandeis University, 2007); Leila Nadya Sadat, "The Legacy of the International Criminal Tribunal for Rwanda" (paper, Whitney R. Harris World Law Institute, Washington University, St. Louis, MO, 2012).

12. Galina Nelaeva, "The Impact of Transnational Advocacy Networks on The Prosecution of Wartime Rape and Sexual Violence: The Case of the ICTR," *International Social Science Review* 85, nos. 1–2 (2010); Prosecutor v. Jean-Paul Akayesu, Case No. ICTR 96-4-T, Judgment (Sept. 2, 1998).

13. Phillip Weiner, "The Evolving Jurisprudence of the Crime of Rape in International Criminal Law," *Boston College Law Review* 54, no. 3 (2013).

14. See Nelaeva, "Impact."

15. Nicholas A. Jones, *The Courts of Genocide: Politics and the Rule of Law in Rwanda and Arusha* (New York: Routledge, 2009); Luc Reydams, "The ICTR Ten Years On: Back to the Nuremberg Paradigm?," *Journal of International Criminal Justice* 3, no. 4 (2005); Sadat, "Legacy."

16. Rupert Skilbeck, "Funding Justice: The Price of War Crimes Trials," *Human Rights Brief* 15, no. 3 (2008); United Nations International Residual Mechanism for Criminal Tribunals, "The ICTR in Brief," http://unictr.unmict.org/en/tribunal (accessed October 2018).

17. Priscilla B. Hayner, *Unspeakable Truths: Confronting State Terror and Atrocity* (New York: Routledge, 2001); Minow, *Between Vengeance and Forgiveness*; Claire Moon, "Healing Past Violence: Traumatic Assumptions and Therapeutic Interventions in War and Reconciliation." *Journal of Human Rights* 8, no. 1 (2009); National Unity and Reconciliation Commission, "National Unity and Reconciliation Commission," (2014). http://www.nurc.gov.rw/index.php?id=69.

18. See Claire Moon's work on the South African Truth Commission, especially Claire Moon, *Narrating Political Reconciliation* (Lanham, MD: Lexington, 2009).

19. James L. Gibson, *Overcoming Apartheid: Can Truth Reconcile a Divided Nation?* (Cape Town, South Africa: HSRC Press, 2004).

20. Hayner, *Confronting*.

21. Hayner, *Confronting*.

22. Onur Bakiner, "Truth Commission Impact: An Assessment of How Commissions Influence Politics and Society," *International Journal of Transitional Justice* 8, no. 1 (2014); Karen Brounéus, "The Trauma of Truth Telling: Effects of Witnessing in the Rwandan Gacaca Courts on Psychological Health," *Journal of Conflict Resolution* 54, no. 3 (2010).

23. See Beth Goldblatt and Shiela Meintjes, "Dealing with the Aftermath: Sexual Violence and the Truth and Reconciliation Commission," *Agenda: Empowering Women for Gender Equity* (1998); Lyn Graybill, "The Contribution of the Truth and Reconciliation Commission toward the Promotion of Women's Rights in South Africa," *Women's Studies International Forum* 24, no. 1 (2001); Karen Brounéus, "Truth-Telling as Talking Cure? Insecurity and Retraumatization in the Rwandan Gacaca Courts," *Security Dialogue* 39, no. 1 (2008).

24. Elazar Barkan and Alexander Karn, eds., *Taking Wrongs Seriously: Apologies and Reconciliation* (Stanford: Stanford University Press, 2006); James L. Gibson, "The Contributions of Truth to Reconciliation: Lessons from South Africa," *Journal of Conflict Resolution* 50, no. 3 (2006); Gibson, *Overcoming*.

25. Donna E. Arzt, "Views on the Ground: The Local Perception of International Criminal Tribunals in the Former Yugoslavia and Sierra Leone," *Annals of the American Academy of Political and Social Science*, no. 603 (2006); Barkan and Karn, *Taking Wrongs Seriously*; Phil Clark and Zachary D. Kaufman, *After Genocide: Transitional Justice, Post-Conflict Reconstruction and Reconciliation in Rwanda and Beyond* (New York: Columbia University Press, 2009); David M. Engel and Frank W. Munger, "Rights, Remembrance, and the Reconciliation of Difference," *Law & Society Review* 30, no. 1 (1996).

26. Canada's truth commission addresses the forced assimilation of indigenous children, which resulted in a comprehensive settlement, including compensation and survivor-led commemoration events and memorialization initiatives. These projects ranged from "traditional and virtual quilts, monuments and memorials, traditional medicine gardens, totem pole and canoe carving, oral history, community ceremonies and feasts, land-based culture and language camps, cemetery restoration, film and digital storytelling, commemorative walking trails, and theatre or dance productions." See the summary report: Truth and Reconciliation Commission of Canada, *Honouring the Truth, Reconciling for the Future: Summary of the Final Report of the Truth and Reconciliation Commission of Canada* (University of Manitoba: Truth and Reconciliation Commission of Canada, 2015), 284.

27. Barsalou and Baxter, "Urge to Remember." The International Center for Transitional Justice is an exception with projects on memory and justice in several different

countries. See International Center for Truth and Justice, "Truth and Memory," accessed December 2018, https://www.ictj.org/our-work/transitional-justice-issues/truth-and -memory.

28. Hayner, *Confronting*.

29. United Nations, Human Rights Office of the High Commissioner, "Basic Principles and Guidelines on the Right to a Remedy and Reparation for Victims of Gross Violations of International Human Rights Law and Serious Violations of International Humanitarian Law," December 2005, http://www.ohchr.org/EN/Profession alInterest/Pages/RemedyAndReparation.aspx.

30. Artemis Christodulou, *Memorials and Transitional Justice*, Sierra Leone Truth and Reconciliation Commission Final Report by the Sierra Leone Truth and Reconciliation Commission, Appendix 1: Part 4, 2004.

31. George Herbert Mead, *The Nature of the Past* (New York: Henry Holt, 1929), 238.

32. Jeffrey K. Olick and Joyce Robbins, "Social Memory Studies: From Collective Memory to the Historical Sociology of Mnemonic Practices," *Annual Review of Sociology* 24 (1998); Eviatar Zerubavel, "Social Memories: Steps to a Sociology of the Past," *Qualitative Sociology* 19, no. 3 (1996); Eviatar Zerubavel, *Time Maps: Collective Memory and the Social Shape of the Past* (Chicago: University of Chicago Press, 2003).

33. On this range of issues, see the following: Janet L. Jacobs, *Memorializing the Holocaust: Gender, Genocide, and Collective Memory* (New York: I.B. Tauris, 2010); Annie E. Coombes, *History after Apartheid: Visual Culture and Public Memory in a Democratic South Africa* (Durham, NC: Duke University Press, 2003); Francesca Polletta, "Legacies and Liabilities of an Insurgent Past: Remembering Martin Luther King, Jr., on the House and Senate Floor," *Social Science History* 22, no. 4 (1998); Vered Vinitzky-Seroussi, "Commemorating a Difficult Past: Yitzhak Rabin's Memorial," *American Sociological Review* 67, no. 1 (2002); Robin Wagner-Pacifici and Barry Swartz, "The Vietnam Veterans Memorial: Commemorating a Difficult Past," *American Journal of Sociology* 97, no. 2 (1991).

34. Pat Caplan, "'Never Again': Genocide Memorials in Rwanda," *Anthropology Today* 23, no. 1 (2007); Patrick Hagopian, *The Vietnam War in American Memory: Veterans, Memorials and the Politics of Healing* (Boston: University of Massachusetts Press, 2009); Janet Jacobs, "Memorializing the Sacred: Kristallnacht in German National Memory," *Journals for the Scientific Study of Religion* 47, no. 3 (2008); James Tatum, "Memorials of the American War in Vietnam," *Critical Inquiry*, no. 22 (1996); Vinitzky-Seroussi, "Commemorating"; Wagner-Pacifici and Swartz, "Vietnam"; Lars Waldorf, "Revisiting Hotel Rwanda: Genocide Ideology, Reconciliation, and Rescuers," *Journal of Genocide Research* 11, no. 1 (2009); James E. Young, *The Texture of Memory: Holocaust Memorials and Meaning* (New Haven, C: Yale University Press, 1993).

35. Caplan, "Genocide Memorials"; Piotr Cieplak, *Death, Image, Memory: The Genocide in Rwanda and its Aftermath in Photography and Documentary Film* (London: Palgrave Macmillan, 2017); Amy Sodaro, *Exhibiting Atrocity: Memorial Museums and the Politics of Past Violence* (New Brunswick, NJ: Rutgers University Press, 2018); Véronique

Tadjo, "Genocide: The Changing Landscape of Memory in Kigali," *African Identities* 8, no. 4 (2010).

36. Olick and Robbins, "Social Memory."

37. Maurice Halbwachs, *On Collective Memory* (Chicago: University of Chicago Press, 1992).

38. Karl Marx, *The Eighteenth Brumaire of Louis Bonaparte, Surveys from Exile: Political Writings* (London: Verso, 1852): 15.

39. Halbwachs, *Collective Memory*.

40. Jeffrey Olick, "Collective Memory: Two Cultures," *Sociological Theory* 17, no. 3 (1999).

41. Barbara Zelizer, "Reading the Past against the Grain: The Shape of Memory Studies," *Critical Studies in Mass Communication* 12, no. 2 (1999).

42. Olick, "Collective Memory," 338.

43. Olick, "Collective Memory," 342.

44. Halbwachs, *Collective Memory*, 40.

45. Olick, "Collective Memory," 335.

46. Karl Mannheim, "The Problems of Generations," in *Essays in the Sociology of Knowledge*, ed. Karl Mannheim (London: Routledge, 1952).

47. Mannheim, "Problems," 298.

48. See Lynne Chisholm, "Mannheim Revisited: Youth, Generation and Life-Course" (paper presented at the International Sociological Association World Congress of Sociology, Brisbane, Australia, 2002); Larry J. Griffin, "'Generations and Collective Memory' Revisited: Race, Region, and Memory of Civil Rights," *American Sociological Review* 69, no. 4 (2004); Camille Peugny and Cécile Van de Velde, "Re-Thinking Inter-Generational Inequality," *Revue Française de Sociologie* 54, no. 4 (2013); Howard Schuman and Jacqueline Scott, "Generations and Collective Memories," *American Sociological Review* 54, no. 3 (1989): 359; Howard Schuman and Cheryl Rieger, "Historical Analogies, Generational Effects, and Attitudes Toward War," *American Sociological Review*, no. 57 (1992). On generations bonding over shared national events, see Griffin, "Civil Rights"; Jeff A. Larson and Omar Lizardo, "Generations, Identities, and the Collective Memory of Che Guevara," *Sociological Forum* 22, no. 4 (2007); Schuman and Scott, "Generations"; Frederick D. Weil, "Cohorts, Regimes, and the Legitimation of Democracy: West Germany since 1945," *American Sociological Review* 52, no. 3 (1987).

49. Zerubavel, "Social Memories," 289.

50. Benedict Anderson, *Imagined Communities: Reflections on the Origins and Spread of Nationalism*, 2nd ed. (New York: Verso, 1991): 7; Eric Hobsbawm and Terrence Ranger, eds., *The Invention of Tradition* (New York: Cambridge University Press, 1983).

51. Reinhart Koselleck, *The Practice of Conceptual History: Timing History, Spacing Concepts* (Stanford: Stanford University Press, 2002).

52. Edward S. Casey, *Remembering: A Phenomenological Study*, 2nd ed. (Bloomington: Indiana University Press, 2000), 250.

53. Paul Connerton, *How Societies Remember* (New York: Cambridge University Press, 1989), 43.

54. Connerton, *Societies*, 61.

55. Joachim Savelsberg and Ryan King, "Institutionalizing Collective Memories of Hate: Law and Law Enforcement in Germany and the United States," *American Journal of Sociology* III, no. 2 (2005); Richard Ashby Wilson, *The Politics of Truth and Reconciliation in South Africa: Legitimizing the Post-Apartheid State* (Cambridge: Cambridge University Press, 2001).

56. See Wagner-Pacifici and Swartz, "Vietnam." See also Griffin, "Civil Rights"; Robert S. Jansen, "Resurrection and Appropriation: Reputational Trajectories, Memory Work, and the Political Use of Historical Figures," *American Journal of Sociology* 112, no. 4 (2007); Jeffrey K. Olick, *The Politics of Regret: On Collective Memory and Historical Responsibility* (New York: Routledge, 2007); Francesca Polletta, *It Was Like a Fever: Storytelling in Protest and Politics* (Chicago: University of Chicago Press, 2006).

57. Vinitzky-Seroussi, "Commemorating."

58. Peter Ehrenhaus, "Commemorating the Unwon War: On Not Remembering Vietnam," *Journal of Communication*, no. 39 (1989); Hagopian, *Vietnam War*; Arthur G. Neal, *National Trauma and Collective Memory: Extraordinary Events in the American Experience* (Armonk, NY: M. E. Sharpe, 2005); Marita Sturken, *Tangled Memories: The Vietnam War, the AIDS Epidemic, and the Politics of Remembering* (Berkeley: University of California Press, 1997); Tatum, "Memorials."

59. Young, *Texture*.

60. Anup Shekar Chakraborty, "Memory of a Lost Past, Memory of Rape: Nostalgia, Trauma and the Construction of Collective Social Memory Among the Zo Hnahthlak," *Identity, Culture and Politics* 11, no. 2 (2010); Francesca Declich, "When Silence Makes History: Gender and Memories of War Violence from Somalia," in *Anthropology of Violence and Conflict*, ed. Bettina Schmudt and Ingo Schroeder (New York: Routledge, 2001); Jacobs, *Memorializing*; Jayne S. Werner, "Between Memory and Desire: Gender and the Remembrance of War in Doi Moi Vietnam," *Gender, Place and Culture* 13, no. 3 (2006).

61. Miriam Cooke, *Women and the War Story* (Berkeley: University of California Press, 1996); Jacobs, *Memorializing*; Barbara Zelizer, *Visual Culture and the Holocaust* (New Brunswick, NJ: Rutgers University Press, 2001).

62. Jacobs, *Memorializing*.

63. Barsalou and Baxter, *Urge*.

64. Memorials and collective memory projects can have profound institutional effects in law, law enforcement, and public policy. For example, based on their national collective memories, the United States and Germany have dealt with hate crimes very differently. Germany, with memories of the Holocaust and a failed state, has instituted specific hate crime law around groups that were formally targeted by the Nazis, while the US legislature has drawn primarily on foreign human rights abuses rather than national ones (Savelsberg and King, "Institutionalizing").

65. Nicole Fox, "'Oh, Did the Women Suffer, They Suffered so Much': Impacts of Gender-Based Violence on Kinship Networks in Rwanda," *International Journal of*

Sociology of the Family 37, no. 2 (2011); Nicole Fox and Carla De Ycaza, "Narratives of Mass Violence: The Role of Memory and Memorialization in Addressing Human Rights Violations in Post-Conflict Rwanda and Uganda," *Societies without Borders* 8, no. 3 (2013).

66. See the appendix for a discussion on secondary trauma and research dilemmas and ethics when conducting qualitative research in postconflict communities.

Chapter 1. The Context of Violence in Rwanda

1. Tom Goodfellow and Alyson Smith, "From Urban Catastrophe to 'Model' City? Politics, Security and Development in Post-Conflict Kigali," *Urban Studies* 50, no. 15 (2013). Often it is in these very moments of rapid growth after conflict that countries face an increase or resurgence of violence and insecurity—not the contrary. Jack A. Goldstone, "Population and Security: How Demographic Change Can Lead to Violent Conflict," *Journal of International Affairs* 56, no. 1 (2002).

2. Ine Cottyn, "Small Towns and Rural Growth Centers as Strategic Spaces of Control in Rwanda's Post-Conflict Trajectory," *Journal of Eastern African Studies* 12, no. 2 (2018): 329.

3. For Rwanda's Master Plan, see "Kigali Master Plan Update," 2018, https://gcca .eu/sites/default/files/documents/2019-10/17.10%20Session%203.%20Fred%20Mugi sha%20Kigali%20Master%20Plan_0.pdf. For analysis on the impact of the Master Plan on variously situated communities in Rwanda, including the urban poor, see Tom Goodfellow, "Rwanda's Political Settlement and the Urban Transition: Expropriation, Construction and Taxation in Kigali," *Journal of Eastern African Studies* 8, no. 2 (2014); Goodfellow and Smith, "Urban Catastrophe"; Samuel Shearer, "The City Is Burning! Street Economies and the Juxtacity of Kigali, Rwanda," *Urban Forum* (2020). On Kigali as a model city, see Goodfellow and Smith, "Urban Catastrophe."

4. Laura Mann and Marie Berry, "Understanding the Political Motivations That Shape Rwanda's Emergent Developmental State," *New Political Economy* 21, no. 1 (2016). Aid to Rwanda reached almost US$1 billion annually in 2010. Goodfellow and Smith, "Urban Catastrophe." See also Peter Uvin, *Aiding Violence: The Development Enterprise in Rwanda* (Hartford, CT: Kumarian Press, 1998).

5. For more on state efforts to dismantle and reorganize the street economy, with both economic and gendered outcomes, see Shearer, "Street Economies." For more on how state policies have impacted the way poor people can access urban space—for example, the country's mandate that everyone must wear shoes in public (i.e., barefoot individuals are excluded from public spaces and official government functions)—see Ingelaere, "Life after Genocide."

6. Quote from participant in 2012.

7. René Lemarchand, *Burundi Ethnic Conflict and Genocide* (New York: Woodrow Wilson Center, 1996).

8. Anuradha Chakravarty, *Investing in Authoritarian Rule: Punishment and Patronage in Rwanda's Gacaca Courts for Genocide Crimes* (New York: Cambridge University Press, 2016), 52–53.

9. For a detailed analysis of these categories, see J. J. Carney, *Rwanda before the Genocide: Catholic Politics and Ethnic Discourse in the Late Colonial Era* (New York: Oxford University Press, 2013).

10. Catharine Newbury, *The Cohesion of Oppression: Clientship and Ethnicity in Rwanda, 1860–1960* (New York: Columbia University Press, 1988).

11. Helen Codere, *The Biography of an African Society: Rwanda, 1900–1960* (Tervuren: MRAC, 1973); Jacques Maquet, *The Premise of Inequality in Ruanda: A Study of Political Relations in a Central African Kingdom* (New York: Oxford University Press, 1961). See also Susan Thomson's important critique of Maquet's hierarchal perspective of Rwandan Society: *Rwanda: From Genocide to Precarious Peace* (New Haven, CT: Yale University Press, 2018), 42–43.

12. Villia Jefremovas, "Contested Identities: Power and the Fictions of Ethnicity, Ethnography and History in Rwanda," *Anthropologica* 39, no. 1/2 (1997); C. Newbury, *Cohesion*.

13. For more on these systems and inequality prior to the arrival of colonial powers, see Johan Pottier, *Re-imagining Rwanda: Conflict, Survival and Disinformation in the Late Twentieth Century* (New York: Cambridge University Press, 2002); Andrea Purdeková, "Building a Nation in Rwanda? De-ethnicisation and Its Discontents," *Studies in Ethnicity & Nationalism* 8, no. 3 (2008); Jan Vansina, *Antecedents to Modern Rwanda: The Nyiginya Kingdom* (Madison: University of Wisconsin Press, 2004).

14. Carney, *Rwanda*, 23; David Newbury, *The Land beyond the Mists: Essays on Identity and Authority in Precolonial Congo and Rwanda* (Athens: Ohio University Press, 2009), 334.

15. Timothy Longman, *Christianity and Genocide in Rwanda* (New York: Cambridge University Press, 2010).

16. For examples of Germans who reiterated aspects of the Hamitic myth, see Nigel Eltringham, "'Invaders Who Have Stolen the Country': The Hamitic Hypothesis, Race, and the Rwandan Genocide," *Social Identities* 12, no. 4 (2006). See also chapter 3 of Mahmood Mamdani, *When Victims Become Killers: Colonialism, Nativism, and the Genocide in Rwanda* (Princeton, NJ: Princeton University Press, 2001).

17. Rangira Béa Gallimore, "Militarism, Ethnicity, and Sexual Violence in the Rwandan Genocide," *Feminist Africa*, no. 10 (2008); Mamdani, *When Victims Become Killers*.

18. Mamdani, *When Victims Become Killers*, 80.

19. Longman, *Christianity*.

20. Alison Des Forges, *Leave None to Tell the Story: Genocide in Rwanda*, 2nd ed. (New York: Human Rights Watch, 1999); Mamdani, *When Victims Become Killers*.

21. Mamdani, *When Victims Become Killers*, 88.

22. See Carney's discussion of Catholic priest Leon Classe's role in expanding Catholic missions recruiting Tutsi elites, and his assertion of Tutsi nobility and natural leadership (*Rwanda*, 31–36).

23. Carney, *Rwanda*; Des Forges, *Leave None*; Gallimore, "Militarism"; Mamdani, *When Victims Become Killers*; Gérard Prunier, *The Rwanda Crisis: History of a Genocide* (New York: Columbia University Press, 1995).

24. Longman, *Christianity*. For a discussion on the association of Catholic missionary projects and the draw of Western modernizations (schooling, health, and the creation of a Catholic identity for Rwandans), see Carney, *Rwanda*, 36–39.

25. Alison Bashford and Philippa Levine (eds), *The Oxford Handbook of the History of Eugenics* (Oxford: Oxford University Press, 2010).

26. Carney, *Rwanda*.

27. Carney, *Rwanda*.

28. C. Newbury, *Cohesion*.

29. Jefremovas, "Contested Identities."

30. Thomson, *Rwanda*.

31. Catharine Newbury, "Ethnicity and the Politics of History in Rwanda," *Africa Today* 45, no. 1 (1998). Susan Thomson makes an important point that because ethnicity was the marker of oppression, it became the marker of liberation: "for the majority Hutu, ethnic categories became the sole avenue to democratic emancipation." "Ethnicity," 45.

32. C. Newbury, "Ethnicity."

33. Buckley-Zistel, "Nation."

34. Prunier, *Rwanda Crisis*.

35. Carney, *Rwanda*.

36. Des Forges, *Leave None*.

37. Thomson, *Rwanda*, 48.

38. Lee Ann Fujii, *Killing of Neighbors: Webs of Violence in Rwanda* (Ithaca, NY: Cornell University Press, 2009); Longman, *Christianity*, 88.

39. Prunier, *Rwanda Crisis*.

40. One of Habyarimana's development projects was the institution of *umuganda*—required weekly work (repairing infrastructure) for the public good; if individuals missed participation in this civic duty, they were fined. See Thomson, *Rwanda*, 53.

41. Catharine Newbury, "Background to Genocide: Rwanda," *Issue: A Journal of Opinion* 23, no. 2 (1995); Uvin, *Aiding Violence*.

42. Des Forges, *Leave None*.

43. Catharine Newbury and David Newbury, "Rwanda: The Politics of Turmoil," *Africa Notes* (1994).

44. Longman, *Christianity*.

45. Jonathan R. Beloff and Samantha Lakin, "Peace and Compromise, Idealism and Constraint: The Case of the Arusha Peace Accords in Rwanda and Burundi," *Genocide Studies and Prevention: An International Journal* 13, no. 2 (2019); Des Forges, *Leave None*.

46. Des Forges, *Leave None*; Scott Straus, *The Order of Genocide: Race, Power, and War in Rwanda* (Ithaca, NY: Cornell University Press, 2006).

47. Fujii, *Killing*, 50.

48. Straus, *Order of Genocide*.

49. John A. Berry and Carol Pott Berry, *Genocide in Rwanda: A Collective Memory* (Washington, DC: Howard University Press, 1999); Des Forges, *Leave None*.

50. Berry and Berry, *Genocide*, 115.

51. Lee Ann Fujii, "Transforming the Moral Landscape: The Diffusion of a Genocidal Norm in Rwanda," *Journal of Genocide Research* 6, no. 1 (2004).

52. Hutu hardliners were those of the Coalition pour la Défense de la République (CDR, Coalition for the Defense of the Republic) and MRND party who worked together, with CDR being the more extreme of the two parties. Hutu hardliners in both groups saw the extinction of the Tutsi population (and those who supported them) as the solution to all national problems. Hutu moderates were those in the general Hutu population, many of whom interacted daily with Tutsi due to familial, occupational, or economic relations.

53. Jones reports that Hutu hardliners, and specifically a network of senior clan-family members holding high institutional positions throughout Rwanda (known as the *akazu*), "offered large bribes, loan forgiveness, and promises of future benefit in state positions to many within the government and opposition parties—people who had signed onto the Arusha process—in an attempt to turn them against the Arusha deal." Bruce D. Jones, "Rwanda," in *United Nations Interventionism 1991–2004*, ed. Mats Berdal and Spyros Economides (Cambridge: Cambridge University Press, 2007), 144.

54. Straus, *Order of Genocide*, 26.

55. Phillip Verwimp, "Machetes and Firearms: The Organization of Massacres in Rwanda," *Journal of Peace Research* 43, no. 1 (2006).

56. Dallaire and others assert that these weapons serve as evidence that planning for the genocide began as early as 1992. However, the counterargument is that any country experiencing military invasion would be likely to import weapons in preparation for an escalation of war. Still, there was clearly a shift from what could be characterized as a counterguerilla military strategy to a genocidal one in which all Tutsi were framed in media and political discourse as collaborators and conspirators with the RPF. Roméo Dallaire, *Shake Hands with the Devil: The Failure of Humanity in Rwanda* (New York: Carroll & Graf, 2004).

57. Human Rights Watch, "Arming Rwanda: The Arms Trade and Human Rights Abuses in the Rwandan War," *New York* 6, no. 1 (January 1994). See also Kathi Austin, "Light Weapons and Conflict in the Great Lakes Region of Africa," in *Light Weapons and Civil Conflict*, ed. Jeffrey Boutwell and Michael T. Klare (Lanham, MD: Rowman & Littlefield, 1999), 31, 34.

58. Whether someone was killed by a firearm, grenade, or machete was dependent on an interaction of factors including the population density where the person lived, the victim's age, and the point in time when the violence erupted in the victim's community. See Verwimp, "Machetes," for details on patterns of death and weapon use.

59. B. Jones, "Rwanda."

60. B. Jones, "Rwanda."

61. B. Jones, "Rwanda," 144.

62. For a detailed analysis of the actors, timeline, agreements, and what ultimately went wrong, see Bruce D. Jones, *Peacemaking in Rwanda: Dynamics of a Failure* (Boulder, CO: Lynne Rienner, 2001).

63. Michael N. Barnett, *Eyewitness to a Genocide: The United Nations and Rwanda* (Ithaca, NY: Cornell University Press, 2002).

64. The *akazu* ("little house") was an elite social circle of Hutu extremists who supported Habyarimana. It consisted mainly of Hutu from Habyarimana's home region and Madame Habyarimana's relatives. They played a major role in genocidal propaganda, mobilizing outrage over the Arusha Accords, the development of the civilian self-defense, and, ultimately, genocidal killings (Des Forges, *Leave None*).

65. Barnett, *Eyewitness*, 78.

66. Alan J. Kuperman, *The Limits of Humanitarian Intervention: Genocide in Rwanda* (Washington, DC: Brookings Institution, 2001), 88, 105.

67. Dallaire, *Shake Hands*.

68. Des Forges, *Leave None*.

69. *Genocidaires* is the term used in Rwanda to refer to those who perpetrated genocidal violence during the 1994 genocide against the Tutsi. This term is often used interchangeably with the term Interahamwe (in Kinyarwanda, "those who work together"), which denoted the Hutu youth paramilitary. When discussing actors in genocide, it is common to reference perpetrators, victims, and bystanders. However, these categories and the dynamics of genocide can often be more complicated and fluid than such terminology allows, as one could be both a perpetrator and a victim, and so on. For a discussion on this, see Hollie Nyseth Brehm and Nicole Fox, "Narrating Genocide: Time, Memory, and Blame," *Sociological Forum* 32, no. 1 (2016); Bradley Campbell, "Contradictory Behavior during Genocides," *Sociological Forum* 25, no. 2 (2010); Fujii, *Killing*; Aliza Luft, "Toward a Dynamic Theory of Action at the Micro-Level of Genocide: Killing, Desistance, and Saving in 1994 Rwanda," *Sociological Theory* 33, no. 2 (2015).

70. The reported number of people killed in the genocide varies significantly. The UN (1999) reports 800,000 deaths, as does Gérard Prunier (1998) in *Rwanda Crisis*. The Association des Etudiants et Elèves Rescapés du Genocide (AERG, Association of Student Survivors of the Genocide), a Rwandan government agency, reports almost two million, which seems too high given the Tutsi population in the 1991 census. The most rigorous analysis, conducted by Marijke Verpoorten, estimates that 562,000 to 662,000 Tutsi died in the genocidal campaign directed against them (with a death rate of 70–80 percent among Tutsi in 1994). The same analysis gives a wide range of estimated Hutu deaths—between 212,000 and 1,300,000. These numbers suggest that 800,000 is a conservative estimate of the total number of deaths. See Marijke Verpoorten, "The Death Toll of the Rwandan Genocide: A Detailed Analysis for Gikongoro Province," *Population* 60, no. 4 (2005); Marijke Verpoorten, "How Many Died in Rwanda?," *Journal of Genocide Research* 22, no. 1 (2020).

71. Christopher C. Taylor, "The Cultural Face of Terror in the Rwandan Genocide of 1994," in *Annihilating Difference: The Anthropology of Genocide*, ed. Alexander Laban Hinton (Berkeley: University of California Press, 2002).

72. Des Forges, *Leave None*; Fujii, *Killing*.

73. The murder of Prime Minister Agathe Uwilingiyimana is often mentioned in descriptions of the early days of the genocide because her death was significant for a

number of reasons. Uwilingiyimana, who on July 18, 1993, became the first woman to serve as prime minister, was outspoken and therefore did not win the hearts of traditional male leaders (Andre Guichaoua, *From War to Genocide: Criminal Politics in Rwanda, 1990–1994* [Madison: University of Wisconsin Press, 2015]). After the previous president's plane was shot down, Uwilingiyimana was next in line to be president (although there was no precedent for the peaceful transfer of power). Some objected, including Théoneste Bagosora (named one of the masterminds of the genocide), who told General Dallaire that she did not "enjoy the confidence of the Rwandan people and was incapable of governing the nation" (see Dallaire, *Shake Hands*, 224). Late at night on April 6, disagreements among the crisis committee members and Bagosora emerged, with some asserting that as the prime minister, Uwilingiyimana was the legitimate head of state and should be consulted in all decisions on how to move forward (see Dallaire, *Shake Hands*, 227). While these conversations were occurring, Uwilingiyimana was at home, terrified for her safety and requesting more protection from military headquarters; this protection ultimately never reached her (Des Forges, *Leave None*). In the middle of the night, she arranged for UNAMIR to escort her to the radio station on the morning of April 7, 1994, so she could ensure the Rwandan people that she was still dedicated to the Arusha Accords and to stay calm. Fifteen UNAMIR peacekeepers arrived at her home at 5:30 a.m. in four different jeeps, and immediately Rwandan soldiers opened fire on them, taking all fifteen hostage at the Kigali military camp a few meters away from the prime minister's house. When they reached Kigali military camp, the Rwandan soldiers separated out the five Ghanaian peacekeepers in order to murder the ten Belgian ones. With the Rwandan army surrounding Prime Minister Uwilingiyimana and her family, shortly before noon, she and her husband surrendered from their hiding place in order to protect their five children, who were hiding in her home (and did indeed survive). The prime minister was instantly shot in the face and later found naked, with a beer bottle pushed inside her vagina (Des Forges, *Leave None*). Uwilingiyimana's death demonstrates key dynamics of the genocidal violence: brutal violence against women, the impossible choices parents had to make in hopes of saving their children, the power that the masterminds of the genocide did indeed have in the early days, and the limitations of a poorly backed UNAMIR mission. Finally, the murders of the Belgian soldiers who were tasked with protecting her proved a successful tactic of the *genocidaires* to get the UN to remove the little support they had provided in Rwanda.

74. Barnett, *Eyewitness*; Dallaire, *Shake Hands*. The Battle of Mogadishu in Somalia, later known as Black Hawk Down (and made famous by the 2001 film), was part of a UN mission known as Operation Gothic Serpent that was part of broader intervention in the Somali Civil War. In October 1993, what was supposed to be a one-hour, straightforward mission resulted in a standoff and the death of several UN soldiers and thousands of Somalis, ultimately shaping the UN's reluctance to intervene in Rwanda. For more on the Battle of Mogadishu and UN intervention policy, see Robert G. Patman, "Disarming Somalia: The Contrasting Fortunes of the United States and Australian Peacekeepers during the United Nations Intervention, 1992–1993," *African*

Affairs 96, no. 385 (1997); Major Roger N. Sangvic, *Battle of Mogadishu: Anatomy of a Failure* (Royal Oak, New Zealand: Pickle Partners, 2015); Ramesh Thakur, "From Peacekeeping to Peace Enforcement: The UN Operation in Somalia," *Journal of Modern African Studies* 32, no. 3 (1994). For more on Somalia's effect on Rwanda, see the chapter titled "The Somalia Hangover" in Jared Cohen, *One Hundred Days of Silence: America and the Rwanda Genocide* (Lanham, MD: Rowman & Littlefield, 2007).

75. Cohen, *One Hundred Days*.

76. See Guichaoua, *Criminal Politics*; Straus, *Order of Genocide*; Philip Verwimp, *Peasants in Power: The Political Economy of Development and Genocide in Rwanda* (New York: Springer, 2013).

77. Dallaire, *Shake Hands*; Fujii, *Killing*; Verwimp, *Peasants in Power*.

78. Dallaire, *Shake Hands*; Des Forges, *Leave None*; Longman, *Christianity*.

79. Mamdani, *When Victims Become Killers*, 5.

80. Women also participated in killings, lootings, and espionage. Nicole Hogg, "Women's Participation in the Rwandan Genocide: Mothers or Monsters?," *International Review of the Red Cross* 92, no. 877 (2010); Adam Jones, "Gender and Genocide in Rwanda," *Journal of Genocide Research* 4, no. 1 (2002); Lisa Sharlach, "Gender and Genocide in Rwanda: Women as Agents and Objects of Genocide," *Journal of Genocide Research* 1, no. 3 (1999). Overall, women were far more likely to participate in property crimes. For analysis of the demographics of those charged at Gacaca for perpetrating crime, see Hollie Nyseth Brehm, Christopher Uggen, and Jean-Damascène Gasanabo, "Age, Gender, and the Crime of Crimes: Toward a Life-Course Theory of Genocide Participation," *Criminology* 54, no. 4 (2016).

81. For more information on the motivations of the killers, characteristics of attacks, and why perpetrators say they committed genocide, see Fujii, *Killing*; Fujii, "Transforming"; Straus, *Order of Genocide*.

82. Estimates vary significantly. See Scott Straus, "How Many Perpetrators Were There in the Rwandan Genocide? An Estimate," *Journal of Genocide Research* 6, no. 1 (2004). Note that Straus does not include property damage as a form of genocidal violence in this estimate.

83. For more information on what variables impacted the levels and temporal onset of violence, especially factors such as the degree of elite state control and ethnic segregation, see Omar S. McDoom, "Predicting Violence within Genocide: A Model of Elite Competition and Ethnic Segregation from Rwanda," *Political Geography* 42 (2014).

84. Hollie Nyseth Brehm, "Subnational Determinants of Genocide in Rwanda," *Criminology* 55, no. 1 (2017).

85. Damian De Walque and Philip Verwimp, "The Demographic and Socio-Economic Distribution of Excess Mortality during the 1994 Genocide in Rwanda: Policy Research Working Paper 4850," World Bank, 2009; Straus, *Order of Genocide*.

86. For more on how the church supported genocidal violence, see Emmanuel Katongole and Jonathan Wilson-Hartgrove, *Mirror to the Church: Resurrecting Faith after Genocide in Rwanda* (Grand Rapids, MI: Zondervan, 2009); Longman, *Christianity*;

Timothy Longman, "Church Politics and the Genocide in Rwanda," *Journal of Religion in Africa* 31, no. 2 (2001); Mamdani, *When Victims Become Killers*; Hugh McCullum, *The Angels Have Left Us: The Rwandan Tragedy and the Churches* (Geneva: World Council of Churches, 1996); Carol Rittner, John K. Roth, and Wendy Whitworth, *Genocide in Rwanda: Complicity of the Churches?* (St. Paul, MN: Paragon House, 2004).

87. For what I consider the best analysis for numbers, see Catrien Bijleveld, Aafke Morssinkhof, and Alette Smeulers, "Counting the Countless: Rape Victimization during the Rwandan Genocide," *International Criminal Justice Review* 19, no. 2 (2009). The issue of numbers and genocidal rape is also discussed in more detail in chapter 5 of this book. See also Amnesty International, *Rwanda: "Marked for Death," Rape Survivors Living with HIV/AIDS in Rwanda* (New York: Amnesty International, 2004); Christopher W. Mullins, "'He Would Kill Me with His Penis': Genocidal Rape in Rwanda as a State Crime," *Critical Criminology* 17, no. 1 (2009); Christopher W. Mullins, "'We Are Going to Rape You and Taste Tutsi Women': Rape during the 1994 Rwandan Genocide," *British Journal of Criminology* 49, no. 6 (2009). For important work on the resilience of rape survivors and the experience of mothers who had children out of rape, see Maggie Zraly's work. Maggie Zraly and Laetitia Nyirazinyoye, "Don't Let the Suffering Make You Fade Away: An Ethnographic Study of Resilience among Survivors of Genocide-Rape in Southern Rwanda," *Social Science & Medicine* 70, no. 10 (2010); Maggie Zraly, Sarah E. Rubin, and Donatilla Mukamana, "Motherhood and Resilience among Rwandan Genocide-Rape Survivors," *Ethos* 41, no. 4 (2013).

88. Des Forges, *Leave None*; Christopher C. Taylor, *Sacrifice as Terror: The Rwandan Genocide* (Oxford: Berg, 1999).

89. For stories of survivors of gender-based violence, see Anne-Marie De Brouwer and Sandra Chu, *The Men Who Killed Me: Rwandan Survivors of Sexual Violence* (Vancouver: Douglas & McIntyre, 2009); Fox, "Impacts"; A. Jones, "Gender and Genocide"; Mullins, "Genocidal Rape"; Catharine Newbury and Hannah Baldwin, *Aftermath: Women in Post-Genocide Rwanda* (New York: USAID, 2000); Binaifer Nowrojee, "Shattered Lives," in *H. R. Watch* (New York: Human Rights Watch, 1996).

90. Brounéus, "Truth-Telling," and personal communication, 2012.

91. Des Forges, *Leave None*; Helen M. Hintjens, "Explaining the 1994 Genocide in Rwanda," *Journal of Modern African Studies* 37, no. 2 (1999); Elisa von Joeden-Forgey, "The Devil in the Details: 'Life Force Atrocities' and the Assault on the Family in Times of Conflict," *Genocide Studies and Prevention* 5, no. 1 (2010).

92. Des Forges, *Leave None*, 216.

93. Mamdani, *When Victims Become Killers*.

94. Amnesty International, *Rwanda*; Des Forges, *Leave None*; Prunier, *Rwanda Crisis*.

95. Eric Irivuzumugabe and Tracey D. Lawrence, *My Father, Maker of the Trees: How I Survived the Rwandan Genocide* (Grand Rapids, MI: Baker Books, 2009); Stephen Rwembeho, "Over 10,000 Tutsi Perished in Lake Muhazi during the Genocide," *New Times*, April 24, 2014.

96. Personal communication, March 2012.

97. The refugee situation in the Kivu region was intensified by an already divisive history within Eastern Congo. See chapter 8 of Mamdani's *When Victims Become Killers* for a thorough explanation of how the local conflict in Kivu collided with the volatile postgenocide dynamic in Rwanda and the insidious role of international actors in the creation of a large-scale humanitarian crisis. See also Filip Reyntjens, "Waging (Civil) War Abroad: Rwanda and the DRC," in Straus and Waldorf, *Remaking Rwanda*.

98. Kisangani N. F. Emizet, "The Massacre of Refugees in Congo: A Case of UN Peacekeeping Failure and International Law," *Journal of Modern African Studies* 38, no. 2 (2000).

99. Des Forges, *Leave None*; C. Newbury and Baldwin, *Aftermath*.

100. For example, see Thomson's chapter 4 discussion of the Gersony report that was silenced by several high-power institutions and individuals, including UN Secretary General Kofi Annan, who directed the UN High Commissioner for Refugees to embargo the report describing killings and mass human rights abuses on civilians (Thomson, *Rwanda*).

101. Filip Reyntjens, *Political Governance in Post-Genocide Rwanda* (New York: Cambridge University Press, 2013); Pottier, *Re-imagining Rwanda*; Thomson, *Rwanda*.

102. Kevin O'Halloran, *Pure Massacre: Aussie Soldiers Reflect on the Rwandan Genocide* (New York: Simon & Schuster, 2020), 16. For details from the perspective of Australian Defense Force Medics, who were part of the Australian contingent of UNAMIR, see Paul Jordan, "Witness to Genocide: A Personal Account of the 1995 Kibeho Massacre," *Australian Army Journal* 1, no. 1 (June 2003); Terry Pickard, *Combat Medic: An Eyewitness Account of the Kibeho Massacre* (Sydney: Big Sky, 2010).

103. O'Halloran, *Pure Massacre*, 164.

104. Thus began a long pattern of impunity toward human rights abuses by Rwanda. See Reyntjens, *Governance*.

105. Amnesty International, "Rwanda: Civilians Trapped in Armed Conflict. The Dead Can No Longer Be Counted," *AI Index AFR* 47/043/1997 (December 1997); Amnesty International, "Rwanda: Sharp Increase in Killings Could Plunge Rwanda Back into a Cycle of Violence," *AI Index AFR* 47/17/1996 (August 1996); United Nations, Economic and Social Council, Commission on Human Rights, *Report on the Situation of Human Rights in Rwanda*, Mr. René Deqni-Séqui, Special Rapporteur of the Commission on Human Rights, under paragraph 20 of resolution S-3/1 of 25 May 1994. For information on the wars and human rights abuses in the DRC, see the chapter "Mass Murder in Eastern Congo: 1996–1997" in René Lemarchand, *Forgotten Genocides: Oblivion, Denial, and Memory* (Philadelphia: University of Pennsylvania Press, 2011); Gérard Prunier, *Africa's World War: Congo, the Rwandan Genocide, and the Making of a Continental Catastrophe* (New York: Oxford University Press, 2009); Filip Reyntjens, *The Great African War: Congo and Regional Geopolitics, 1996–2006* (Cambridge: Cambridge University Press, 2009); Jason Stearns, *Dancing in the Glory of Monsters: The Collapse of the Congo and the Great War of Africa* (New York: Public Affairs, 2012).

106. Personal contact, 2011.

107. Paul Bolton, "Local Perceptions of the Mental Health Effects of the Rwandan Genocide," *Journal of Nervous & Mental Disease* 189, no. 4 (2001); Atle Dyregrov Leila Gupta, Rolf Gjestad, and Eugenie Mukanoheli, "Trauma Exposure and Psychological Reactions to Genocide among Rwandan Children," *Journal of Traumatic Stress* no. 13 (2000); Heide Rieder and Thomas Elbert, "Rwanda—Lasting Imprints of a Genocide: Trauma, Mental Health and Psychosocial Conditions in Survivors, Former Prisoners and Their Children," *Conflict and Health* 7, no. 1 (2013); Susanne Schaal et al., "Rates and Risks for Prolonged Grief Disorder in a Sample of Orphaned and Widowed Genocide Survivors," *BMC Psychiatry* 10, no. 55 (2010); Susanne Schaal et al., "Rates of Trauma Spectrum Disorders and Risks of Posttraumatic Stress Disorder in a Sample of Orphaned and Widowed Genocide Survivors," *European Journal of Psychotraumatology* 2 (2011); Susanne Schaal and Thomas Elbert, "Ten Years after the Genocide: Trauma Confrontation and Posttraumatic Stress in Rwandan Adolescents," *Journal of Traumatic Stress* 19, no. 1 (2006).

108. The majority of survivors have not actually been clinically diagnosed; given the paucity of services to address mental health in Rwanda, scholars can only speculate as to the scope of mental health problems in the wake of the genocide. See Dyregrov et al., "Trauma Exposure"; Phuong N. Pham, Harvey M. Weinstein, and Timothy Longman, "Trauma and PTSD Symptoms in Rwanda: Implications for Attitudes toward Justice and Reconciliation," *Journal of the American Medical Association* 292, no. 5 (2004). See chapter 4 of this book for more on the aftermath of mass trauma and Rwandan trauma responses.

109. Human Rights Watch, *Rwanda's Lasting Wounds: Consequences of Genocide and War for Rwanda's Children* (New York: Human Rights Watch, 2003).

110. Richard Neugebauer et al., "Post-Traumatic Stress Reactions among Rwandan Children and Adolescents in the Early Aftermath of Genocide," *International Journal of Epidemiology* 38, no. 4 (2009).

111. Suzanne Kaplan, "Child Survivors of the 1994 Rwandan Genocide and Trauma-Related Affect," *Journal of Social Issues* 69, no. 1 (2013).

112. Schaal and Elbert, "Ten Years."

113. UNICEF, "Ten Years after Genocide, Rwandan Children Suffer Lasting Impact" (New York, 2004); Angela Veale et al., "Struggling to Survive: Orphans and Community Dependent Children in Rwanda" (Kigali: UNICEF, 2001); Tonya Renee Thurman et al., "Barriers to the Community Support of Orphans and Vulnerable Youth in Rwanda," *Social Science & Medicine* 66, no. 7 (2008).

114. Neil W. Boris et al., "Infants and Young Children Living in Youth-Headed Households in Rwanda: Implications of Emerging Data," *Infant Mental Health Journal* 27, no. 6 (2006).

115. Chitra Nagarajan, "An Appraisal of Rwanda's Response to Survivors Who Experienced Sexual Violence in 1994," *Wagadu* 10 (2012); C. Newbury and Baldwin, *Aftermath*.

116. Boris et al., "Infants."

117. Shortly after the genocide, Rwandan feminists actively sought to change property and land laws in which only women who were married (and officiated by the state) could inherit their husbands' land, leaving the vast majority of widows propertyless and unable to inherit the land of their deceased husband. Saskia Van Hoyweghen, "The Urgency of Land and Agrarian Reform in Rwanda," *African Affairs* 98, no. 392 (1999).

118. Mullins, "Genocidal Rape."

119. Marie E. Berry, "From Violence to Mobilization: War, Women, and Threat in Rwanda," *Mobilization: An International Quarterly* 20, no. 2 (2015); C. Newbury and Baldwin, *Aftermath*; Women's Commission for Refugee Women and Children, *Rwanda's Women and Children: The Long Road to Reconciliation: A Field Report Assessing the Protection and Assistance Needs of Rwandan Women and Children* (New York: Women's Commission for Refugee Women and Children, 1997).

120. Nagarajan, "Appraisal," 111.

121. For more information on women's organizing, including the types of organizations that emerged during the postgenocide era, what factors impact organizations' success, and the types of services and projects women's organizations undertake, see Marie E. Berry, *War, Women, and Power: From Violence to Mobilization in Rwanda and Bosnia-Herzegovina* (New York: Cambridge University Press, 2018); C. Newbury and Baldwin, *Aftermath*. On the number of Rwandan women in parliament, see Nagarajan, "Appraisal," 111.

122. Reinventing the country has included a range of reeducation efforts nationwide, as well as policy reforms, including a new constitution and national symbols (the flag and national colors). Susan Thomson, "Re-education for Reconciliation: Participant Observations on Ingando," in Straus and Waldorf, *Remaking Rwanda*.

123. Centers for Disease Control and Prevention, Division of Tuberculosis Elimination, *DTBE in Rwanda* (Atlanta Division of Tuberculosis, 2012); Stephen Rulisa et al., "Malaria Prevalence, Spatial Clustering and Risk Factors in a Low Endemic Area of Eastern Rwanda: A Cross Sectional Study," *Public Library of Science* 8, no. 7 (2013).

124. Personal communication, 2013. For a historical account of how development was defined, managed, and implemented pre-1994 in ways that impacted the genocide, see Peter Uvin, *Aiding Violence.*

125. For country statistics, see https://www.cia.gov/library/publications/the-world-factbook/geos/rw.html (retrieved in March 2018 for this chapter).

126. Policies around urbanization and development have resulted in the forced relocation of much of the urban poor (see Goodfellow and Smith, "Urban Catastrophe"; Shearer, "Street Economies"). For a discussion on how growth and political control go hand in hand, see Mann and Berry, "Political Motivations." For a discussion on how modernization policies have increased demands, stress, and costly obligations for rural populations, see chapter 6 in Reyntjens, *Governance.* Thomson's work complements Reyntjens's chapter with a discussion on the production of good citizens and poverty reduction programs. See chapter 9 in Thomson, *Rwanda.*

127. Lars Waldorf, "Instrumentalizing Genocide: The RPF's Campaign against 'Genocide Ideology,'" in *Remaking Rwanda: State Building and Human Rights after*

Mass Violence, ed. Scott Straus and Lars Waldorf (Madison: University of Wisconsin Press, 2011).

128. Buckley-Zistel, "Nation"; Sarah Warshauer-Freedman, Harvey M. Weinstein, K. L. Murphy, and Timothy Longman, "Teaching History in Post-Genocide Rwanda," in Straus and Waldorf, *Remaking Rwanda*; Jennifer G. Cooke, *Rwanda: Assessing Risks to Stability*, A Report from the CSIS Africa Program: Center for Strategic and International Studies, 2011. For information on the restrictions of free speech and journalists, see Anjan Sundaram, *Bad News: Last Journalists in a Dictatorship* (New York: Knopf Doubleday, 2016).

129. For a discussion on how *ingando* camps are an effective civic education tool for nationalism and instilling a culture of *ubumwe* (unity) through fear, discipline, and power, see Chi Mgbako, "Ingando Solidarity Camps: Reconciliation and Political Indoctrination in Post-Genocide Rwanda," *Harvard Human Rights Journal*, no. 18 (2005); chapter 8 in Andrea Purdeková, *Making Ubumwe: Power, State and Camps in Rwanda's Unity-Building Project* (New York: Berghahn Books, 2015); Thomson, "Re-education."

130. Freedman et al., "Teaching History." Regarding how these narratives shape reconciliation and unity, see Buckley-Zistel, "Nation."

131. See J. Cooke, *Assessing Risks*; Des Forges, *Leave None*; Prunier, *Continental Catastrophe*; Filip Reyntjens, "Rwanda, Ten Years On: From Genocide to Dictatorship," *African Affairs* no. 103 (2004); Stearns, *Dancing*; Straus and Waldorf, *Remaking Rwanda*. Also, for more information on assassination attempts of Rwandan dissidents and the challenges faced by researchers who have critiqued the government, see Jennie E. Burnet, *Genocide Lives in Us: Women, Memory and Silence in Rwanda* (Madison: University of Wisconsin Press, 2012); J. Cooke, *Assessing Risks*; Christian Davenport and Allan Stam, "GenoDynamics: Understanding Rwandan Political Violence in 1994" (2000); Timothy Longman, "Rwanda: Achieving Equality or Serving an Authoritarian State?," in *Women in African Parliaments*, ed. Gretchen Bauer and Hannah E. Britton (London: Lynne Rienner, 2006); Jens Meierhenrich, "Topographies of Remembering and Forgetting: The Transformation of Lieux De Memoire in Rwanda," in Straus and Waldorf, *Remaking Rwanda*; Jens Meierhenrich, "The Transformation of Lieux de Memoire: The Nyabarongo River in Rwanda, 1992–2009," *Anthropology Today* 25, no. 5 (2009); Victor Peskin, "Victor's Justice Revisited: Rwandan Patriotic Front Crimes and the Prosecutorial Endgame at the ICTR," in Straus and Waldorf, *Remaking Rwanda*; Joseph Sebarenzi and Laura Mullane, *God Sleeps in Rwanda: A Journey of Transformation* (New York: Atria Books, 2009); Thomson, "Re-education."

132. Nagarajan, "Appraisal"; Alana Erin Tiemessen, "After Arusha: Gacaca Justice in Post-Genocide Rwanda," *African Studies Quarterly* 8, no. 1 (2004).

133. United Nations Security Council, Resolution 955 (1994) Adopted by the Security Council at its 3453rd meeting, November 8, 1994, http://unscr.com/en/resolutions/doc/955.

134. Alison Des Forges and Timothy Longman, "Legal Responses to Genocide in Rwanda," in *My Neighbor, My Enemy: Justice and Community in the Aftermath of Mass*

Atrocity, ed. Eric Stover and Harvey M. Weinstein (Cambridge: Cambridge University Press, 2004).

135. United Nations International Criminal Tribunal for the former Yugoslavia, Timeline, https://www.icty.org/en/features/timeline.

136. Des Forges and Longman, "Legal Responses."

137. See Amnesty International, *Rwanda*; Mullins, "We Are Going."

138. Rosemary Nagy, "Traditional Justice and Legal Pluralism in Transitional Context: The Case of Rwanda's Gacaca Courts," in *Reconciliation(s): Transitional Justice in Postconflict Societies*, ed. Joanna R. Quinn (Quebec: McGill-Queen's University Press, 2009).

139. For more summary statistics on the ICTR, see http://unictr.unmict.org/en/tribunal.

140. Bert Ingelaere, *Inside Rwanda's "Gacaca" Courts: Seeking Justice after Genocide* (Madison: University of Wisconsin Press, 2016).

141. Kristin Conner Doughty, *Remediation in Rwanda Grassroots Legal Forums* (Philadelphia: University of Pennsylvania Press, 2016).

142. Urusaro Alice Karekezi, Alphonse Nshimiyimana, and Beth Mutamba, "Localizing Justice: Gacaca Courts in Post-Genocide Rwanda," in Stover and Weinstein, *My Neighbor*.

143. Doughty, *Remediation*.

144. Genocide crimes were divided into three categories. Category one was reserved for organizers of the genocide, including officials, and leaders who participated or incited others to participate, as well as those who committed rape and sexual torture. Some of these cases were reserved for the ICTR. Category two suspects were those who killed or attempted to kill under the direction of others, those who tortured others or defiled their bodies, and those who served as accomplices. Category three involved property crimes that had not yet been resolved with victims or authorities before the law took effect. For details on gacaca and the appeals process, see Hollie Nyseth Brehm, Christopher Uggen, and Jean-Damascéne Gasanabo, "Genocide, Justice, and Rwanda's Gacaca Courts," *Journal of Contemporary Criminal Justice* 30, no. 3 (2014); Doughty, *Remediation*; Nicola Palmer, *Courts in Conflict: Interpreting the Layers of Justice in Post-Genocide Rwanda* (Oxford: Oxford University Press, 2015).

145. Lars Waldorf, "'Like Jews Waiting for Jesus': Posthumous Justice in Post-Genocide Rwanda," in *Localizing Transitional Justice: Interventions and Priorities after Mass Violence*, ed. Rosalind Shaw, Lars Waldorf, and Pierre Hazan (Stanford: Stanford University Press, 2010).

146. As Timothy Longman states, "even as *gacaca* has held thousands of individuals accountable for crimes against humanity, allowed communities to develop accounts of the past, and encouraged dialogue about what went wrong in 1994, *gacaca* has also been used by the government to assert its authority and to guarantee the dominance of its main constituency." Timothy Longman, "An Assessment of Rwanda's Gacaca Courts," *Peace Review* 21, no. 3 (2009): 304. Scholars have made similar arguments about gacaca's imposition of the victors' justice and contributions to social complicity and

authoritarian rule. See Chakravarty, *Investing*; Allison Corey and Sandra F. Joireman, "Retributive Justice: The Gacaca Courts in Rwanda," *African Affairs* 103, no. 410 (2004); Bert Ingelaere, "'Does the Truth Pass across the Fire without Burning?' Locating the Short Circuit in Rwanda's Gacaca Courts," *Journal of Modern African Studies* 47, no. 4 (2009). For an important analysis on gender, trauma, and gacaca, see Brounéus, "Trauma"; Brounéus, "Truth-Telling."

147. Nyseth Brehm, Uggen, and Gasanabo, "Genocide"; Palmer, *Courts*.

148. In some gacaca cases, perpetrators described where bodies were buried. In the final years of gacaca, as Rwanda embarked on intense urban development projects, locating bodies after confessions became increasingly more challenging because bodies were often buried beneath new urban centers and homes. For example, a friend of mine explained that in her previous home, she answered the door one day to a gacaca representative who stated that a perpetrator had confessed to burying bodies in what was now her backyard. Excavation started immediately, and the bodies were exhumed, but the vivid memory of the experience is still traumatic for her nearly decades later. Gacaca's performative functions have had both positive and negative effects. For more, see Carla De Ycaza, "Performative Functions of Genocide Trials in Rwanda: Reconciliation Through Restorative Justice?," *African Journal on Conflict Resolution* 10, no. 3 (2010).

149. For scholarship on the psychosocial effects of gacaca, see Brounéus, "Truth-Telling"; Patrick Kanyangaraab et al., "Trust, Individual Guilt, Collective Guilt and Dispositions toward Reconciliation among Rwandan Survivors and Prisoners before and after Their Participation in Postgenocide Gacaca Courts in Rwanda," *Journal of Social and Political Psychology* 2, no. 1 (2014); Bernard Rimé et al., "The Impact of Gacaca Tribunals in Rwanda: Psychosocial Effects of Participation in a Truth and Reconciliation Process after a Genocide," *European Journal of Social Psychology* 41 (2011).

150. Ariel Meyerstein, "Between Law and Culture: Rwanda's Gacaca and Postcolonial Legacy," *Law and Society Inquiry* 32, no. 2 (2007).

151. See Jennie E. Burnet, "(In)Justice: Truth, Reconciliation and Revenge in Rwanda's Gacaca," in *Transitional Justice: Global Mechanisms and Local Realities after Genocide and Mass Violence*, ed. Alexander Laban Hinton (New Brunswick, NJ: Rutgers University Press, 2010); Human Rights Watch, "Rwanda: Human Rights Overview," in *World Report 2006* (New York: Human Rights Watch, 2007); Ingelaere, "Locating"; Lars Waldorf, "Rwanda's Failing Experiment in Restorative Justice," in *Handbook of Restorative Justice: A Global Perspective*, ed. Dennis Sullivan and Larry Tifft (London: Routledge, 2006).

152. Chakravarty argues that the gacaca tribunals were strategically used to strengthen authoritarian rule in Rwanda by enforcing a system of clientelism, in which those who demonstrated allegiance with the current administration were rewarded by resources, power, and prestige positions in government (Chakravarty, *Investing*). For more on gacaca, see Brounéus, "Truth-Telling"; Anuradha Chakravarty, "Gacaca Courts in Rwanda: Explaining Divisions within the Human Rights Community," *Yale Journal of International Affairs* 1, no. 2 (2006); Phil Clark, "The Rules (and Politics) of

Engagement: The Gacaca Courts and Post-Genocide Justice, Healing and Reconciliation in Rwanda," in *After Genocide: Transitional Justice, Post-Conflict Reconstruction and Reconciliation in Rwanda and Beyond*, ed. Phil Clark and Zachary D. Kaufman (New York: Columbia University Press, 2009); Des Forges and Longman, "Legal Responses"; Karekezi, Nshimiyimama, and Mutamba, "Localizing Justice"; Meyerstein, "Between Law and Culture"; Nagy, "Traditional Justice"; Pham, Weinstein, and Longman, "Trauma"; Tiemessen, "After Arusha"; Idi Gaparayi Tuzinde, "Justice and Social Reconstruction in the Aftermath of Genocide in Rwanda: An Evaluation of the Possible Role of the Gacaca Tribunals," in *Law* (Pretoria: University of Pretoria, South Africa, 2000).

Chapter 2. Memory Landscapes after Human Rights Violations

1. I define survivors as those who were persecuted and feared for their lives during the 1994 genocide against the Tutsi. The term is used here to denote those who were targeted for being Tutsi, for having relations with Tutsi, or for trying to protect Tutsi. Additionally, survivors as defined here were located within the Rwandan national boundaries during some part of the approximately one hundred days of the genocide against the Tutsi (some were able to escape). This distinction rules out Tutsi who were persecuted in Burundi, Democratic Republic of the Congo (then Zaire), or other East African countries during 1994. This usage may not be consistent with the definitions and practices of all institutions or organizations within Rwanda or serving Rwandans abroad. Scholars have documented that after the 1994 genocide against the Tutsi, the government of Rwanda and some survivor-serving NGOs implemented a hierarchy of survivorship (either directly or in practice) in which certain groups of victims were considered worthier of resources and public acknowledgment than others. See Marie E. Berry, "Barriers to Women's Progress after Atrocity: Evidence from Rwanda and Bosnia-Herzegovina," *Gender & Society* 31, no. 6 (2017); Jennie E. Burnet, "Whose Genocide? Whose Truth? Representations of Victim and Perpetrator in Rwanda," in *Genocide: Truth Memory and Representation*, ed. Alexander Laban Hinton and Kevin Lewis O'Neill (Durham, NC: Duke University Press, 2009); Thomson, "Re-education." Berry argues that such a process of ranking occurred after genocidal violence in both Rwanda and Bosnia when political elites "mobilized ethnically defined social groups and elevated certain groups as those 'most victimized.' These efforts created hierarchies of victimhood that facilitated new social divisions and undermined the possibility of a cross-cutting women's movement" ("Barriers," 837). For example, scholars have found that some Hutu women who were raped by Hutu militias during the war or genocide have not had access to the same resources that Tutsi rape victims received. See M. Berry, *War*; Burnet, *Genocide Lives*; Doris E. Buss, "Rethinking 'Rape as a Weapon of War,'" *Feminist Legal Studies* 17, no. 2 (2009). According to the larger discourse on survivorship that filters down to service providers, these victims' experience of sexual violence does not fall within the bounds of genocidal rape and is treated as interpersonal violence, which translates into less access to resources and less public acknowledgment of the crimes against them (M. Berry, *War*).

2. Stefan Lovgren, "Documenting Cambodia's Genocide, Survivor Finds Peace," *National Geographic News*, December 2, 2005.

3. Jennie Burnet poignantly compares the magnitude of Kagame's commemoration speech to the US state of the union address ("Genocide," 95).

4. Burnet found that some survivors critiqued the process of providing testimony "to strangers" at commemorations or in memorials, for it was believed that no one but an individual's own family could really understand that person's pain (*Genocide Lives*, 116). Survivors I spoke with also critiqued testimonies; their objection was not to the inclusion of testimonies in commemorations but to the process of choosing whose voices would be heard (see chapters 4 and 5).

5. Burnet, *Genocide Lives*, 95. Burnet also describes the development and changes in memorialization over time. She explains amplified silence on pages 112 and 126.

6. Denise Bentrovato, *Narrating and Teaching the Nation: The Politics of Education in Pre- and Post-Genocide Rwanda* (Göttingen: V&R Unipress, 2015).

7. Johan Pottier, *Re-imagining Rwanda*.

8. Timothy Longman, *Memory and Justice in Post-Genocide Rwanda* (New York: Cambridge University Press, 2017), 318.

9. Bridget Conley-Zilkic, "Rights on Display: Museums and Human Rights Claims," in *The Human Rights Paradox: Universality and Its Discontents*, ed. Steve Stern and Scott Straus (Madison: University of Wisconsin Press, 2014), 75.

10. Jackie Feldman, "Between Yad Vashem and Mt. Herzl: Changing Inscriptions of Sacrifice on Jerusalem's 'Mountain of Memory,'" *Anthropological Quarterly* 80, no. 4 (2007); Amos Goldberg, "The 'Jewish Narrative' in the Yad Vashem Global Holocaust Museum," *Journal of Genocide Research* 14, no. 2 (2012); Marouf Hasian Jr., "Remembering and Forgetting the 'Final Solution': A Rhetorical Pilgrimage through the U.S. Holocaust Memorial Museum," *Critical Studies in Media Communication* 21, no. 1 (2004); Peter Jan Margry and Cristina Sánchez-Carretero, *Grassroots Memorials: The Politics of Memorializing Traumatic Death* (New York: Berghahn Books, 2011).

11. Paul Connerton, *Societies*, 7.

12. Jay Winter, *Sites of Memory, Sites of Mourning: The Great War in European Cultural History* (Cambridge: Cambridge University Press, 1995).

13. Rachel Ibreck, "The Politics of Mourning: Survivor Contributions to Memorials in Post-Genocide Rwanda," *Memory Studies* 3, no. 4 (2010): 330.

14. Ibreck, "Politics." For countermemories, see Claire Whitlinger, "From Countermemory to Collective Memory: Acknowledging the 'Mississippi Burning' Murders," *Sociological Forum*, no. 30 (2015).

15. Survivors most certainly took a leadership role in memorialization projects during the first months and even years after the genocide. While survivors still play an active present-day role in aspects of memorialization and commemoration (varying in centrality depending on the memorial site), their leadership control has diminished over time, beginning as early as 1995, when the government of Rwanda began its campaign to exhume bodies for memorial mass graves. See Erin Jessee, "Promoting Reconciliation through Exhuming and Identifying Victims in the 1994 Genocide," Policy

Brief: CIGI & Africa Initiative Policy, Brief Series (2010). Government control on memorials tightened formally in 2007 with the founding of the government entity the National Commission for the Fight Against Genocide (which goes by its French acronym, CNLG [Commission Nationale de Lutte contre le Génocide]), established by Law Nº09/2007 on February 16, 2007, when CNLG was given control of all national memorials and commemoration events. See https://cnlg.gov.rw/index.php?id=10.

16. Ibreck "Politics," 110.

17. See Laura Mann and Marie Berry's important work on how economic development in particular has been a tool of regime entrenchment and power consolidation: "The development of Rwandan capitalism is bound up in the process of state (re)formation. Transformation extends beyond industrial policies to encompass a reordering of the physical, ideological, and social infrastructure of the country. This reordering is driven not only by a real desire to grow the economy but also by a parallel desire to maintain control" ("Political Motivations," 138).

18. Emmanuel Ntirenganya, "Myumbu, Home to Rwanda's First Genocide Memorial," *New Times*, April 21, 2017.

19. It would be inaccurate to assert that those buried in memorials were always killed by the Interahamwe. Undoubtedly, victims of the RPF and dead Interahamwe were also included among the remains. For examples, see Burnet, *Genocide Lives*.

20. Burnet, *Genocide Lives*.

21. See Longman (*Memory*) for a critique of the display of bones to manufacture horror about the genocide—the inverse of the feeling of peace that is supposed to be felt with a proper burial. Burnet found that some survivors did not approve of the display of bones because it deprived victims of a proper burial. Burnet, *Genocide Lives*, 107.

22. Sara Guyer, "Rwanda's Bones," *Boundary 2*, 36, no. 2 (2009); Meierhenrich, "Topographies." Critiques arose from scholars as well as their interviewees. On the one hand, scholars and survivors have asserted that "Rwanda's genocide memorials are raw and macabre. They are uncomfortable—physically, emotionally, and intellectually" and generate this discomfort to remind visitors of the enormity of genocide and the risk genocide ideology poses to humanity (Guyer, "Bones," 158). On the other hand, "Others argue that the memorials should be dismantled and that the bones in them must be buried; their gruesome visibility—and more than visibility, stench—must be removed from the landscape, whether as a gesture of respect for the dead or for the living, whether as a way of dealing with the past or of imagining a future" (Guyer, "Bones," 158). In interviews, participants in my study did not critique the display of bones (but had other critiques, which I discuss in chapters 4–6). The display of skeletal remains and clothes of victims is not unique to Rwanda but is a practice implemented in genocide memorials around the globe. See Paul Williams, *Memorial Museums: The Global Rush to Commemorate Atrocities* (New York: Oxford International, 2007), 41.

23. "Mass Graves," Kigali Memorial Centre, accessed January 15, 2021, http://www.kigalimemorialcentre.org/centre/massgraves.html.

24. One significantly understudied area, the argument that missing persons create a serious barrier to reconciliation, is explored in more detail in chapter 6 and case

studies ranging from Bosnia-Herzegovina to Kosovo. See, for example, Janine Natalya Clark, "Missing Persons, Reconciliation and the View from Below: A Case Study of Bosnia-Hercegovina," *Southeast European and Black Sea Studies* 10, no. 4 (2010); Jose Pablo Baraybar, Valerie Brasey, and Andrew Zadel, "The Need for a Centralised and Humanitarian-Based Approach to Missing Persons in Iraq: An Example from Kosovo," *International Journal of Human Rights* 11, no. 3 (2007). See also Jenny Edkins, *Missing: Persons and Politics* (Ithaca, NY: Cornell University Press, 2011).

25. For a description of the emotional labor of conducting qualitative interviews in a postconflict zone and the ethical challenges of inquiring about a painful past, please see the appendix of this book.

26. For a thoughtful and accurate description of the process of exhumation and separating the bones from clothing, see work by Erin Jessee and Laura Major: Jessee, "Reconciliation"; Laura Major, "Unearthing, Untangling and Re-articulating Genocide Corpses in Rwanda," *Critical African Studies* 7, no. 2 (2015).

27. From what I was told, deliberately moving bodies from mass graves where they were discovered to memorials was not an organic process spearheaded by survivors. Rather, survivors organized the particular church-turned-memorial spaces and requested that remains found on-site be buried there. However, an organized effort on the part of the Rwandan government to move remains to mass graves at memorial sites began as early as 1995.

28. Jessee, "Reconciliation," 13. Beyond PHR's cultural incompetency and communication problems, the warm weather in Rwanda made large-scale DNA analysis years after the genocide futile even though such efforts might have been successful in colder climates. See Susan Ladika, "Laying Ghosts to Rest in Bosnia," *Science* 293, no. 5534 (2001).

29. After the ethnic cleansing that occurred in Bosnia and Herzegovina, the government partnered with ICMP, resulting in approximately 70 percent of missing persons being accounted for, as well as "legislation to safeguard the rights of families . . . [including] systematic forensic methods, including the use of DNA, upholding rule of law-based processes that have ensured the provision of evidence to domestic courts and the ICTY, and facilitating the active engagement of the families of the missing" ("Bosnia and Herzegovina," ICMP, accessed January 15, 2021, https://www.icmp .int/where-we-work/europe/western-balkans/bosnia-and-herzegovina/). For a technical overview of ICMP's DNA testing and training, see Edwin Huffine et al., "Mass Identification of Persons Missing from the Break-Up of the Former Yugoslavia: Structure, Function, and Role of the International Commission on Missing Persons," *Forensic Sciences* 42, no. 3 (2001); Thomas J. Parsons et al., "Large Scale DNA Identification: The ICMP Experience," *Forensic Science International: Genetics* 38 (2019).

30. These services are not extended to all survivors of violence during the genocide (see Burnet, "Genocide"). However, because the survivors in this study fell under the umbrella of those eligible for such resources, interviewees did not discuss restrictions on resources beyond those related to SES or geographical location (such as the difficulty of traveling to Kigali among those living in rural areas).

31. I believe that this survivor used the term "students" to mean orphans who spend their time studying, preparing for exams, and socializing outside school at memorials.

32. Returning refugees are Rwandans who fled in the 1950s, 1970s, or early 1990s because of massacres in neighboring countries such as Uganda, Burundi, or DRC. They returned to Rwanda in 1994 after the genocide.

33. Regarding claims that conditions for the recovery process were unprecedented, see Laura Major's work on how body exhumers consistently reminded her that what they were doing was "new" work: "Informants at the exhumation sites consistently reminded me that the routine exhumation of human remains and the transformation of the recovered bodies that accompanied this process were 'new' work. All were ardent that there had been no history of this kind of handling of corpses prior to the genocide, and they were adamant that the genocide was unequivocally to blame" (Major, "Unearthing," 169).

Chapter 3. The Role of Memory Work in Violence Prevention

1. All survivors I interviewed for this project worked at memorials or lived in rural areas in close proximity to the memorials. This meant that unlike the diverse population of survivors in Rwanda, this particular group of survivors was very dedicated to and engaged with memory work. In this respect, their perspectives are likely different from those of survivors who do not have regular interactions with memorials.

2. The similarities between these individuals' perspectives and official narratives are even evident on a linguistic level, in phrases such as "bright future" or "divisionist ideology." See Marie E. Berry, "When 'Bright Futures' Fade: Paradoxes of Women's Empowerment in Rwanda," *Signs: Journal of Women in Culture and Society* 41, no. 1 (2014); Purdeková, "Building."

3. It should be noted that this assertion is not that unusual for post-atrocity societies more generally: museums around the globe dedicated to the Holocaust, apartheid, various wars, and imperialism also echo versions of "never again" and assert the notion that if people understand the past and experience empathy, they will do everything in their power to "never again" let it happen.

4. This process resembles the social construction of reality. See Peter L. Berger and Thomas Luckmann, *The Social Construction of Reality: A Treatise in the Sociology of Knowledge* (New York: Random House, 1966); Crystal L. Park and Amy L. Ai, "Meaning Making and Growth: New Directions for Research on Survivors of Trauma," *Journal of Loss & Trauma* 11, no. 5 (2006).

5. I understand the dynamics of meaning-making and narrative formation as two deeply intertwined and dialectical social processes that occur when an individual (or group) creates meaning or makes sense of a tragedy or atrocity to give order to the story of the event. In the creation of meaning, and ordering disorder, a narrative that can be told and retold is formed. Through the retelling of life (or atrocity/hardship) narratives, with individuals bearing witness and social actors engaging with the telling, new

meaning is produced and in turn reshapes the narrative. This process continues cognitively and socially as new information is garnered and new life events are processed.

6. See Lidwien Kapteijns and J. M. Richters, *Mediations of Violence in Africa: Fashioning New Futures from Contested Pasts* (Boston: Brill, 2010), especially the chapter by Naomi van Stapele, titled "Testimonies of Suffering and Recasting the Meanings of Memories of Violence in Post-War Mozambique."

7. This process is also evident in other cases of significant loss when the individual can make sense of the tragedy in the midst of grief. See J. M. Holland, J. M. Currier, and R. A. Neimeyer, "Meaning Reconstruction in the First Two Years of Bereavement: The Role of Sense-Making and Benefit-Finding," *Omega: Journal of Death & Dying* 53, no. 3 (2006).

8. Marilyn Armour, "Meaning Making in Survivorship: Application to Holocaust Survivors," *Journal of Human Behavior in the Social Environment* 20, no. 4 (2010): 441; J. M. Iorio and W. Parnell, *Meaning Making in Early Childhood Research: Pedagogies and the Personal* (New York: Taylor & Francis, 2017); Ani Kalayjian and Dominque Eugene, *Mass Trauma and Emotional Healing around the World: Rituals and Practices for Resilience and Meaning-Making* (Santa Barbara, CA: Praeger, 2010); Park and Ai, "Meaning."

9. Armour, "Meaning Making," 441.

10. Corina Sas and Alina Coman, "Designing Personal Grief Rituals: An Analysis of Symbolic Objects and Actions," *Death Studies* 40, no. 9 (2016). Cultural anthropologist Renato Rosaldo argues that dilemmas grew for the group he was observing when the practices for dealing with grief were "blocked" and it was "agonizing to live." See Renato Rosaldo, "Grief and Headhunter's Rage," in *Death, Mourning, and Burial: A Cross-Cultural Reader*, ed. Antonius C. G. M. Robben (Oxford: Blackwell, 2004), 169.

11. Rosaldo, "Grief," 176.

12. Young, *Texture*, 3.

13. This has most certainly been true for wars and atrocity in the US and Europe. The slow and unimpressive memorialization of Korean War veterans in American commemorative history demonstrates an intentional forgetting of the Korean War, in contrast to the celebration of America's role in World War II through monuments and museums. See Christine Knauer, "Their Forgotten War: Veterans and the Korean War in American Memory," in *War Memories: Commemoration, Recollections, and Writings on War*, ed. Stéphanie A. H. Bélanger and Renée Dickason (Montreal: McGill-Queen's University Press, 2017). On Eastern Europe's strategy of "memory-through-forgetting" of Nazi collaborators, nationalist strategic catering to ex-Nazis, and the "general disabling of the memory of war," see Richard S. Esbenshade, "Remembering to Forget: Memory, History, National Identity in Postwar East-Central Europe," *Representations*, no. 49 (1995), 79.

14. As Andrea Purdeková states, "Written history was always used to justify contemporary political objectives, and according to the particular ideological appropriation, it served either to comfort the aristocracy, or legitimated its contrary, populism" ("Building," 508). Patterns of historical narratives that support state efforts are present

in US cases of collective memory projects ranging from the use of political figures (Polletta, "Legacies"; Barry Schwartz, "Social Change and Collective Memory: The Democratization of George Washington," *American Sociological Review* 56, no. 2 [1991]), to Holocaust memorials (Young, *Texture*), to public speeches (Christina Simko, *The Politics of Consolation: Memory and the Meaning of September 11* [New York: Oxford University Press, 2015]).

15. Buckley-Zistel, "Nation," 31.

16. No doubt, colonial powers exacerbated inequality and racialized Hutu, Tutsi, and Twa identities. However, historians have extensively documented the inaccuracies of this narrative, documenting complex power dynamics throughout Rwandan precolonial history. See chapter 1 of this book for an overview of various points of inequality throughout Rwandan history. For more complex histories of Rwanda that demonstrate economic and political tensions and inequality that were evident prior to colonialism, see Alison Des Forges, *Defeat Is the Only Bad News* (Madison: University of Wisconsin Press, 2011); D. Newbury, *Land beyond the Mists*; Vansina, *Antecedents*.

17. Warshauer-Freedman et al., "Teaching History," 675.

18. See Erin Jessee's work on the state narrative and how variously situated social actors narrate different versions of it: Erin Jessee, *Negotiating Genocide in Rwanda: The Politics of History* (Basingstoke, UK: Palgrave Macmillan, 2017).

19. Pottier, *Re-imagining*.

20. The RPF government is officially called "the government of national unity and reconciliation." See Purdeková, *Making*.

21. Buckley-Zistel, "Nation," 675.

22. Phil Clark, "Negotiating Reconciliation in Rwanda: Popular Challenges to the Official Discourse of Post-Genocide National Unity," *Journal of Intervention and State-Building* 8, no. 4 (2014); Purdeková, "Building"; Purdeková, *Making*; Filip Reyntjens, "(Re-)Imagining a Reluctant Post-Genocide Society: The Rwandan Patriotic Front's Ideology and Practice," *Journal of Genocide Research* 18, no. 1 (2016); Warshauer-Freedman et al., "Teaching History"; Eugenia Zorbas, "What Does Reconciliation after Genocide Mean? Public Transcripts and Hidden Transcripts in Post-Genocide Rwanda," *Journal of Genocide Research* 11, no. 1 (2009).

23. Jeffremovas, "Contested Identities"; Mamdani, *When Victims Become Killers*.

24. C. Newbury, *Cohesion*.

25. Nyseth Brehm and Fox, "Narrating"; Susan Thomson, *Whispering Truth to Power: Everyday Resistance to Reconciliation in Postgenocide Rwanda* (Madison: University of Wisconsin Press, 2013).

26. See Jessee, *Negotiating*; Warshauer-Freedman et al., "Teaching History"; Nyseth Brehm and Fox, "Narrating."

27. The narrative of the past in which Rwandans once lived in social harmony is not unlike nostalgic narratives arising after instances of significant social change. See Shirley Y. Y. Cheng et al., "The Good Old Days and a Better Tomorrow: Historical Representations and Future Imaginations of China during the 2008 Olympic Games," *Asian Journal of Social Psychology* 13, no. 2 (2010); Anouk Smeekes, Maykel Verkuyten,

and Borja Martinovic, "Longing for the Country's Good Old Days: National Nostalgia, Autochthony Beliefs, and Opposition to Muslim Expressive Rights," *British Journal of Social Psychology* 54, no. 3 (2015).

28. Anderson, *Imagined Communities*, quoted in Akhil Gupta and James Ferguson, "Beyond 'Culture': Space, Identity, and the Politics of Difference," *Cultural Anthropology* 7, no. 1 (1992): 10.

29. See chapters 2 and 6 of this book for a discussion on survivors who never found the remains of their loved ones and the impact of that on the survivors' ability to heal and be part of the reconciliation process.

30. For an example of how tightly controlled the state narrative is, especially as it pertains to Rwandan social science/historical material used for education, see Warshauer-Freedman et al., "Teaching History." See also Reyntjens, who states that "official narrative is open to replication but closed to debate. This closure of the debate on the interpretation of the past is actively policed by the regime" ("[Re-]Imagining," 64).

Chapter 4. Trauma and the Stratification of Collective Memory

1. For more on the process of conducting qualitative research in postconflict zones, please see the appendix in this book, where I discuss the challenges and ethical questions I faced and my research methods.

2. The word "trauma" is used here to denote a range of physical, emotional and psychological responses to a disturbing or distressing event, such as genocidal violence. The term "traumatizing," however, is the English word used by Rwandans to reference an extreme response to trauma or flashbacks that sometimes afflicts survivors, particularly during commemorative events.

3. Cheryl McEwan, "Building a Postcolonial Archive? Gender, Collective Memory and Citizenship in Post-Apartheid South Africa," *Journal of Southern African Studies* 29, no. 3 (2003).

4. Michelle Kelso and Daina S. Eglitis, "Holocaust Commemoration in Romania: Roma and the Contested Politics of Memory and Memorialization," *Journal of Genocide Research*, 16, no. 4 (2014).

5. Harold Kerbo, "Social Stratification," in *The Wiley-Blackwell Encyclopedia of Social Theory*, edited by Bryan S. Turner et al. (Hoboken, NJ: John Wiley & Sons, 2017), 1–4.

6. Touraj Ayazi et al., "What Are the Risk Factors for the Comorbidity of Post-traumatic Stress Disorder and Depression in a War-Affected Population? A Cross-Sectional Community Study in South Sudan," *BMC Psychiatry* 12, no. 175 (2012). It is important to note that trauma response and PTSD are not interchangeable terms. PTSD is a diagnostic term that requires a series of symptoms and duration of such symptoms to be present, all of which are analyzed and then diagnosed by a mental health professional (DSM-5 Criteria for PTSD, American Psychiatric Association, 2013). While those experiencing "traumatizing" may indeed be strong candidates for a PTSD diagnosis, some argue that the diagnosis and even the treatment commonly

prescribed in the West would not be culturally appropriate in the Rwandan context. See Derek Summerfield's (1999) critique of the West's trend of spending millions of dollars in mental health programs to treat PTSD. Derek Summerfield, "A Critique of Seven Assumptions behind Psychological Trauma Programmes in War-Affected Areas," *Social Science & Medicine* 48, no. 10 (1999). This may especially be true for rape survivors. See Holly Porter, *After Rape: Violence, Justice and Social Harmony in Uganda* (New York: Cambridge University Press, 2017).

7. Jasmina Spasojević, Robert W. Heffer, and Douglas K. Snyder, "Effects of Posttraumatic Stress and Acculturation on Marital Functioning in Bosnian Refugee Couples," *Journal of Traumatic Stress* 13, no. 2 (2000).

8. G. A. Bonanno and A. D. Mancini, "The Human Capacity to Thrive in the Face of Potential Trauma," *Pediatrics* 121, no. 2 (2008); F. Fan et al., "Longitudinal Trajectories of Post-Traumatic Stress Disorder Symptoms among Adolescents after the Wenchuan Earthquake in China," *Psychological Medicine* 45, no. 13 (2015); S. Y. Tam, S. Houlihan, and G. J. Melendez-Torres. "A Systematic Review of Longitudinal Risk and Protective Factors and Correlates for Posttraumatic Stress and Its Natural History in Forcibly Displaced Children," *Trauma, Violence, & Abuse* 18, no. 4 (2015).

9. L. Gupta, *1998 Rwanda: Follow-up Survey of Rwandan Children's Reactions to War Related Violence from the 1994 Genocide* (New York: UNICEF, 1998).

10. Sameera Nayak, Sowmya Kshtriya, and Richard Neugebauer, "Trauma Alleviation Treatment for Unaccompanied Children after the Rwandan Genocide: A Cautionary Tale," *Intervention* 17, no. 1 (2019): 24.

11. Nayak, Kshtriya, and Neugebauer, "Trauma Alleviation Treatment."

12. Derek Summerfield, "The Invention of PTSD and the Social Usefulness of a Psychiatric Category," *BMJ* (Clinical research ed.) 322 (2001).

13. Summerfield, "Assumptions," 1449.

14. Nayak, Kshtriya, and Neugebauer, "Trauma Alleviation Treatment," 28.

15. Collective trauma may also require more collective forms of trauma treatment rather than individually focused psychological help. For a US example, see T. Wicke and R. C. Silver, "A Community Responds to Collective Trauma: An Ecological Analysis of the James Byrd Murder in Jasper, Texas," *American Journal Community Psychology* 44, nos. 3–4 (2009). Furthermore, scholars have argued that Western psychological approaches to trauma may not be appropriate for a range of cases outside the West, especially in the aftermath of mass atrocity and collective communal or national trauma. See Rochelle Ann Burgess and Laura Fonseca, "Re-Thinking Recovery in Post-Conflict Settings: Supporting the Mental Well-Being of Communities in Colombia," *Global Public Health* 15, no. 2 (2020); Katriona Taylor and Gerald H. Burgess, "Views of Non-Western Trainee or Recently-Qualified Practitioner Psychologists on the Import of Western Psychology into Their Indigenous Non-Western Cultures," *International Journal of Mental Health* 48, no. 4 (2019); Rachel Tribea, "Culture, Politics and Global Mental Health," *Disability and the Global South* 1, no. 2 (2014). See also Holly Porter's important work on justice and social harmony after rape in Northern Uganda (Porter, *After Rape*).

16. UNICEF, "Ten Years."

17. This exact scenario played out at the CFC: men died on the hills trying to protect their families, and women and children died inside the church on a fateful day when the men miscalculated the location of the perpetrators.

18. There is evidence of a gender differences in PTSD diagnoses in Western contexts as well, including a similar discussion to the effect that the higher prevalence of PTSD found in women could be attributed to their experiences of sexual violence. Carlos I. Pérez Benitez et al., "Epidemiology of Trauma, PTSD and Other Psychiatric Disorders in a Representative Population 145 of Chile," *Salud Mental* 32, no. 2 (2009); Leah M. Blain, Tara E. Galovski, and Tristan Robinson, "Gender Differences in Recovery from Posttraumatic Stress Disorder: A Critical Review," *Aggression and Violent Behavior* 15 no. 6 (2010); Bonnie S. Dansky et al., "Victimization and PTSD in Individuals with Substance Use Disorders: Gender and Racial Differences," *American Journal of Drug and Alcohol Abuse* 22, no. 1 (1996); Tara E. Galovski et al., "Gender Differences in the Clinical Presentation of PTSD and Its Concomitants in Survivors of Interpersonal Assault," *Journal of Interpersonal Violence* 26, no. 4 (2011); Elizabeth Ann Lee and Sue A. Theus, "Lower Heart Rate Variability Associated with Military Sexual Trauma Rape and Posttraumatic Stress Disorder," *Biological Research for Nursing* 14, no. 4 (2012); Kim Steven Betts et al., "Exploring the Female Specific Risk to Partial and Full PTSD Following Physical Assault," *Journal of Traumatic Stress* 26, no. 1 (2013).

19. A *moto* is a motorcycle taxi.

20. Participants also explained that this is in some part due to a problem the WHO has called the "treatment gap," where there are not enough trained mental health professionals to care for populations that need assistance. For more details, see Stefan Jansen et al., "The 'Treatment Gap' in Global Mental Health Reconsidered: Sociotherapy for Collective Trauma in Rwanda," *European Journal of Psychotraumatology* 6, no. 1 (2015).

21. Priscilla B. Hayner, *Unspeakable Truths: Transitional Justice and the Challenge of Truth Commissions*, 2nd ed. (New York: Routledge, 2011); Judith Herman, *Trauma and Recovery: The Aftermath of Violence—From Domestic Abuse to Political Terror* (New York: Basic Books, 1997); Minow, *Between*.

22. M. Berry, "Women's Empowerment"; Uvin, *Aiding*.

23. Nicole Fox, "'God Must Have Been Sleeping': Faith as an Obstacle and a Resource for Rwandan Genocide Survivors in the United States," *Journal for the Scientific Study of Religion* 51, no. 1 (2012).

Chapter 5. Gendered Violence and the Politics of Remembering and Forgetting

Portions of this chapter appeared in an earlier form in Nicole Fox, "Memory in Interaction: Gender-Based Violence, Genocide, and Commemoration," *Signs: Journal of Women in Culture and Society* 45, no. 1 (2019).

1. For a number of reasons, it is difficult to obtain accurate estimates of SGBV, and rape in particular, during war and genocide. While we know that rape can occur during all kinds of political conflicts (including election violence—see Jana Krause,

"Restrained or Constrained? Elections, Communal Conflicts, and Variation in Sexual Violence," *Journal of Peace Research* 57, no. 1 [2020]), the majority of studies on SGBV have been qualitative in nature because it is so difficult to implement quantitative and big data projects on rape victimization. Researchers conducting large-scale studies may have to contend with factors such as environments where conflict is ongoing, lack of reliable data, methodological challenges, minimal access to victims and perpetrators, and the shame and stigma surrounding sexual violence. For more on these hurdles, see Catrien Bijleveld, "Missing Pieces: Methodological Issues in the Study of International Crimes and Gross Human Rights Violations," in *Supranational Criminology: Towards a Criminology of International Crimes*, ed. A. Smeulers and R. H. Haveman (Antwerp, Belgium: Intersentia, 2008); D. Lisak and P. M. Miller, "Repeat Rape and Multiple Offending among Undetected Rapists," *Violence & Victims* 17 (2002). Furthermore, some scholars have argued that the actual numbers do not matter and can cause problems in hierarchies of victimhood or atrocity. For a discussion on this, see Catrien Bijleveld, Aafke Morssinkhof, and Alette Smeulers, "Counting the Countless: Rape Victimization during the Rwandan Genocide," *International Criminal Justice Review* 19, no. 2 (2009). However, by knowing the numbers of those affected by a particular atrocity, variously situated social actors can learn the scope of victimization and allocate the resources needed to alleviate the impacts of such violence and facilitate healing. This is why I include the most accurate estimate that I have found on the number of rapes. See the work of Bijleveld, Morssinkhof, and Smeulers, who detail their methodology for the 350,000 estimate and lay out how they tested the reliability limits of their estimate (Bijleveld, Morssinkhof, and Smeulers, "Counting").

2. Christopher W. Mullins and Dawn Rothe, *Blood, Power, and Bedlam: Violations of International Criminal Law in Post-colonial Africa* (New York: Peter Lang, 2008). World Health Organization (WHO), *World Report on Violence and Health*, Geneva, 2002.

3. Susan Brownmiller, *Against Our Will: Men, Women, and Rape* (New York: Fawcett Columbine, 1975); Catharine MacKinnon, "Rape, Genocide, and Women's Human Rights," *Harvard Women's Law Journal*, no. 17 (1994); Phillip Weiner, "The Evolving Jurisprudence of the Crime of Rape in International Criminal Law," *Boston College Law Review* 54, no. 3 (2013). For the first individual conviction of rape as a crime against humanity, see Prosecutor v. Akayesu, Case No. ICTR 96-4-T, Judgment, ¶ 598 (September 2, 1998), http://www.internationalcrimesdatabase.org/Case/50/Akayesu/.

4. Nowrojee, "Shattered"; F. Nduwimana, *The Right to Survive: Sexual Violence, Women and HIV/AIDS* (Montreal: International Centre for Human Rights and Democratic Development, 2004); von Joeden-Forgey, "Devil."

5. Fox, "Impacts."

6. Fox, "Impacts," 280.

7. R. Charli Carpenter, *Forgetting Children Born of War: Setting the Human Rights Agenda in Bosnia and Beyond* (New York: Columbia University Press, 2010); Janine Natalya Clark, "A Crime of Identity: Rape and Its Neglected Victims," *Journal of Human Rights* 13, no. 2 (2014).

8. C. Twagiramariya and M. Turshen, "'Favours' to Give and 'Consenting' Victims: The Sexual Politics of Survival in Rwanda," in *What Women Do in Wartime: Gender and Conflict in Africa*, edited by M. Turshen and C. Twagiramariya (New York: Zed Books, 1998).

9. For a discussion on forced impregnation as a form of biological warfare, see Beverly Allen, *Rape Warfare: The Hidden Genocide in Bosnia-Herzegovina and Croatia* (Minneapolis: University of Minnesota, 1996).

10. R. Charli Carpenter, "Surfacing Children: Limitations of Genocidal Rape Discourse," *Human Rights Quarterly* 22, no. 1 (2000): 449.

11. R. Charli Carpenter, "Recognizing Gender-Based Violence against Civilian Men and Boys in Conflict Situations," *Security Dialogue* 37, no. 1 (2006); Gabrielle Ferrales, Hollie Nyseth Brehm, and Suzy McElrath, "Gender-Based Violence against Men and Boys in Darfur: The Gender-Genocide Nexus," *Gender & Society* 30, no. 4 (2016); Paul Kirby, "How Is Rape a Weapon of War? Feminist International Relations, Modes of Critical Explanation and the Study of Wartime Sexual Violence," *European Journal of International Relations* 19, no. 4 (2013).

12. Anne McClintock, "Family Feuds: Gender, Nationalism and the Family," *Feminist Review* 44, no. 1 (1993): 61.

13. Nira Yuval-Davis, *Gender & Nation* (London: SAGE, 1997).

14. Yuval-Davis, *Gender*; Nira Yuval-Davis, *The Politics of Belonging: Intersectional Contestations* (London: SAGE, 2011).

15. Yuval-Davis, *Gender*.

16. Swanee Hunt, *This Was Not Our War: Bosnian Women Reclaiming Peace* (Durham, NC: Duke University Press, 2004).

17. Patricia Albanese, "Nationalism, War, and Archaization of Gender Relations in the Balkans," *Violence against Women* 7, no. 9 (2001): 1000.

18. Carole Pateman, *The Disorder of Women: Democracy, Feminism, and Political Theory* (Stanford: Stanford University Press, 1989).

19. For analysis on mental health care for Rwandan survivors of SGBV, see Maggie Zraly, Julia Rubin-Smith, and Theresa Betancourt, "Primary Mental Health Care for Survivors of Collective Sexual Violence in Rwanda," *Global Public Health* 6, no. 3 (2011). Holly Porter's work on social harmony and justice after rape in Northern Uganda is also relevant (Porter, *After Rape*).

20. This position ignores the fact that victimization can result in resiliency. See Zraly, Rubin, and Mukamana, "Motherhood"; Zraly and Nyirazinyoye, "Ethnographic Study."

21. See Coombes, *History*; James Hawdon and John Ryan, "Social Relations That Generate and Sustain Solidarity after a Mass Tragedy," *Social Forces* 89, no. 4 (2011); Michael Lewis and Jacqueline Serbu, "Kommemorating the Ku Klux Klan," *Sociological Quarterly* 40, no. 1 (1999); Claire Whitlinger, *Between Remembrance and Repair: Commemorating Racial Violence in Philadelphia, Mississippi* (Chapel Hill: University of North Carolina Press, 2020). See also Judith Herman, *Trauma and Recovery*; Rhoda E.

Howard-Hassmann, "Getting to Reparations: Japanese American and African Americans," *Social Forces* 83, no. 2 (2004). On truth commissions, see Hayner, *Transitional Justice*.

22. MacKinnon, "Rape," 5.

23. Carpenter, *Forgetting*; Carpenter, "Surfacing."

24. Hilary Charlesworth, "Not Waving but Drowning: Gender Mainstreaming and Human Rights in the United Nations," *Harvard Human Rights Journal*, no. 18 (2005); Anne Gallagher, "Ending the Marginalization: Strategies for Incorporating Women into the United Nations Human Rights System," *Human Rights Quarterly* 19, no. 2 (1997).

25. Ministry of Gender and Family Promotion, Republic of Rwanda, "Mission and Vision," 2015, http://migeprof.gov.rw/index.php?id=186.

26. Sara E. Brown, "Female Perpetrators of the Rwandan Genocide," *International Feminist Journal of Politics* 16, no. 3 (2014); Sharlach, "Gender"; Des Forges, *Leave None*. Rwandan women were often with their children during executions or abductions, staying close to the village and home, while men often took the role of manning defensive positions outside the village premises. This was evident in this study when survivors spoke of their survival stories, especially at the CFC (described in more detail below). Gendercide is defined as killings that target a specific sex. Like other genocides, the perpetrators in the Rwandan case began with the targeted killings of men and boys in the early months of genocidal violence and then moved on to women, girls, and the elderly (Jones, "Gender").

27. Nagarajan, "Appraisal," 111. The word *inyenzi* (Kinyarwanda for "cockroach") was used to refer to the RPF but over time became a derogatory ethnic slur for all Tutsis.

28. Des Forges, *Leave None*.

29. Des Forges, *Leave None*.

30. Des Forges, *Leave None*; Mamdami, *When Victims Become Killers*.

31. Jones, "Gender." "Hutu moderates" is the term used to describe Hutus who did not believe in the genocidal agenda, intermarried with Tutsis, or had friendly relations with Tutsis. While the genocidal regime targeted Hutu moderates, it is important to note that stereotypical physical markings of Hutu (short stature and flatter noses) and Tutsi (tall stature and thinner noses) were not always reliable, especially since Hutu and Tutsi were once class categories and not ethnic identities (see chapter 1). This means that some Hutu-identified people were killed because they had physical markings associated with Tutsi, and some Tutsi were spared because they were perceived as Hutu. However, because communities were tightly knit, this generally only happened to individuals who had traveled or escaped from other villages: in their own communities they would easily be identified as Hutu or Tutsi by people who knew them—or by their identity cards.

32. Erin K. Baines, "Body Politics and the Rwandan Crisis," *Third World Quarterly* 24, no. 3 (2003); Scharlach, "Gender."

33. Sharlach, "Gender," 394.

34. Mary Ann Tetreault and Sita Ranchod-Nilsson, eds., *Women, States and Nationalism: At Home in the Nation?* (New York: Routledge, 2000).

35. De Brouwer and Chu, *Men*.

36. See Jennie Burnet's work on amplified silences and Lee Ann Fujii's discussion on "meta-data"—also discussed in the appendix on listening to silences when conducting interviews (Burnet, *Genocide*; Fujii, "Shades").

37. Catharine MacKinnon, "Genocide's Sexuality," in *Political Exclusion and Domination*, ed. Stephen Macedo and Melissa Williams (New York: New York University Press, 2004); Weiner, "Evolving."

38. Baines, "Body Politics."

39. De Brouwer and Chu, *Men*.

40. Buss, "Rethinking."

41. Nagarajan, "Appraisal"; Schaal et al., "Prolonged Grief"; Zraly and Nyirazinyoye, "Ethnographic Study." Scholars have also found that those who are impregnated from rape suffer particularly high rates of suicidal thoughts and severe depression. See Vera Folnegovic-Small, "Psychiatric Aspects of the Rapes in the War against the Republics of Croatia and Bosnia-Herzegovina," in *Mass Rape*, ed. Alexandra Stiglmayer (Lincoln: University of Nebraska Press, 1993), 174, 177.

42. Arden B. Levy, "International Prosecution of Rape in Warfare: Nondiscriminatory Recognition and Enforcement," *UCLA Women's Law Journal* 4, no. 2 (1994); Anne Tierney Goldstein, *Recognizing Forced Impregnation as a War Crime under International Law: A Special Report of the International Program* (New York: Center for Reproductive Law & Policy, 1993), 14–15.

43. Newbury and Baldwin, *Aftermath*.

44. Marie E. Berry, "Mobilization"; Thomson, *Whispering*.

45. Longman, "Rwanda."

46. M. Berry, "From Violence"; Jennie E. Burnet, "Gender Balance and the Meanings of Women in Governance in Post-Genocide Rwanda," *African Affairs* 107, no. 428 (2008).

47. Burnet, "Genocide," 372.

48. Catherine Bolzendahl and Clem Brooks, "Women's Political Representation and Welfare State Spending in 12 Capitalist Democracies," *Social Forces* 85, no. 4 (2007); Liam Swiss, Kathleen M. Fallon, and Giovani Burgos, "Does Critical Mass Matter? Women's Political Representation and Child Health in Developing Countries," *Social Forces* 91, no. 2 (2012).

49. Burnet, "Gender Balance."

50. Burnet, "Gender Balance."

51. Longman, "Rwanda," 149.

52. M. Berry, "Mobilization," 3.

53. Nicole Fox, field notes, 2012.

54. Fox, field notes.

55. Fox, field notes; Schmidt, "Deaths."

56. On children born out of rape, see Mariana Torgovnick, "Rereading 'The Iliad' in Times of War," *PMLA* 124, no. 5 (2009).

57. Fox, field notes.

58. Andrea Dworkin, "The Unremembered: Searching for Women at the Holocaust Memorial Museum," *Ms. Magazine* 5, no. 3 (1994).

59. Carpenter, "Recognizing"; Ferrales, Nyseth Brehm, and McElrath, "Gender-Based Violence"; Nicola Henry, "Theorizing Wartime Rape: Deconstructing Gender, Sexuality, and Violence," *Gender & Society* 30, no. 1 (2016).

60. Arrizón and Forster-Towne argue for framing rape during political violence as a form of terrorism. Forster-Towne explicitly states: "Although there is a plethora of definitions for terrorism, many share certain commonalities, namely, terrorism is strategic, targeted at noncombatants, violent in nature and likely to be politically motivated. . . . Women are often, although not always, non-combatants of war, they are strategically chosen because defacing a woman is used as a deliberate way to undermine men and their masculinity, thereby slowly debasing the entire community" (iv). Gendered-based violence in Rwanda was strategic, targeted civilians, was violent and politically motivated. Alicia Arrizón, "'Invisible Wars': Gendered Terrorism in the US Military and the Juárez Feminicidio," in *Gender, Globalization, and Violence: Postcolonial Conflict Zones*, ed. Sandra Ponzanesi (New York: Routledge, 2014); Claudia Forster-Towne, *Exploring the Plausibility of Linking Notions of Terrorism and Sexual Violence by Using the Great Lakes Region as a Case Study* (Pretoria, South Africa: African Books Collective, 2011).

61. William James Booth, *Communities of Memory: On Witness, Identity and Justice* (Ithaca, NY: Cornell University Press, 2006), 73.

62. Booth, *Communities*, 91.

63. MacKinnon, "Rape," 12.

Chapter 6. Survivors' Lived Experiences of Reconciliation

1. I find Lederach's definition of reconciliation to be the most open-ended and able to capture both top-down and bottom-up peace efforts: "Reconciliation is best understood as the bringing together of justice and mercy in the context of fractured relationships. It assumes the proactive engagement of people in restoring what has been lost and starting anew." J. P. Lederach, *Preparing for Peace: Conflict Transformation across Cultures* (Syracuse: Syracuse University Press, 1996), 20.

2. It is productive to consider how dynamics of reconciliation fall on a larger continuum: on one end is a community that experiences nonlethal coexistence, and on the other is complete social harmony. Nonlethal coexistence entails former enemies no longer killing one another or violating each other's basic human rights. This, of course, is much easier to accomplish than social harmony, which entails total reconciliation between wrongdoers and their victims. Nobel Peace Prize winner Desmond Tutu, based on his experiences with the TRC, argues that social harmony is the highest level and most promising form of reconciliation; in other words, it is an end result rather

than a process. Desmond Tutu, *No Future without Forgiveness* (New York: Random House, 1999).

3. Please see the appendix for details on the methodology of this project as well as the ethical challenges of conducting qualitative work in postconflict zones.

4. Jean de Dieu explained that the formula occurred after a gacaca trial in which the perpetrator publicly acknowledged the crime he had committed and then privately asked for forgiveness from the victims. Jean de Dieu also stated that the perpetrator attended commemorations and memorials as a form of apology, accepting that he had wronged his entire community as well as the specific victims.

5. Institute for Economics and Peace, "Structures of Peace: Identifying What Leads to Peaceful Societies," 2011, http://www.operationspaix.net/DATA/DOCUMENT/64 40~v~Structures_of_Peace__Identifying_What_Leads_to_Peaceful_Societies.pdf.

6. United Nations Development Programme, "Human Development Reports: Human Development Index (HDI)," http://hdr.undp.org/en/content/human-develop ment-index-hdi.

7. See Martin Cooke et al., "Indigenous Well-Being in Four Countries: An Application of the UNDP'S Human Development Index to Indigenous Peoples in Australia, Canada, New Zealand, and the United States," *BMC International Health and Human Rights* 7, no. 1 (2007): 9.

8. Ralph Sundberg and Erik Melander, "Introducing the UCDP Georeferenced Event Dataset," *Journal of Peace Research* 50, no. 4 (2013). For a comparison of these two datasets, see Kristine Eck, "In Data We Trust? A Comparison of UCDP GED and ACLED Conflict Events Datasets," *Cooperation and Conflict* 47, no. 1 (2012).

9. For a comparison of national reconciliation barometers across multiple nations, see Elizabeth A. Cole and Pamina Firchow, "Reconciliation Barometers: Tools for Post-Conflict Policy Design," *International Journal of Transitional Justice* 13, no. 3 (2019).

10. For Australia's recent report on their National Reconciliation Barometer, see Reconciliation Australia, *2018 Australian Reconciliation Barometer*, https://www.recon ciliation.org.au/wp-content/uploads/2019/02/ra_2019-barometer-brochure_web.sin gle.page_.pdf. For South Africa's 2019 report on their National Reconciliation Barom-eter, see Institute for Reconciliation and Justice, *SA Reconciliation Barometer 2019*, https://www.ijr.org.za/portfolio-items/sa-reconciliation-barometer-2019/.

11. Pamina Firchow and Roger MacGinty, "Measuring Peace: Comparability, Com-mensurability, and Complementarity Using Bottom-Up Indicators," *International Stud-ies Review* 19, no. 1 (2017): 22.

12. See Brewer's call for a more sociological (and human-focused) approach to accounts of peace. J. Brewer, *Peace Processes: A Sociological Approach* (Cambridge: Polity Press, 2010). See also Lee Jarvis and Michael Lister's call for research of the vernacular of international relations, "Vernacular Securities and Their Study: A Qualitative Anal-ysis and Future Research Agenda," *International Relations* 27, no. 2 (2013); and Patricia Justino, Tilman Brück, and Philip Verwimp's call for more micro-level approaches to conflict, violence, and development, *A Micro Level Perspective on the Dynamics of Conflict, Violence, and Development* (Oxford: Oxford University Press, 2013).

13. Brewer, *Peace*; R. MacGinty and O. Richmond, "The Local Turn in Peace-building: A Critical Agenda for Peace," *Third World Quarterly* 34, no. 5 (2013); Justino, Brück, and Verwimp, *Perspective*; Elisa Randazzo, "The Paradoxes of the 'Everyday': Scrutinising the Local Turn in Peacebuilding," *Third World Quarterly* 37, no. 8 (2016).

14. See Everyday Peace Indicators, accessed June 1, 2020, https://everydaypeacein-dicators.org/; Pamina Firchow, *Reclaiming Everyday Peace: Local Voices in Measurement and Evaluation after War* (Cambridge: Cambridge University Press, 2018).

15. See Varshney's important work on how interethnic mundane interactions re-duced violent conflict in some parts of India: Ashutosh Varshney, *Ethnic Conflict and Civic Life: Hindus and Muslims in India* (New Haven, CT: Yale University Press, 2002).

16. M. Abu-Nimer, "Toward the Theory and Practice of Positive Approaches to Peacebuilding," in *Positive Approaches to Peacebuilding*, ed. C. Sampson, M. Abu-Nimer, C. Liebler, and D. Whitney (Washington, DC: PACT Publications, 2003); Susan Brison, "Trauma Narratives and the Remaking of the Self," in *Acts of Memory: Cultural Recall in the Present*, ed. Mieke Bal, Jonathan V. Crewe, and Leo Spitzer (Hanover, NH: University Press of New England, 1999); Sara Cobb, *Speaking of Violence: The Politics and Poetics of Narrative Dynamics in Conflict Resolution* (New York: Oxford University Press, 2013); Barry Hart and Edita Colo, "Psychosocial Peacebuilding in Bosnia and Herzegovina: Approaches to Relational and Social Change," *Intervention* 12, no. 1 (2014); Jennifer Mason, "Personal Narratives, Relational Selves: Residential His-tories in the Living and Telling," *Sociological Review* 52, no. 2 (2004); H. H. Saunders, *A Public Peace Process: Sustained Dialogue to Transform Racial and Ethnic Conflicts* (New York: Palgrave, 2001).

17. Benedict Anderson, *Imagined Communities*.

18. Susan Brison explains that "survivors of trauma frequently remark that they are not the same people they were before they were traumatized. . . . The undoing of the self in trauma involves a radical disruption of memory, a severing of past from present and, typically, an inability to envision a future. And yet trauma survivors often eventually find ways to reconstruct themselves and carry on with reconfigured lives." Brison, "Trauma," 39.

19. Polletta et al., "Sociology," 117; Robert Zussman, "Autobiographical Occasions," *Contemporary Sociology* 25, no. 2 (1996).

20. Polletta et al., "Sociology"; Ronald J. Berger and Richard Quinney, eds., *Story-telling Sociology: Narrative as Social Inquiry* (Boulder, CO: Lynne Rienner, 2004).

21. As discussed in chapter 2, the mourning period in Rwanda begins on April 7 every year and lasts one hundred days, marking the one hundred days of the genocidal violence.

22. One of the major goals of the gacaca courts, explained in chapter 1, was to bring restorative justice to communities by sentencing perpetrators to perform services for their victims' families, such as rebuilding houses or restoring property. Described in more depth in the introduction and chapter 1, restorative justice is an approach to justice and crime that focuses on the needs of the victim rather than legal discourse.

Victims are active in this process and offenders are assumed to make right by repairing the harm they did to the victims and their communities through community service, apologies, or paying debt. Yvon Dandurand and Curt T. Griffith, *United Nations Handbook on Restorative Justice Programmes* (Vienna: United Nations, 2006); Brandon Hamber and Richard A. Wilson, "Symbolic Closure through Memory, Reparation and Revenge in Post-Conflict Societies," *Journal of Human Rights* 1, no. 1 (2002). On the importance of truth-telling, see Brounéus, "Truth-Telling"; Hayner, *Transitional Justice*; Teresa Phelps, *Shattered Voices: Language, Violence and the Work of Truth Commissions* (Pennsylvania: University of Pennsylvania Press, 2004); Gearoid Millar, "Assessing Local Experiences of Truth-Telling in Sierra Leone: Getting to 'Why' through a Qualitative Case Study Analysis," *International Journal of Transitional Justice* 4, no. 3 (2010). On restorative practices, see J. Clark, "Rules"; Ingelaere, *Inside*; Nyseth Brehm, Uggen, and Gasanabo, "Genocide."

23. See chapters 2 and 3 of this book for a discussion on survivors' desire to locate the remains of their loved ones; see also the conclusion for why locating remains should be a peacebuilding priority. The desire to know where loved ones' bodies are buried is a recurring theme in postgenocide Rwanda and beyond. See P. Clark, "Missing"; Pablo Baraybar, Brasey, and Zadel, "Need"; Angela Soler and Jared S. Beatrice, "Expanding the Role of Forensic Anthropology in a Humanitarian Crisis: An Example from the USA-Mexico Border," in *Sociopolitics of Migrant Death and Repatriation: Perspectives from Forensic Science*, ed. Krista E. Latham and Alyson J. O'Daniel (Cham: Springer International, 2018); Sharika Thiranagama, "Claiming the State: Postwar Reconciliation in Sri Lanka," *Humanity: An International Journal of Human Rights, Humanitarianism, and Development* 4, no. 1 (2013).

24. Halbwachs, *Collective Memory*; Schwartz, "Social Change"; Howard Schuman, Vered Vinitzky-Seroussi, and Amiram D. Vinokur, "Keeping the Past Alive: Memories of Israeli Jews at the Turn of the Millennium," *Sociological Forum* 18, no. 1 (2003); Chana Teeger, "Collective Memory and Collective Fear: How South Africans Use the Past to Explain Crime," *Qualitative Sociology* 37, no. 1 (2014).

25. The reconciliation formula was also present in Western media during the coverage of the twentieth anniversary of the 1994 genocide against the Tutsi. See Susan Dominus, "Portraits of Reconciliation: 20 Years after the Genocide in Rwanda, Reconciliation Still Happens One Encounter at a Time," *New York Times Magazine*, April 5, 2014; Jason Straziuso, "Rwanda Genocide: Man and Victim Now Friends," *ABC News*, April 6, 2014.

26. In April 2014, two decades after the 1994 genocide against the Tutsi, the *New York Times* printed a photo essay titled "Portraits of Reconciliation: 20 Years after the Genocide in Rwanda Reconciliation Still Happens One Encounter at a Time," by South African photographer Pieter Hugo and *Times* staff writer Susan Dominus. The photographs show perpetrators posing side by side with victims of their crimes; all but one photograph show a male perpetrator and a female victim holding hands or embracing. The text contains a quote from each person explaining what the perpetrator did and how he asked for forgiveness. The pairs photographed were noted as having

participated in a reconciliation program facilitated by the Association Modeste et Innocent (AMI), a nonprofit organization under the umbrella organization Peace Direct, an international NGO with offices in the UK and the US.

27. Alexander Beresford, Marie E. Berry, and Laura Mann, "Liberation Movements and Stalled Democratic Transitions: Reproducing Power in Rwanda and South Africa through Productive Liminality," *Democratization* 25, no. 7 (2018); Jonathan Goodhand, "Sri Lanka in 2011: Consolidation and Militarization of the Post-War Regime," *Asian Survey* 52, no. 1 (2011); Zorbas, "Reconciliation."

28. Moon, *Narrating*, 6.

29. See Claire Moon's work on how this functioned in South Africa. Claire Moon, "Prelapsarian State: Forgiveness and Reconciliation in Transitional Justice," *International Journal for the Semiotics of Law* 17, no. 2 (2004).

30. Sara Cobb, "Empowerment and Mediation: A Narrative Perspective," *Negotiation Journal* 9, no. 3 (1993).

31. Minow, *Between*, 5.

32. Prabha S. Chandra et al., "Do Men and Women with HIV Differ in Their Quality of Life? A Study from South India," *AIDS and Behavior* 13, no. 1 (2009); John Maltby, Ann Macaskill, and Raphael Gillett, "The Cognitive Nature of Forgiveness: Using Cognitive Strategies of Primary Appraisal and Coping to Describe the Process of Forgiving," *Journal of Clinical Psychology* 63, no. 6 (2007); Robert J. Sidelinger, Brandi N. Frisby, and Audra L. McMullen, "The Decision to Forgive: Sex, Gender, and the Likelihood to Forgive Partner Transgressions," *Communication Studies* 60, no. 2 (2009); Loren Toussaint and Jon R. Webb, "Gender Differences in the Relationship between Empathy and Forgiveness," *Journal of Social Psychology* 145, no. 6 (2005).

33. This sentiment is echoed by the government in an effort to educate young people about Rwandan history and genocide ideology, cultivating ideal citizens. Some of this motivation is reflective of country-wide demographics. In 2001, 61 percent of Rwandans were under the age of twenty-four, so to consolidate power and disseminate specific narratives, it made sense to invest in this youth-directed campaign. See S. Garnett Russell, *Becoming Rwandan: Education, Reconciliation, and the Making of a Post-Genocide Citizen* (New Brunswick, NJ: Rutgers University Press, 2020); Thomson, *Rwanda* (chapter 11 in particular).

34. This is not a new finding per se, but it is worth mentioning as it is dynamic sometimes overlooked. See the conclusion in this book for policy and agenda recommendations related to basic needs and forensic technologies to assist in locating missing persons and remains.

Conclusion

1. Susan Brison writes of trauma and remaking the self in its aftermath, underscoring the communal dynamics of healing: "In order to construct self-narratives we need not only the words with which to tell our stories, but also an audience able and willing to hear us and to understand our words as we intend them. This aspect of

remaking a self in the aftermath of trauma highlights the dependency of the self on others and helps to explain why it is so difficult for survivors to recover when others are unwilling to listen to what they endured" ("Trauma," 46).

2. Sturken, *Tangled Memories*, 1; Olick and Robbins, "Social Memory"; Savelsberg and King, "Institutionalizing"; Wilson, *Politics*.

3. Émile Durkheim, *The Elementary Forms of the Religious Life*, trans. Joseph Ward Swain (New York: Free Press, 1965).

4. Robin Wagner-Pacifici, "Memories in the Making: The Shapes of Things That Went," *Qualitative Sociology* 19, no. 3 (1996): 303.

5. Wagner-Pacifici, "Memories," 312.

6. Chakravarty, "Gacaca Courts"; P. Clark, "Rules"; Des Forges and Longman, "Legal Responses"; Nagy, "Traditional Justice"; National Unity and Reconciliation Commission, "National Unity and Reconciliation Commission," 2014, http://www.nurc.gov.rw/index.php?id=69.

7. M. Cherif Bassiouni, "Searching for Peace and Achieving Justice: The Need for Accountability," *Law and Contemporary Problems* 59, no. 4 (1996); David Bloomfield, Terri Barnes, and Lucien Huyse, *Reconciliation after Violent Conflict: A Handbook* (Stockholm: International Institute for Democracy and Electoral Assistance, 2003); Elizabeth Kiss, "Moral Ambition within and beyond Political Constraints," in *Truth v. Justice: The Morality of Truth Commissions*, ed. Robert I. Rotberg and Dennis Thompson (Princeton, NJ: Princeton University Press, 2000).

8. Hayner, *Transitional*; Minow, *Between*.

9. David Mendeloff, "Truth-Seeking, Truth-Telling, and Postconflict Peacebuilding: Curb the Enthusiasm?," *International Studies Review* 6, no. 3 (2004).

10. Hayner, *Transitional*; Nahla Valji, *Gender Justice and Reconciliation: Dialogue on Globalization* (Berlin: Friedrich-Ebert-Stiftung [FES], 2007).

11. Robyn K. Autry, "Memory, Materiality, and the Apartheid Past," *Contexts* 9, no. 3 (2010); Burnet, "Whose Genocide"; Coombes, *History*; Jacobs, *Memorializing*; Young, *Texture*.

12. Barry Schwartz and Howard Schuman, "History, Commemoration, and Belief: Abraham Lincoln in American Memory: 1945–2001," *American Sociological Review* 70, no. 2 (2005); Teeger, "Collective."

13. Olick and Robbins, "Social Memory," 133–34.

14. Iwona Irwin-Zarecka, *Frames of Remembrance: The Dynamics of Collective Memory* (New Brunswick, NJ: Transaction, 1994); Olick and Robbins, "Social Memory"; Savelsberg and King, "Institutionalizing"; Wilson, *Politics*.

15. David Thelen, ed., *Memory and American History* (Bloomington: University of Indiana Press, 1989), 127.

16. Michel Foucault, *Language, Counter-memory, Practice: Selected Essays and Interviews* (Ithaca, NY: Cornell University Press, 1977), 126.

17. Hannah Arendt, *Eichmann in Jerusalem: A Report on the Banality of Evil* (New York: Penguin Books, 1977).

18. See Brewer's call for a more sociological (and human-focused) approach to our accounts of peace (Brewer, *Peace*); Jarvis and Lister's call for research in interest in the vernacular of international relations (Jarvis and Lister, "Vernacular"); and Justino, Brück, and Verwimp's call for more micro-level approaches to conflict, violence, and development (Justino, Brück, and Verwimp, *Perspective*). Scholars on Rwanda have also asserted the need for more local-level research. See Bert Ingelaere, who writes, "Large-scale research projects of all sorts exist, but what is lacking is local-level research and analysis of the micro-level processes at work in smaller communities" ("Life after Genocide," 47). See also Buckley-Zistel, "Nation." Schwartz and Schuman argue that individuals must be brought back into research on collective memory. The literature has largely viewed memory as collective once it exists outside an individual's mind rather than examining the dialectical relationship between history, commemoration, and individual belief (Schwartz and Schuman, "History," 184).

19. This is a consistent theme raised by survivors in a range of postconflict cases, including Bosnia (J. Clark, "Missing"); Kosovo (Pablo Baraybar, Brasey, and Zadel, "Need"); South Africa (Jay D. Aronson, "The Strengths and Limitations of South Africa's Search for Apartheid-Era Missing Persons," *International Journal of Transitional Justice* 5, no. 2 [2011]; Thiranagama, "Claiming"); see also, among others, D. Congram, *Missing Persons: Multidisciplinary Perspectives on the Disappeared* (Toronto: Canadian Scholars' Press, 2016).

20. Everyday Peace Indicators, accessed June 1, 2020, https://everydaypeaceindicators.org/.

21. Firchow, *Reclaiming*; Varshney, *Ethnic*.

22. Firchow and MacGinty, "Measuring"; Varshney, *Ethnic*.

23. See also Morton Deutsch, "Reconciliation after Destructive Intergroup Conflict," in *Social Psychology of Intergroup Reconciliation: From Violent Conflict to Peaceful Co-Existence*, ed. Arie Nadler, Thomas E. Malloy, and Jeffrey D. Fisher (New York: Oxford University Press, 2008); J. P. Lederach, *Building Peace: Sustainable Reconciliation in Divided Societies* (Washington, DC: United States Institute of Peace, 1998).

24. National Memorial for Peace and Justice, accessed April 26, 2018, https://museumandmemorial.eji.org/memorial.

25. Sasha Ingber, "Mass Graves Discovered 24 Years after Rwandan Genocide," NPR, April 26, 2018, https://www.npr.org/sections/thetwo-way/2018/04/26/6061053 47/mass-graves-discovered-24-years-after-rwandan-genocide.

Appendix

1. R. Charli Carpenter, "'You Talk of Terrible Things So Matter-of-Factly in This Language of Science': Constructing Human Rights in the Academy," *Perspectives on Politics* 10, no. 2 (2012); Sherryl Kleinman, "Fieldworkers' Feelings: What We Felt, Who We Are, How We Analyze," in *Experiencing Fieldwork: An Inside View of Qualitative Research*, ed. William B. Shaffir and Robert A. Stebbins (SAGE, London, 1991).

2. Rosaldo, "Grief," 172.

3. Rosaldo, "Grief," 176.

4. United Nations, "General Assembly Designates 7 April International Day of Reflection on 1994 Genocide against Tutsi in Rwanda, Amending Title of Annual Observance," January 2018, https://www.un.org/press/en/2018/ga12000.doc.htm.

5. I also asked the Rwandan research assistants and translators with whom I was working on a different project. They had the most varied responses. Two said I should use the official UN title, while one said, "Whatever I call it, whoever is in the title, you should just make sure you use the word 'genocide.'" Another research assistant said I did not need to use Tutsi in the title, another said I should, and others declared it did not matter so long as I used Rwanda and genocide. None were as insistent as the Tutsi survivors and Hutu rescuers to whom I had previously spoken. While opinions in this group were not as strong as those of the survivors I interviewed, they were younger than the sample interviewed for this book: all were either born after 1994 or were infants in the mid-1990s.

6. Fox, "Faith as an Obstacle"; Fox, "Impacts."

7. This was no small feat! For more on the challenges of conducting research in a highly politicized research setting such as Rwanda, see Larissa R. Begley, "The Other Side of Fieldwork: Experiences and Challenges of Conducting Research in the Border Area of Rwanda/Eastern Congo," *Anthropology Matters Journal* 11, no. 2 (2009); Ingelaere, "Life after Genocide"; Erin Jessee, "Conducting Fieldwork in Rwanda," *Canadian Journal of Development Studies / Revue canadienne d'études du développement* 33, no. 2 (2012); Elisabeth King, "From Data Problems to Data Points: Challenges and Opportunities of Research in Post-Genocide Rwanda," *African Studies Review* 52, no. 3 (2009); Cyanne E. Loyle, "Overcoming Research Obstacles in Hybrid Regimes: Lessons from Rwanda," *Social Science Quarterly* 97, no. 4 (2016).

8. Bert Ingelaere, "Learning 'To Be' Kinyarwanda in Postgenocide Rwanda: Immersion, Iteration, and Reflexivity in Times of Transition," *Canadian Journal of Law and Society* 30, no. 2 (2015).

9. Fujii, "Shades," 240.

10. Kathy Charmaz, *Constructing Grounded Theory: A Practical Guide through Qualitative Analysis* (London: SAGE, 2006).

11. Susanne Friese, *Qualitative Data Analysis with ATLAS.ti* (London: SAGE, 2014).

12. Janet L. Jacobs, "Women, Genocide, and Memory: The Ethics of Feminist Ethnography in Holocaust Research," *Gender and Society* 18, no. 2 (2004).

13. Fujii, "Shades," 231.

14. Liisa H. Malkki, *Purity and Exile: Violence, Memory, and National Cosmology among Hutu Refugees in Tanzania* (Chicago: University of Chicago Press, 1995).

15. Jennifer Pals and Dan McAdams, "The Transformed Self: A Narrative Understanding of Posttraumatic Growth," *Psychological Inquiry* 15, no. 1 (2004); Lucia De Haene, Hans Grietens, and Karine Verschueren, "Holding Harm: Narrative Methods in Mental Health Research on Refugee Trauma," *Qualitative Health Research* 20, no. 12 (2010): 1670.

16. De Haene, Grietens, and Verschueren. "Holding," 1670.

17. Elaine Scarry, *The Body in Pain: The Making and Unmaking of the World* (New York: Oxford University Press, 1985).

18. Ntwari is a pseudonym, not his actual name.

19. Lee Ann Fujii, *Interviewing in Social Science Research* (New York: Routledge, 2018), 4.

20. Gayle Letherby, "Dangerous Liaisons: Auto/biography in Research and Research Writing," in *Danger in the Field: Ethics and Risks in Social Research*, ed. Geraldine Lee-Treweek and Stephanie Linkogle (London: Routledge, 2000).

21. See Mary Maynard and June Purvis, eds., *Researching Women's Lives from a Feminist Perspective* (London: Taylor & Francis, 1994); Letherby, "Dangerous Liaisons"; Dorothy E. Smith, *The Everyday as Problematic: Feminist Sociology* (Boston: Northeastern University Press, 1987).

22. Fujii, *Interviewing*, 8.

23. Rebecca Campbell, *Emotionally Involved: The Impact of Researching Rape* (New York: Psychology Press, 2002), 68.

24. Michele J. Burman, Susan A. Batchelor, and Jane A. Brown, "Researching Girls and Violence: Facing the Dilemmas of Fieldwork," *British Journal of Criminology* 41, no. 3 (2001).

25. Steve Smith, "Singing Our World into Existence: International Relations Theory and September 11," *International Studies Quarterly* 48, no. 3 (2004): 500.

26. Ingelaere, "Learning."

27. Fujii, *Interviewing*, xv.

28. Jan Coles et al., "A Qualitative Exploration of Researcher Trauma and Researchers' Responses to Investigating Sexual Violence," *Violence against Women* 20, no. 1 (2014): 100.

29. Campbell, *Emotionally Involved*.

30. Campbell, *Emotionally Involved*, 39.

31. Olivera Simic, "Feminist Research in Transitional Justice Studies: Navigating Silences and Disruptions in the Field," *Human Rights Review* 17, no. 1 (2016): 96.

32. Nicole Fox, "'Their History Is Part of Me': Third Generation American Jews and Intergenerational Transmission of Memory, Trauma and History," *Moreshet: Journal for the Study of the Holocaust and Anti-Semitism* 8 (2010).

33. Linda R. Stoler, "Researching Childhood Sexual Abuse: Anticipating Effects on the Researcher," *Feminism & Psychology* 12, no. 2 (2002).

34. Coles et al., "Qualitative Exploration."

35. Sergio is a pseudonym, not his actual name.

36. Allison Pugh, "What Good Are Interviews for Thinking about Culture? Demystifying Interpretive Analysis," *American Journal of Cultural Sociology* 1, no. 1 (2013): 48.

Bibliography

Abu-Nimer, M. "Toward the Theory and Practice of Positive Approaches to Peace-building." In *Positive Approaches to Peacebuilding*, edited by C. Sampson, M. Abu-Nimer, C. Liebler, and D. Whitney, 13–23. Washington, DC: PACT Publications, 2003.

Albanese, Patricia. "Nationalism, War, and Archaization of Gender Relations in the Balkans." *Violence against Women* 7, no. 9 (2001): 999–1023.

Allen, Beverly. *Rape Warfare: The Hidden Genocide in Bosnia-Herzegovina and Croatia.* Minneapolis: University of Minnesota, 1996.

Amnesty International. "Rwanda: Civilians Trapped in Armed Conflict. The Dead Can No Longer Be Counted." *AI Index AFR* 47/043/1997 (December 1997).

Amnesty International. *Rwanda: "Marked for Death," Rape Survivors Living with HIV/AIDS in Rwanda.* New York: Amnesty International, 2004.

Amnesty International. "Rwanda: Sharp Increase in Killings Could Plunge Rwanda Back into a Cycle of Violence." *AI Index AFR* 47/17/96 (August 1996).

Anderson, Benedict. *Imagined Communities: Reflections on the Origins and Spread of Nationalism.* 2nd ed. New York: Verso, 1991.

Appel, Hilary. "Anti-Communist Justice and Founding the Post-Communist Order: Lustration and Restitution in Central Europe." *East European Politics and Societies* 19, no. 3 (2005): 379–405.

Arendt, Hannah. *Eichmann in Jerusalem: A Report on the Banality of Evil.* New York: Penguin Books, 1977.

Armour, Marilyn. "Meaning Making in Survivorship: Application to Holocaust Survivors." *Journal of Human Behavior in the Social Environment* 20, no. 4 (2010): 440–68.

Aronson, Jay D. "The Strengths and Limitations of South Africa's Search for Apartheid-Era Missing Persons." *International Journal of Transitional Justice* 5, no. 2 (2011): 262–81.

Arrizón, Alicia. "'Invisible Wars': Gendered Terrorism in the US Military and the Juárez Feminicidio." In *Gender, Globalization, and Violence: Postcolonial Conflict Zones*, edited by Sandra Ponzanesi, 257–86. New York: Routledge, 2014.

Arzt, Donna E. "Views on the Ground: The Local Perception of International Criminal Tribunals in the Former Yugoslavia and Sierra Leone." *Annals of the American Academy of Political and Social Science*, no. 603 (2006): 226–39.

Austin, Kathi. "Light Weapons and Conflict in the Great Lakes Region of Africa." In *Light Weapons and Civil Conflict*, edited by Jeffrey Boutwell and Michael T. Klare, 29–47. Lanham, MD: Rowman & Littlefield, 1999.

Autry, Robyn K. "Memory, Materiality, and the Apartheid Past." *Contexts* 9, no. 3 (2010): 46–51.

Ayazi, Touraj, Lars Lien, Arne H. Eide, Majok Malek Ruom, and Edvard Hauff. "What Are the Risk Factors for the Comorbidity of Posttraumatic Stress Disorder and Depression in a War-Affected Population? A Cross-Sectional Community Study in South Sudan." *BMC Psychiatry* 12, no. 175 (2012): 1–12.

Baines, Erin K. "Body Politics and the Rwandan Crisis." *Third World Quarterly* 24, no. 3 (2003): 479–93.

Bakiner, Onur. "Truth Commission Impact: An Assessment of How Commissions Influence Politics and Society." *International Journal of Transitional Justice* 8, no. 1 (2014): 6–30.

Barkan, Elazar, and Alexander Karn, eds. *Taking Wrongs Seriously: Apologies and Reconciliation*. Stanford: Stanford University Press, 2006.

Barnett, Michael N. *Eyewitness to a Genocide: The United Nations and Rwanda*. Ithaca, NY: Cornell University Press, 2002.

Barsalou, Judy, and Victoria Baxter. *The Urge to Remember: The Role of Memorials in Social Reconstruction and Transitional Justice*. Stabilization and Reconstruction Series 5. Washington, DC: United States Institute for Peace, 2007.

Bashford, Alison, and Philippa Levine, eds. *The Oxford Handbook of the History of Eugenics*. Oxford: Oxford University Press, 2010.

Bassiouni, M. Cherif. "Searching for Peace and Achieving Justice: The Need for Accountability." *Law and Contemporary Problems* 59, no. 4 (1996): 9–28.

Begley, Larissa R. "The Other Side of Fieldwork: Experiences and Challenges of Conducting Research in the Border Area of Rwanda/Eastern Congo." *Anthropology Matters Journal* 11, no. 2 (2009): 1–11.

Bell, Duncan S. "Mythscapes: Memory, Mythology, and National Identity." *British Journal of Sociology* 54 (2003): 63–81.

Beloff, Jonathan R., and Samantha Lakin. "Peace and Compromise, Idealism and Constraint: The Case of the Arusha Peace Accords in Rwanda and Burundi." *Genocide Studies and Prevention: An International Journal* 13, no. 2 (2019): 129–47.

Bentrovato, Denise. *Narrating and Teaching the Nation: The Politics of Education in Pre- and Post-Genocide Rwanda*. Göttingen: V&R Unipress, 2015.

Beresford, Alexander, Marie E. Berry, and Laura Mann. "Liberation Movements and Stalled Democratic Transitions: Reproducing Power in Rwanda and South Africa through Productive Liminality." *Democratization* 25, no. 7 (2018): 1231–50.

Berger, Peter L., and Thomas Luckmann. *The Social Construction of Reality: A Treatise in the Sociology of Knowledge*. New York: Random House, 1966.

Berger, Ronald J., and Richard Quinney, eds. *Storytelling Sociology: Narrative as Social Inquiry.* Boulder, CO: Lynne Rienner, 2004.

Berry, John A., and Carol Pott Berry. *Genocide in Rwanda: A Collective Memory.* Washington, DC: Howard University Press, 1999.

Berry, Marie E. "Barriers to Women's Progress after Atrocity: Evidence from Rwanda and Bosnia-Herzegovina." *Gender & Society* 31, no. 6 (2017): 830–53.

Berry, Marie E. "From Violence to Mobilization: War, Women, and Threat in Rwanda." *Mobilization: An International Quarterly* 20, no. 2 (2015): 135–56.

Berry, Marie E. *War, Women, and Power: From Violence to Mobilization in Rwanda and Bosnia-Herzegovina.* New York: Cambridge University Press, 2018.

Berry, Marie E. "When 'Bright Futures' Fade: Paradoxes of Women's Empowerment in Rwanda." *Signs: Journal of Women in Culture and Society* 41, no. 1 (2014): 1–27.

Bijleveld, Catrien. "Missing Pieces: Methodological Issues in the Study of International Crimes and Gross Human Rights Violations." In *Supranational Criminology: Towards a Criminology of International Crimes*, edited by A. Smeulers and R. H. Haveman, 77–100. Antwerp, Belgium: Intersentia, 2008.

Bijleveld, Catrien, Aafke Morssinkhof, and Alette Smeulers. "Counting the Countless: Rape Victimization during the Rwandan Genocide." *International Criminal Justice Review* 19, no. 2 (2009): 208–24.

Blain, Leah M., Tara E. Galovski, and Tristan Robinson. "Gender Differences in Recovery from Posttraumatic Stress Disorder: A Critical Review." *Aggression and Violent Behavior* 15, no. 6 (2010): 463–74.

Bloomfield, David, Terri Barnes, and Lucien Huyse. *Reconciliation after Violent Conflict: A Handbook.* Stockholm: International Institute for Democracy and Electoral Assistance, 2003.

Bolton, Paul. "Local Perceptions of the Mental Health Effects of the Rwandan Genocide." *Journal of Nervous & Mental Disease* 189, no. 4 (2001): 243–48.

Bolzendahl, Catherine, and Clem Brooks. "Women's Political Representation and Welfare State Spending in 12 Capitalist Democracies." *Social Forces* 85, no. 4 (2007): 1509–34.

Bonanno, G. A., and A. D. Mancini. "The Human Capacity to Thrive in the Face of Potential Trauma." *Pediatrics* 121, no. 2 (2008): 369–75.

Booth, William James. *Communities of Memory: On Witness, Identity and Justice.* Ithaca, NY: Cornell University Press, 2006.

Boris, Neil W., Tonya R. Thurman, Leslie Snider, Erin Spencer, and Lisanne Brown. "Infants and Young Children Living in Youth-Headed Households in Rwanda: Implications of Emerging Data." *Infant Mental Health Journal* 27, no. 6 (2006): 584–602.

Brewer, J. *Peace Processes: A Sociological Approach.* Cambridge: Polity Press, 2010.

Brison, Susan. "Trauma and Narratives and the Remaking of the Self." In *Acts of Memory: Cultural Recall in the Present*, edited by Mieke Bal, Jonathan V. Crewe, and Leo Spitzer, 39–54. Hanover, NH: University Press of New England, 1999.

Brounéus, Karen. "The Trauma of Truth Telling: Effects of Witnessing in the Rwandan Gacaca Courts on Psychological Health." *Journal of Conflict Resolution* 54, no. 3 (2010): 408–37.

Brounéus, Karen. "Truth-Telling as Talking Cure? Insecurity and Retraumatization in the Rwandan Gacaca Courts." *Security Dialogue* 39, no. 1 (2008): 55–76.

Brown, Sara E. "Female Perpetrators of the Rwandan Genocide." *International Feminist Journal of Politics* 16, no. 3 (2014): 448–69.

Brownmiller, Susan. *Against Our Will: Men, Women, and Rape.* New York: Fawcett Columbine, 1975.

Buckley-Zistel, Susanne. "Nation, Narration, Unification? The Politics of History Teaching after the Rwandan Genocide." *Journal of Genocide Research* 11, no. 1 (2009): 31–53.

Burgess, Rochelle Ann, and Laura Fonseca. "Re-Thinking Recovery in Post-Conflict Settings: Supporting the Mental Well-Being of Communities in Colombia." *Global Public Health* 15, no. 2 (2020): 200–219.

Burman, Michele J., Susan A. Batchelor, and Jane A. Brown. "Researching Girls and Violence: Facing the Dilemmas of Fieldwork." *British Journal of Criminology* 41, no. 3 (2001): 443–59.

Burnet, Jennie E. "Gender Balance and the Meanings of Women in Governance in Post-Genocide Rwanda." *African Affairs* 107, no. 428 (2008): 361–86.

Burnet, Jennie E. *Genocide Lives in Us: Women, Memory and Silence in Rwanda.* Madison: University of Wisconsin Press, 2012.

Burnet, Jennie E. "(In)Justice: Truth, Reconciliation and Revenge in Rwanda's Gacaca." In *Transitional Justice: Global Mechanisms and Local Realities after Genocide and Mass Violence,* edited by Alexander Laban Hinton, 95–118. New Brunswick, NJ: Rutgers University Press, 2010.

Burnet, Jennie E. "Whose Genocide? Whose Truth? Representations of Victim and Perpetrator in Rwanda." In *Genocide: Truth Memory and Representation,* edited by Alexander Laban Hinton and Kevin Lewis O'Neill, 80–110. Durham, NC: Duke University Press, 2009.

Buss, Doris E. "Rethinking 'Rape as a Weapon of War.'" *Feminist Legal Studies* 17, no. 2 (2009): 145–63.

Campbell, Bradley. "Contradictory Behavior during Genocides." *Sociological Forum* 25, no. 2 (2010): 296–314.

Campbell, Rebecca. *Emotionally Involved: The Impact of Researching Rape.* New York: Psychology Press, 2002.

Caplan, Pat. "'Never Again': Genocide Memorials in Rwanda." *Anthropology Today* 23, no. 1 (2007): 20–22.

Carney, J. J. *Rwanda before the Genocide: Catholic Politics and Ethnic Discourses in the Late Colonial Era.* New York: Oxford University Press, 2013.

Carpenter, R. Charli. *Forgetting Children Born of War: Setting the Human Rights Agenda in Bosnia and Beyond.* New York: Columbia University Press, 2010.

Carpenter, R. Charli. "Recognizing Gender-Based Violence against Civilian Men and Boys in Conflict Situations." *Security Dialogue* 37, no. 1 (2006): 83–103.

Carpenter, R. Charli. "Surfacing Children: Limitations of Genocidal Rape Discourse." *Human Rights Quarterly* 22, no. 1 (2000): 428–77.

Carpenter, R. Charli. "'You Talk of Terrible Things So Matter-of-Factly in This Language of Science': Constructing Human Rights in the Academy." *Perspectives on Politics* 10, no. 2 (2012): 363–83.

Casey, Edward S. *Remembering: A Phenomenological Study.* 2nd ed. Bloomington: Indiana University Press, 2000.

Centers for Disease Control and Prevention, Division of Tuberculosis Elimination. *DTBE in Rwanda.* Atlanta Division of Tuberculosis, 2012.

Chakraborty, Anup Shekar. "Memory of a Lost Past, Memory of Rape: Nostalgia, Trauma and the Construction of Collective Social Memory Among the Zo Hnahthlak." *Identity, Culture and Politics* 11, no. 2 (2010): 87–104.

Chakravarty, Anuradha. "Gacaca Courts in Rwanda: Explaining Divisions within the Human Rights Community." *Yale Journal of International Affairs* 1, no. 2 (2006): 132–45.

Chakravarty, Anuradha. *Investing in Authoritarian Rule: Punishment and Patronage in Rwanda's Gacaca Courts for Genocide Crimes.* New York: Cambridge University Press, 2016.

Chandra, Prabha S., Veena A. Satyanarayana, P. Satishchandra, K. S. Satish, and Mahendra Kumar. "Do Men and Women with HIV Differ in Their Quality of Life? A Study from South India." *AIDS and Behavior* 13, no. 1 (2009): 110–17.

Charlesworth, Hilary. "Not Waving but Drowning: Gender Mainstreaming and Human Rights in the United Nations." *Harvard Human Rights Journal*, no. 18 (2005): 1–18.

Charmaz, Kathy. *Constructing Grounded Theory: A Practical Guide through Qualitative Analysis.* London: SAGE, 2006.

Cheng, Shirley Y. Y. et al. "The Good Old Days and a Better Tomorrow: Historical Representations and Future Imaginations of China During the 2008 Olympic Games." *Asian Journal of Social Psychology* 13, no. 2 (2010): 118–27.

Chisholm, Lynne. "Mannheim Revisited: Youth, Generation and Life-Course." Paper presented at the International Sociological Association World Congress of Sociology, Brisbane, Australia, 2002.

Christodulou, Artemis. *Memorials and Transitional Justice.* Sierra Leone Truth and Reconciliation Commission Final Report by the Sierra Leone Truth and Reconciliation Commission, Appendix 1: Part 4, 2004.

Cieplak, Piotr. *Death, Image, Memory: The Genocide in Rwanda and Its Aftermath in Photography and Documentary Film.* London: Palgrave Macmillan, 2017.

Clark, Janine Natalya. "A Crime of Identity: Rape and Its Neglected Victims." *Journal of Human Rights* 13, no. 2 (2014): 146–69.

Clark, Janine Natalya. "Missing Persons, Reconciliation and the View from Below: A Case Study of Bosnia-Hercegovina." *Southeast European and Black Sea Studies* 10, no. 4 (2010): 425–42.

Clark, Phil. "Negotiating Reconciliation in Rwanda: Popular Challenges to the Official Discourse of Post-Genocide National Unity." *Journal of Intervention and State-Building* 8, no. 4 (2014): 303–20.

Clark, Phil. "The Rules (and Politics) of Engagement: The Gacaca Courts and Post-Genocide Justice, Healing and Reconciliation in Rwanda." In *After Genocide: Transitional Justice, Post-Conflict Reconstruction and Reconciliation in Rwanda and Beyond*, edited by Phil Clark and Zachary D. Kaufman, 297–320. New York: Columbia University Press, 2009.

Clark, Phil, and Zachary D. Kaufman, eds. *After Genocide: Transitional Justice, Post-Conflict Reconstruction and Reconciliation in Rwanda and Beyond*. New York: Columbia University Press, 2009.

Cobb, Sara. "Empowerment and Mediation: A Narrative Perspective." *Negotiation Journal* 9, no. 3 (1993): 245–60.

Cobb, Sara. *Speaking of Violence: The Politics and Poetics of Narrative Dynamics in Conflict Resolution*. New York: Oxford University Press, 2013.

Codere, Helen. *The Biography of an African Society: Rwanda, 1900–1960*. Tervuren: MRAC, 1973.

Cohen, Jared. *One Hundred Days of Silence: America and the Rwanda Genocide*. Lanham, MD: Rowman & Littlefield, 2007.

Cole, Elizabeth A., and Pamina Firchow. "Reconciliation Barometers: Tools for Post-conflict Policy Design." *International Journal of Transitional Justice* 13, no. 3 (2019): 546–69.

Coles, Jan, Jill Astbury, Elizabeth Dartnall, and Shazneen Limjerwala. "A Qualitative Exploration of Researcher Trauma and Researchers' Responses to Investigating Sexual Violence." *Violence against Women* 20, no. 1 (2014): 95–117.

Congram, D. *Missing Persons: Multidisciplinary Perspectives on the Disappeared*. Toronto: Canadian Scholars' Press, 2016.

Conley-Zilkic, Bridget. "Rights on Display: Museums and Human Rights Claims." In *The Human Rights Paradox: Universality and Its Discontents*, edited by Steve J. Stern and Scott Straus, 61–80. Madison: University of Wisconsin Press, 2014.

Connerton, Paul. *How Societies Remember*. New York: Cambridge University Press, 1989.

Cooke, Jennifer G. *Rwanda: Assessing Risks to Stability*. A Report from the CSIS Africa Program: Center for Strategic and International Studies, 2011.

Cooke, Martin, Francis Mitrou, David Lawrence, Eric Guimond, and Dan Beavon. "Indigenous Well-Being in Four Countries: An Application of the UNDP's Human Development Index to Indigenous Peoples in Australia, Canada, New Zealand, and the United States." *BMC International Health and Human Rights* 7, no. 1 (2007).

Cooke, Miriam. *Women and the War Story*. Berkeley: University of California Press, 1996.

Coombes, Annie E. *History after Apartheid: Visual Culture and Public Memory in a Democratic South Africa*. Durham, NC: Duke University Press, 2003.

Corey, Allison, and Sandra F. Joireman. "Retributive Justice: The Gacaca Courts in Rwanda." *African Affairs* 103, no. 410 (2004): 73–89.

Cottyn, Ine. "Small Towns and Rural Growth Centers as Strategic Spaces of Control in Rwanda's Post-Conflict Trajectory." *Journal of Eastern African Studies* 12, no. 2 (2018): 329–47.

Dallaire, Roméo. *Shake Hands with the Devil: The Failure of Humanity in Rwanda.* New York: Carroll & Graf, 2004.

Daly, Kathleen. "Restorative Justice: The Real Story." *Punishment & Society* 4, no. 1 (2002): 55–79.

Dandurand, Yvon, and Curt T. Griffith. *United Nations Handbook on Restorative Justice Programmes.* Vienna: United Nations, 2006.

Dansky, Bonnie S., Kathleen T. Brady, Michael E. Saladin, Theresa Killeen, Sharon Becker, and John Roitzsch. "Victimization and PTSD in Individuals with Substance Use Disorders: Gender and Racial Differences." *American Journal of Drug and Alcohol Abuse* 22, no. 1 (1996): 75–93.

Davenport, Christian, and Allan Stam. "GenoDynamics: Understanding Rwandan Political Violence in 1994." 2000. http://www.genodynamics.com/.

De Brito, Alexandra Barahona, Carmen Gonzaléz-Enríquez, and Paloma Aguilar, eds. *The Politics of Memory: Transitional Justice in Democratizing Societies.* Oxford: Oxford University Press, 2001.

De Brouwer, Anne-Marie, and Sandra Chu. *The Men Who Killed Me: Rwandan Survivors of Sexual Violence.* Vancouver: Douglas & McIntyre, 2009.

Declich, Francesca. "When Silence Makes History: Gender and Memories of War Violence from Somalia." In *Anthropology of Violence and Conflict*, edited by Bettina Schmudt and Ingo Schroeder, 161–75. New York: Routledge, 2001.

De Haene, Lucia, Hans Grietens, and Karine Verschueren. "Holding Harm: Narrative Methods in Mental Health Research on Refugee Trauma." *Qualitative Health Research* 20, no. 12 (2010): 1664–76.

Des Forges, Alison. *Defeat Is the Only Bad News.* Madison: University of Wisconsin Press, 2011.

Des Forges, Alison. *Leave None to Tell the Story: Genocide in Rwanda.* 2nd ed. New York: Human Rights Watch, 1999.

Des Forges, Alison, and Timothy Longman. "Legal Responses to Genocide in Rwanda." In Stover and Weinstein, *My Neighbor.* Cambridge: Cambridge University Press, 2004.

Deutsch, Morton. "Reconciliation after Destructive Intergroup Conflict." In *Social Psychology of Intergroup Reconciliation: From Violent Conflict to Peaceful Co-Existence*, edited by Arie Nadler, Thomas E. Malloy, and Jeffrey D. Fisher, 471–86. New York: Oxford University Press, 2008.

De Walque, Damian, and Philip Verwimp. "The Demographic and Socio-economic Distribution of Excess Mortality during the 1994 Genocide in Rwanda: Policy Research Working Paper 4850." World Bank, 2009. https://openknowledge.world bank.org/handle/10986/4046.

De Ycaza, Carla. "Performative Functions of Genocide Trials in Rwanda: Reconciliation through Restorative Justice?" *African Journal on Conflict Resolution* 10, no. 3 (2010): 9–28.

Dieng, Adama. "Capacity-Building Efforts of the ICTR: A Different Kind of Legacy." *Northwestern Journal of International Human Rights* 9, no. 3 (2011): 401–22.

Dominus, Susan. "Portraits of Reconciliation: 20 Years after the Genocide in Rwanda, Reconciliation Still Happens One Encounter at a Time." *New York Times Magazine*, April 5, 2014.

Doughty, Kristin Conner. *Remediation in Rwanda Grassroots Legal Forums.* Philadelphia: University of Pennsylvania Press, 2016.

Durkheim, Émile. *The Elementary Forms of the Religious Life.* Translated by Joseph Ward Swain. New York: Free Press, 1965.

Dworkin, Andrea. "The Unremembered: Searching for Women at the Holocaust Memorial Museum." *Ms. Magazine* 5, no. 3 (1994).

Dyregrov, Atle, Leila Gupta, Rolf Gjestad, and Eugenie Mukanoheli. "Trauma Exposure and Psychological Reactions to Genocide among Rwandan Children." *Journal of Traumatic Stress*, no. 13 (2000): 3–21.

Eck, Kristine. "In Data We Trust? A Comparison of UCDP GED and ACLED Conflict Events Datasets." *Cooperation and Conflict* 47, no. 1 (2012): 124–41.

Edkins, Jenny. *Missing: Persons and Politics.* Ithaca, NY: Cornell University Press, 2011.

Ehrenhaus, Peter. "Commemorating the Unwon War: On Not Remembering Vietnam." *Journal of Communication*, no. 39 (1989): 96–107.

Eltringham, Nigel. 2006. "'Invaders Who Have Stolen the Country': The Hamitic Hypothesis, Race, and the Rwandan Genocide." *Social Identities* 12, no. 4 (2006): 425–46.

Emizet, Kisangani N. F. "The Massacre of Refugees in Congo: A Case of UN Peacekeeping Failure and International Law." *Journal of Modern African Studies* 38, no. 2 (2000): 163–202.

Engel, David M., and Frank W. Munger. "Rights, Remembrance, and the Reconciliation of Difference." *Law & Society Review* 30, no. 1 (1996): 7–53.

Esbenshade, Richard S. "Remembering to Forget: Memory, History, National Identity in Postwar East-Central Europe." *Representations*, no. 49 (1995): 72–96.

Everyday Peace Indicators. Accessed June 1, 2020. https://everydaypeaceindicators .org/.

Fan, F., K. Long, Y. Zhou, Y. Zheng, and X. Liu. "Longitudinal Trajectories of Post-Traumatic Stress Disorder Symptoms among Adolescents after the Wenchuan Earthquake in China." *Psychological Medicine* 45, no. 13 (2015): 2885–96.

Feldman, Jackie. "Between Yad Vashem and Mt. Herzl: Changing Inscriptions of Sacrifice on Jerusalem's 'Mountain of Memory.'" *Anthropological Quarterly* 80, no. 4 (2007): 1147–74.

Ferrales, Gabrielle, Hollie Nyseth Brehm, and Suzy McElrath. "Gender-Based Violence against Men and Boys in Darfur: The Gender-Genocide Nexus." *Gender & Society* 30, no. 4 (2016): 565–89.

Firchow, Pamina. *Reclaiming Everyday Peace: Local Voices in Measurement and Evaluation after War.* Cambridge: Cambridge University Press, 2018.

Firchow, Pamina, and Roger MacGinty. "Measuring Peace: Comparability, Commensurability, and Complementarity Using Bottom-Up Indicators." *International Studies Review* 19, no. 1 (2017): 6–27.

Folnegovic-Small, Vera. "Psychiatric Aspects of the Rapes in the War against the Republics of Croatia and Bosnia-Herzegovina." In *Mass Rape,* edited by Alexandra Stiglmayer, 174–79. Lincoln: University of Nebraska Press, 1993.

Forster-Towne, Claudia. *Exploring the Plausibility of Linking Notions of Terrorism and Sexual Violence by Using the Great Lakes Region as a Case Study.* Pretoria, South Africa: African Books Collective, 2011.

Foucault, Michel. *Language, Counter-memory, Practice: Selected Essays and Interviews.* Ithaca, NY: Cornell University Press, 1977.

Fox, Nicole. "'God Must Have Been Sleeping': Faith as an Obstacle and a Resource for Rwandan Genocide Survivors in the United States." *Journal for the Scientific Study of Religion* 51, no. 1 (2012): 65–78.

Fox, Nicole. "Memory in Interaction: Gender-Based Violence, Genocide, and Commemoration." *Signs: Journal of Women in Culture and Society* 45, no. 1 (2019): 123–48.

Fox, Nicole. "'Oh, Did the Women Suffer, They Suffered so Much:' Impacts of Gender-Based Violence on Kinship Networks in Rwanda." *International Journal of Sociology of the Family* 37, no. 2 (2011): 279–305.

Fox, Nicole. "'Their History Is Part of Me': Third Generation American Jews and Intergenerational Transmission of Memory, Trauma and History." *Moreshet: Journal for the Study of the Holocaust and Anti-Semitism,* no. 8 (2010): 7–35.

Fox, Nicole, and Carla De Ycaza. "Narratives of Mass Violence: The Role of Memory and Memorialization in Addressing Human Rights Violations in Post-Conflict Rwanda and Uganda." *Societies without Borders* 8, no. 3 (2013): 344–72.

Freedman, Sarah, Harvey M. Weinstein, Karen Murphy, and Timothy Longman. "Teaching History in Post-Genocide Rwanda." In Straus and Waldorf, *Remaking Rwanda,* 297–315.

Friese, Susanne. *Qualitative Data Analysis with ATLES.ti.* London: SAGE, 2014.

Fujii, Lee Ann. *Interviewing in Social Science Research.* New York: Routledge, 2018.

Fujii, Lee Ann. *Killing of Neighbors: Webs of Violence in Rwanda.* Ithaca, NY: Cornell University Press, 2009.

Fujii, Lee Ann. "Transforming the Moral Landscape: The Diffusion of a Genocidal Norm in Rwanda." *Journal of Genocide Research* 6, no. 1 (2004): 99–114.

Gallagher, Anne. "Ending the Marginalization: Strategies for Incorporating Women into the United Nations Human Rights System." *Human Rights Quarterly* 19, no. 2 (1997): 283–333.

Gallimore, Rangira Béa. "Militarism, Ethnicity, and Sexual Violence in the Rwandan Genocide." *Feminist Africa,* no. 10 (2008): 9–29.

Galovski, Tara E., Juliette Mott, Yinong Young-Xu, and Patricia A. Resick. "Gender Differences in the Clinical Presentation of PTSD and Its Concomitants in Survivors of Interpersonal Assault." *Journal of Interpersonal Violence* 26, no. 4 (2011): 789–806.

Gibson, James L. "The Contributions of Truth to Reconciliation: Lessons from South Africa." *Journal of Conflict Resolution* 50, no. 3 (2006): 409–32.

Gibson, James L. *Overcoming Apartheid: Can Truth Reconcile a Divided Nation?* Cape Town, South Africa: HSRC Press, 2004.

Goldberg, Amos. "The 'Jewish Narrative' in the Yad Vashem Global Holocaust Museum." *Journal of Genocide Research* 14, no. 2 (2012): 187–213.

Goldblatt, Beth, and Shiela Meintjes. "Dealing with the Aftermath: Sexual Violence and the Truth and Reconciliation Commission." *Agenda: Empowering Women for Gender Equity* (1998): 7–18.

Goldstein, Anne Tierney. *Recognizing Forced Impregnation as a War Crime under International Law: A Special Report of the International Program.* New York: Center for Reproductive Law & Policy, 1993.

Goldstone, Jack. "Population and Security: How Demographic Change Can Lead to Violent Conflict." *Journal of International Affairs* 56, no. 1 (2002): 000–000.

Goodfellow, Tom. "Rwanda's Political Settlement and the Urban Transition: Expropriation, Construction and Taxation in Kigali." *Journal of Eastern African Studies* 8, no. 2 (2014): 311–29.

Goodfellow, Tom, and Alyson Smith. "From Urban Catastrophe to 'Model' City? Politics, Security and Development in Post-Conflict Kigali." *Urban Studies* 50, no. 15 (2013): 3185–3202.

Goodhand, Jonathan. "Sri Lanka in 2011: Consolidation and Militarization of the Post-War Regime." *Asian Survey* 52, no. 1 (2012): 130–37.

Graybill, Lyn. "The Contribution of the Truth and Reconciliation Commission toward the Promotion of Women's Rights in South Africa." *Women's Studies International Forum* 24, no. 1 (2001): 1–10.

Griffin, Larry J. "'Generations and Collective Memory' Revisited: Race, Region, and Memory of Civil Rights." *American Sociological Review* 69, no. 4 (2004): 544–57.

Guichaoua, Andre. *From War to Genocide: Criminal Politics in Rwanda 1990–1994.* Madison: University of Wisconsin Press, 2015.

Gupta, Akhil, and James Ferguson. "Beyond 'Culture': Space, Identity, and the Politics of Difference." *Cultural Anthropology* 7, no. 1 (1992): 6–23.

Gupta, L. *Rwanda: Follow-up Survey of Rwandan Children's Reactions to War Related Violence from the 1994 Genocide.* New York: UNICEF, 1998.

Guyer, Sara. "Rwanda's Bones." *Boundary 2*, 36, no. 2 (2009): 155–75.

Hagopian, Patrick. *The Vietnam War in American Memory: Veterans, Memorials and the Politics of Healing.* Boston: University of Massachusetts Press, 2009.

Halbwachs, Maurice. *On Collective Memory.* Chicago: University of Chicago Press, 1992.

Hamber, Brandon, and Richard A. Wilson. "Symbolic Closure through Memory, Reparation and Revenge in Post-conflict Societies." *Journal of Human Rights* 1, no. 1 (2002): 35–53.

Hart, Barry, and Edita Colo. "Psychosocial Peacebuilding in Bosnia and Herzegovina: Approaches to Relational and Social Change." *Intervention* 12, no. 1 (2014): 76–87.

Hasian, Marouf, Jr. "Remembering and Forgetting the 'Final Solution': A Rhetorical Pilgrimage through the U.S. Holocaust Memorial Museum." *Critical Studies in Media Communication* 21, no. 1 (2004): 64–92.

Hawdon, James, and John Ryan. "Social Relations that Generate and Sustain Solidarity after a Mass Tragedy." *Social Forces* 89, no. 4 (2011): 1363–84.

Hayner, Priscilla B. *Unspeakable Truths: Confronting State Terror and Atrocity.* New York: Routledge, 2001.

Hayner, Priscilla B. *Unspeakable Truths: Transitional Justice and the Challenge of Truth Commissions.* 2nd ed. New York: Routledge, 2011.

Henry, Nicola. "Theorizing Wartime Rape: Deconstructing Gender, Sexuality, and Violence." *Gender & Society* 30, no. 1 (2016): 44–56.

Herman, Judith. *Trauma and Recovery: The Aftermath of Violence—From Domestic Abuse to Political Terror.* New York: Basic Books, 1997.

Hintjens, Helen M. "Explaining the 1994 Genocide in Rwanda." *Journal of Modern African Studies* 37, no. 2 (1999): 241–86.

Hinton, Alexander Laban, ed. *Transitional Justice: Global Mechanisms and Local Realities after Genocide and Mass Violence.* New Brunswick, NJ: Rutgers University Press, 2011.

Hobsbawm, Eric, and Terence Ranger, eds. *The Invention of Tradition.* New York: Cambridge University Press, 1983.

Hogg, Nicole. "Women's Participation in the Rwandan Genocide: Mothers or Monsters?" *International Review of the Red Cross* 92, no. 877 (2010): 69–102.

Holland, J. M., J. M. Currier, and R. A. Neimeyer. "Meaning Reconstruction in the First Two Years of Bereavement: The Role of Sense-Making and Benefit-Finding." *Omega: Journal of Death & Dying* 53, no. 3 (2006): 175–91.

Howard-Hassmann, Rhoda E. "Getting to Reparations: Japanese Americans and African Americans." *Social Forces* 83, no. 2 (2004): 823–40.

Huffine, Edwin, John Crews, Brenda Kennedy, Kathryn Bomberger, and Asta Zinbo. "Mass Identification of Persons Missing from the Break-Up of the Former Yugoslavia: Structure, Function, and Role of the International Commission on Missing Persons." *Forensic Sciences* 42, no. 3 (2001): 271–75.

Human Rights Watch. "Arming Rwanda: The Arms Trade and Human Rights Abuses in the Rwandan War." *New York* 6, no. 1 (January 1994): 1–38.

Human Rights Watch. "Rwanda: Human Rights Overview." In *World Report 2006.* New York: Human Rights Watch, 2007.

Human Rights Watch. *Rwanda's Lasting Wounds: Consequences of Genocide and War for Rwanda's Children.* New York: Human Rights Watch, 2003.

Hunt, Swanee. *This Was Not Our War: Bosnian Women Reclaiming Peace.* Durham, NC: Duke University Press, 2004.

Ibreck, Rachel. "The Politics of Mourning: Survivor Contributions to Memorials in Post-genocide Rwanda." *Memory Studies* 3, no. 4 (2010): 330–43.

ICTR. *Symposium on the Legacy of International Criminal Courts and Tribunals in Africa.* Waltham, MA: International Center for Ethics, Justice, and Public Life, Brandeis University, 2007.

Ignatieff, Michael. *The Warrior's Honor: Ethnic War and the Modern Conscience.* New York: Macmillan, 1998.

Ingber, Sasha. "Mass Graves Discovered 24 Years after Rwandan Genocide." NPR, April 26, 2018. https://www.npr.org/sections/thetwo-way/2018/04/26/606105347/mass-graves-discovered-24-years-after-rwandan-genocide.

Ingelaere, Bert. "'Does the Truth Pass across the Fire without Burning?' Locating the Short Circuit in Rwanda's Gacaca Courts." *Journal of Modern African Studies* 47, no. 4 (2009): 507–28.

Ingelaere, Bert. "Do We Understand Life after Genocide? Center and Periphery in the Construction of Knowledge in Postgenocide Rwanda." *African Studies Review* 53, no. 1 (2010): 41–59.

Ingelaere, Bert. *Inside Rwanda's Gacaca Courts: Seeking Justice after Genocide.* Madison: University of Wisconsin Press, 2016.

Ingelaere, Bert. "Learning 'To Be' Kinyarwanda in Postgenocide Rwanda: Immersion, Iteration, and Reflexivity in Times of Transition." *Canadian Journal of Law and Society* 30, no. 2 (2015): 277–92.

Institute for Economics and Peace. "Structures of Peace: Identifying What Leads to Peaceful Societies." 2011. https://www.ethicalmarkets.com/tag/peaceful-societies/.

Institute for Reconciliation and Justice. *SA Reconciliation Barometer 2019.* https://www.ijr.org.za/portfolio-items/sa-reconciliation-barometer-2019/.

International Center for Truth and Justice. "Truth and Memory." Accessed December 1, 2018. https://www.ictj.org/our-work/transitional-justice-issues/truth-and-memory.

International Commission on Missing Persons. "Bosnia and Herzegovina." Accessed May 2, 2020. https://www.icmp.int/where-we-work/europe/western-balkans/bosnia-and-herzegovina/.

Iorio, J. M., and W. Parnell. *Meaning Making in Early Childhood Research: Pedagogies and the Personal.* New York: Taylor & Francis, 2017.

Irivuzumugabe, Eric, and Tracey D. Lawrence. *My Father, Maker of the Trees: How I Survived the Rwandan Genocide.* Grand Rapids, MI: Baker Books, 2009.

Irwin-Zarecka, Iwona. *Frames of Remembrance: The Dynamics of Collective Memory.* New Brunswick, NJ: Transaction, 1994.

Jacobs, Janet L. *Memorializing the Holocaust: Gender, Genocide, and Collective Memory.* New York: I.B. Tauris, 2010.

Jacobs, Janet L. "Memorializing the Sacred: Kristallnacht in German National Memory." *Journal for the Scientific Study of Religion* 47, no. 3 (2008): 485–98.

Jacobs, Janet L. "Women, Genocide, and Memory: The Ethics of Feminist Ethnography in Holocaust Research." *Gender and Society* 18, no. 2 (2004): 223–38.

Jansen, Robert S. "Resurrection and Appropriation: Reputational Trajectories, Memory Work, and the Political Use of Historical Figures." *American Journal of Sociology* 112, no. 4 (2007): 953–1007.

Jansen, Stefan, Ross White, Jemma Hogwood, Angela Jansen, Darius Gishoma, Donatilla Mukamana, and Annemiek Richters. "The 'Treatment Gap' in Global Mental Health Reconsidered: Sociotherapy for Collective Trauma in Rwanda." *European Journal of Psychotraumatology* 6, no. 1 (2015).

Jarvis, Lee, and Michael Lister. "Vernacular Securities and Their Study: A Qualitative Analysis and Future Research Agenda." *International Relations* 27, no. 2 (2013): 157–78.

Jefremovas, Villia. "Contested Identities: Power and the Fictions of Ethnicity, Ethnography and History in Rwanda." *Anthropologica* 39, no. 1/2 (1997): 91–104.

Jessee, Erin. "Conducting Fieldwork in Rwanda." *Canadian Journal of Development Studies / Revue canadienne d'études du développement* 33, no. 2 (2012): 266–74.

Jessee, Erin. *Negotiating Genocide in Rwanda: The Politics of History.* Basingstoke, UK: Palgrave Macmillan, 2017.

Jessee, Erin. "Promoting Reconciliation through Exhuming and Identifying Victims in the 1994 Genocide." Policy Brief: CIGI & Africa Initiative Policy, Brief Series (2010).

Johnson, Nuala. "Cast in Stone: Monuments, Geography, and Nationalism." *Environment and Planning D: Society and Space* 13, no. 1 (1995): 51–65.

Jones, Adam. "Gender and Genocide in Rwanda." *Journal of Genocide Research* 4, no. 1 (2002): 65–94.

Jones, Bruce D. *Peacemaking in Rwanda: Dynamics of a Failure.* Boulder, CO: Lynne Rienner, 2001.

Jones, Bruce D. "Rwanda." In *United Nations Interventionism 1991–2004*, edited by Mats Berdal and Spyros Economides, 139–67. Cambridge: Cambridge University Press, 2007.

Jones, Nicholas A. *The Courts of Genocide: Politics and the Rule of Law in Rwanda and Arusha.* New York: Routledge, 2009.

Jordan, Paul. "Witness to Genocide: A Personal Account of the 1995 Kibeho Massacre." *Australian Army Journal* 1, no. 1 (June 2003): 127–36.

Justino, Patricia, Tilman Brück, and Philip Verwimp, eds. *A Micro Level Perspective on the Dynamics of Conflict, Violence, and Development.* Oxford: Oxford University Press, 2013.

Kalayjian, Ani, and Dominique Eugene. *Mass Trauma and Emotional Healing around the World: Rituals and Practices for Resilience and Meaning-Making.* Santa Barbara, CA: Praeger, 2010.

Kanyangaraab, Patrick, Bernard Rimé, Darío Paéz, and Vincent Yzerby. "Trust, Individual Guilt, Collective Guilt and Dispositions toward Reconciliation among Rwandan Survivors and Prisoners before and after Their Participation in Postgenocide Gacaca Courts in Rwanda." *Journal of Social and Political Psychology* 2, no. 1 (2014): 401–16.

Kaplan, Suzanne. "Child Survivors of the 1994 Rwandan Genocide and Trauma-Related Affect." *Journal of Social Issues* 69, no. 1 (2013): 92–100.

Kapteijns, Lidwien, and J. M. Richters. *Mediations of Violence in Africa: Fashioning New Futures from Contested Pasts.* Boston: Brill, 2010.

Karekezi, Urusaro Alice, Alphonse Nshimiyimana, and Beth Mutamba. "Localizing Justice: Gacaca Courts in Post-genocide Rwanda." In Stover and Weinstein, *My Neighbor*, 69–84.

Katongole, Emmanuel, and Jonathan Wilson-Hartgrove. *Mirror to the Church: Resurrecting Faith after Genocide in Rwanda.* Grand Rapids, MI: Zondervan, 2009.

Kelso, Michelle, and Daina S. Eglitis. "Holocaust Commemoration in Romania: Roma and the Contested Politics of Memory and Memorialization." *Journal of Genocide Research* 16, no. 4 (2014): 487–511.

Kerbo, Harold. "Social Stratification." In *The Wiley-Blackwell Encyclopedia of Social Theory*, edited by Bryan S. Turner et al., 1–4. Hoboken, NJ: John Wiley & Sons, 2017.

King, Elisabeth. "From Data Problems to Data Points: Challenges and Opportunities of Research in Post-genocide Rwanda." *African Studies Review* 52, no. 3 (2009): 127–48.

Kirby, Paul. "How Is Rape a Weapon of War? Feminist International Relations, Modes of Critical Explanation and the Study of Wartime Sexual Violence." *European Journal of International Relations* 19, no. 4 (2013): 797–821.

Kiss, Elizabeth. "Moral Ambition within and beyond Political Constraints." In *Truth v. Justice: The Morality of Truth Commissions*, edited by Robert I. Rotberg and Dennis Thompson, 68–98. Princeton, NJ: Princeton University Press, 2000.

Kleinman, Sherryl. "Fieldworkers' Feelings: What We Felt, Who We Are, How We Analyze." In *Experiencing Fieldwork: An Inside View of Qualitative Research*, edited by William B. Shaffir and Robert A. Stebbins, 184–95. London: SAGE, 1991.

Knauer, Christine. "Their Forgotten War: Veterans and the Korean War in American Memory." In *War Memories: Commemoration, Recollections, and Writings on War*, edited by Stéphanie A. H. Bélanger and Renée Dickason, 11–32. Montreal: McGill-Queen's University Press, 2017.

Koselleck, Reinhart. *The Practice of Conceptual History: Timing History, Spacing Concepts.* Stanford: Stanford University Press, 2002.

Krause, Jana. "Restrained or Constrained? Elections, Communal Conflicts, and Variation in Sexual Violence." *Journal of Peace Research* 57, no. 1 (2020): 185–98.

Kuperman, Alan J. *The Limits of Humanitarian Intervention: Genocide in Rwanda.* Washington, DC: Brookings Institution Press, 2001.

Ladika, Susan. "Laying Ghosts to Rest in Bosnia." *Science* 293, no. 5534 (2001): 1422–23.

Larson, Jeff A., and Omar Lizardo. "Generations, Identities, and the Collective Memory of Che Guevara." *Sociological Forum* 22, no. 4 (2007): 425–51.

Lederach, J. P. *Building Peace: Sustainable Reconciliation in Divided Societies.* Washington, DC: United States Institute of Peace, 1998.

Lederach, J. P. *Preparing for Peace: Conflict Transformation across Cultures.* Syracuse: Syracuse University Press, 1996.

Lee, Elizabeth Ann, and Sue A. Theus. "Lower Heart Rate Variability Associated with Military Sexual Trauma Rape and Posttraumatic Stress Disorder." *Biological Research for Nursing* 14, no. 4 (2012): 412–18.

Lemarchand, René. *Burundi Ethnic Conflict and Genocide*. New York: Woodrow Wilson Center, 1996.

Lemarchand, René. *Forgotten Genocides: Oblivion, Denial, and Memory*. Philadelphia: University of Pennsylvania Press, 2011.

Letherby, Gayle. "Dangerous Liaisons: Auto/biography in Research and Research Writing." In *Danger in the Field: Ethics and Risks in Social Research*, edited by Geraldine Lee-Treweek and Stephanie Linkogle, 91–113. London: Routledge, 2000.

Levy, Arden B. "International Prosecution of Rape in Warfare: Nondiscriminatory Recognition and Enforcement." *UCLA Women's Law Journal* 4, no. 2 (1994): 256–97.

Lewis, Michael, and Jacqueline Serbu. "Kommemorating the Ku Klux Klan." *Sociological Quarterly* 40, no. 1 (1999): 139–58.

Lisak, D., and P. M. Miller. "Repeat Rape and Multiple Offending among Undetected Rapists." *Violence & Victims* 17 (2002): 73–84.

Longman, Timothy. "An Assessment of Rwanda's Gacaca Courts." *Peace Review* 21, no. 3 (2009): 304–12.

Longman, Timothy. *Christianity and Genocide in Rwanda*. New York: Cambridge University Press, 2010.

Longman, Timothy. "Church Politics and the Genocide in Rwanda." *Journal of Religion in Africa* 31, no. 2 (2001): 163–86.

Longman, Timothy. *Memory and Justice in Post-Genocide Rwanda*. New York: Cambridge University Press, 2017.

Longman, Timothy. "Rwanda: Achieving Equality or Serving an Authoritarian State?" In *Women in African Parliaments*, edited by Gretchen Bauer and Hannah E. Britton, 133–50. London: Lynne Rienner, 2006.

Lovgren, Stefan. "Documenting Cambodia's Genocide, Survivor Finds Peace." *National Geographic News*, December 2, 2005.

Loyle, Cyanne E. "Overcoming Research Obstacles in Hybrid Regimes: Lessons from Rwanda." *Social Science Quarterly* 97, no. 4 (2016): 923–35.

Luft, Aliza. "Toward a Dynamic Theory of Action at the Micro-Level of Genocide: Killing, Desistance, and Saving in 1994 Rwanda." *Sociological Theory* 33, no. 2 (2015): 148–172.

MacGinty, R., and O. Richmond. "The Local Turn in Peacebuilding: A Critical Agenda for Peace." *Third World Quarterly* 34, no. 5 (2013): 763–83.

MacKinnon, Catharine. "Genocide's Sexuality." In *Political Exclusion and Domination*, edited by Stephen Macedo and Melissa Williams, 313–56. New York: New York University Press, 2004.

MacKinnon, Catharine. "Rape, Genocide, and Women's Human Rights." *Harvard Women's Law Journal*, no. 17 (1994): 5–16.

Major, Laura. 2015. "Unearthing, Untangling and Re-articulating Genocide Corpses in Rwanda." *Critical African Studies* 7, no. 2 (2015): 164–18.

Malkki, Liisa H. *Purity and Exile: Violence, Memory, and National Cosmology among Hutu Refugees in Tanzania*. Chicago: University of Chicago Press, 1995.

Maltby, John, Ann Macaskill, and Raphael Gillett. "The Cognitive Nature of Forgiveness: Using Cognitive Strategies of Primary Appraisal and Coping to Describe the Process of Forgiving." *Journal of Clinical Psychology* 63, no. 6 (2007): 555–66.

Mamdani, Mahmood. *When Victims Become Killers: Colonialism, Nativism, and the Genocide in Rwanda.* Princeton, NJ: Princeton University Press, 2001.

Mann, Laura, and Marie Berry. "Understanding the Political Motivations that Shape Rwanda's Emergent Developmental State." *New Political Economy* 21, no. 1 (2016): 119–44.

Mannheim, Karl. "The Problems of Generations." In *Essays in the Sociology of Knowledge,* edited by Karl Mannheim, 276–322. London: Routledge, 1952.

Maquet, Jacques J. *The Premise of Inequality in Ruanda: A Study of Political Relations in a Central African Kingdom.* New York: Oxford University Press, 1961.

Margry, Peter Jan, and Cristina Sánchez-Carretero. *Grassroots Memorials: The Politics of Memorializing Traumatic Death.* New York: Berghahn Books, 2011.

Marx, Karl. *The Eighteenth Brumaire of Louis Bonaparte, Surveys from Exile: Political Writings.* London: Verso, 1852.

Mason, Jennifer. "Personal Narratives, Relational Selves: Residential Histories in the Living and Telling." *Sociological Review* 52, no. 2 (2004): 162–79.

Maynard, Mary, and June Purvis, eds. *Researching Women's Lives from a Feminist Perspective.* London: Taylor & Francis, 1994.

McClintock, Anne. "Family Feuds: Gender, Nationalism and the Family." *Feminist Review* 44, no. 1 (1993): 61–80.

McCold, Paul. "Toward a Holistic Vision of Restorative Juvenile Justice: A Reply to the Maximalist Model." *Contemporary Justice Review* 3, no. 4 (2000): 357–414.

McCullum, Hugh. *The Angels Have Left Us: The Rwandan Tragedy and the Churches.* Geneva: World Council of Churches, 1996.

McDoom, Omar S. "Predicting Violence within Genocide: A Model of Elite Competition and Ethnic Segregation from Rwanda." *Political Geography* 42 (2014): 34–45.

McEwan, Cheryl. "Building a Postcolonial Archive? Gender, Collective Memory and Citizenship in Post-Apartheid South Africa." *Journal of Southern African Studies* 29, no. 3 (2003): 739–57.

Mead, George Herbert. *The Nature of the Past.* New York: Henry Holt, 1929.

Meierhenrich, Jens. "Topographies of Remembering and Forgetting: The Transformation of Lieux De Memoire in Rwanda." In Straus and Waldorf, *Remaking Rwanda,* 283–96.

Meierhenrich, Jens. "The Transformation of Lieux de Memoire: The Nyabarongo River in Rwanda, 1992–2009." *Anthropology Today* 25, no. 5 (2009): 13–19.

Mendeloff, David. "Truth-Seeking, Truth-Telling, and Postconflict Peacebuilding: Curb the Enthusiasm?" *International Studies Review* 6, no. 3 (2004): 355–80.

Meyerstein, Ariel. "Between Law and Culture: Rwanda's Gacaca and Postcolonial Legacy." *Law and Society Inquiry* 32, no. 2 (2007): 467–508.

Mgbako, Chi. "Ingando Solidarity Camps: Reconciliation and Political Indoctrination in Post-genocide Rwanda." *Harvard Human Rights Journal,* no. 18 (2005): 201–24.

Millar, Gearoid. "Assessing Local Experiences of Truth-Telling in Sierra Leone: Getting to 'Why' through a Qualitative Case Study Analysis." *International Journal of Transitional Justice* 4, no. 3 (2010): 477–96.

Ministry of Gender and Family Promotion, Republic of Rwanda. "Mission and Vision." 2015. http://migeprof.gov.rw/index.php?id=186.

Minow, Martha. *Between Vengeance and Forgiveness: Facing History after Genocide and Mass Violence.* Boston: Beacon, 1998.

Moon, Claire, "Healing Past Violence: Traumatic Assumptions and Therapeutic Interventions in War and Reconciliation." *Journal of Human Rights* 8, no. 1 (2009): 71–91.

Moon, Claire. *Narrating Political Reconciliation.* Lanham, MD: Lexington, 2009.

Moon, Claire. "Prelapsarian State: Forgiveness and Reconciliation in Transitional Justice." *International Journal or the Semiotics of Law* 17, no. 2 (2004): 185–97.

Mullins, Christopher W. "'He Would Kill Me with His Penis': Genocidal Rape in Rwanda as a State Crime." *Critical Criminology* 17, no. 1 (2009).

Mullins, Christopher W. "'We Are Going to Rape You and Taste Tutsi Women': Rape during the 1994 Rwandan Genocide." *British Journal of Criminology* 49, no. 6 (2009): 719–35.

Mullins, Christopher W., and Dawn Rothe. *Blood, Power, and Bedlam: Violations of International Criminal Law in Post-colonial Africa.* New York: Peter Lang, 2008.

Nagarajan, Chitra. "An Appraisal of Rwanda's Response to Survivors Who Experienced Sexual Violence in 1994." *Wagadu* 10 (2012): 108–30.

Nagy, Rosemary. "Traditional Justice and Legal Pluralism in Transitional Context: The Case of Rwanda's Gacaca Courts." In *Reconciliation(s): Transitional Justice in Post-conflict Societies,* edited by Joanna R. Quinn, 86–115. Montreal: McGill-Queen's University Press, 2009.

National Memorial for Peace and Justice. Accessed April 26, 2018. https://museumandmemorial.eji.org/memorial.

National Unity and Reconciliation Commission. "National Unity and Reconciliation Commission." 2014. http://www.nurc.gov.rw/index.php?id=69.

Nayak, Sameera, Sowmya Kshtriya, and Richard Neugebauer. "Trauma Alleviation Treatment for Unaccompanied Children after the Rwandan Genocide: A Cautionary Tale." *Intervention* 17, no. 1 (2019): 23–30.

Nduwimana, F. *The Right to Survive: Sexual Violence, Women and HIV/AIDS.* Montreal: International Centre for Human Rights and Democratic Development, 2004.

Neal, Arthur G. *National Trauma and Collective Memory: Extraordinary Events in the American Experience.* Armonk, NY: M. E. Sharpe, 2005.

Nelaeva, Galina. "The Impact of Transnational Advocacy Networks on the Prosecution of Wartime Rape and Sexual Violence: The Case of the ICTR." *International Social Science Review* 85, nos. 1–2 (2010): 3–27.

Neugebauer, Richard, Prudence W. Fisher, J. Blake Turner, Saori Yamabe, Julia A. Sarsfield, and Tasha Stehling-Ariza. "Post-Traumatic Stress Reactions among Rwandan Children and Adolescents in the Early Aftermath of Genocide." *International Journal of Epidemiology* 38, no. 4 (2009): 1033–45.

Newbury, Catharine. "Background to Genocide: Rwanda." *Issue: A Journal of Opinion* 23, no. 2 (1995): 12–17.

Newbury, Catharine. *The Cohesion of Oppression: Clientship and Ethnicity in Rwanda, 1860–1960.* New York: Columbia University Press, 1988.

Newbury, Catharine. "Ethnicity and the Politics of History in Rwanda." *Africa Today* 45, no. 1 (1998): 7–24.

Newbury, Catharine, and Hannah Baldwin. *Aftermath: Women in Post-Genocide Rwanda.* New York: USAID, 2000.

Newbury, Catharine, and David Newbury. "Rwanda: The Politics of Turmoil." *Africa Notes* (1994): 1–2.

Newbury, David. *The Land beyond the Mists: Essays on Identity and Authority in Pre-colonial Congo and Rwanda.* Athens: Ohio University Press, 2009.

Nowrojee, Binaifer. "Shattered Lives." In *H. R. Watch.* New York: Human Rights Watch, 1996.

Ntirenganya, Emmanuel. "Myumbu, Home to Rwanda's First Genocide Memorial." *New Times,* April 21, 2017.

Nyseth Brehm, Hollie. "Subnational Determinates of Genocide in Rwanda." *Criminology* 55, no. 1 (2017): 5–31.

Nyseth Brehm, Hollie, and Nicole Fox. "Narrating Genocide: Time, Memory, and Blame." *Sociological Forum* 32, no. 1 (2016): 1–22.

Nyseth Brehm, Hollie, Christopher Uggen, and Jean-Damascéne Gasanabo. "Age, Gender, and the Crime of Crimes: Toward a Life-Course Theory of Genocide Participation." *Criminology* 54, no. 4 (2016): 713–43.

Nyseth Brehm, Hollie, Christopher Uggen, and Jean-Damascéne Gasanabo. "Genocide, Justice, and Rwanda's Gacaca Courts." *Journal of Contemporary Criminal Justice* 30, no. 3 (2014): 333–52.

O'Halloran, Kevin. *Pure Massacre: Aussie Soldiers Reflect on the Rwandan Genocide.* New York: Simon & Schuster, 2020.

Olick, Jeffrey. "Collective Memory: Two Cultures." *Sociological Theory* 17, no. 3 (1999): 333–48.

Olick, Jeffrey K. *The Politics of Regret: On Collective Memory and Historical Responsibility.* New York: Routledge, 2007.

Olick, Jeffrey K., and Joyce Robbins. "Social Memory Studies: From Collective Memory to the Historical Sociology of Mnemonic Practices." *Annual Review of Sociology* 24 (1998): 105–40.

Pablo Baraybar, Jose, Valerie Brasey, and Andrew Zadel. "The Need for a Centralised and Humanitarian-Based Approach to Missing Persons in Iraq: An Example from Kosovo." *International Journal of Human Rights* 11, no. 3 (2007): 265–74.

Palmer, Nicola. *Courts in Conflict: Interpreting the Layers of Justice in Post-genocide Rwanda.* Oxford: Oxford University Press, 2015.

Pals, Jennifer, and Dan McAdams. "The Transformed Self: A Narrative Understanding of Posttraumatic Growth." *Psychological Inquiry* 15, no. 1 (2004): 65–69.

Park, Crystal L., and Amy L. Ai. "Meaning Making and Growth: New Directions for Research on Survivors of Trauma." *Journal of Loss & Trauma* 11, no. 5 (2006): 389–407.

Parsons, Thomas J., Rene M. L. Huel, Zlatan Bajunović, and Adnan Rizvić. "Large Scale DNA Identification: The ICMP Experience." *Forensic Science International: Genetics* 38 (2019): 236–44.

Pateman, Carole. *The Disorder of Women: Democracy, Feminism, and Political Theory.* Stanford: Stanford University Press, 1989.

Patman, Robert G. 1997. "Disarming Somalia: The Contrasting Fortunes of the United States and Australian Peacekeepers during the United Nations Intervention, 1992–1993." *African Affairs* 96, no. 385 (1997): 509–33.

Pérez Benitez, Carlos I., Benjamin Vicente, Caron Zlotnick, Robert Kohn, Jennifer Johnson, Sandra Valdivia, and Pedro Rioseco. "Epidemiology of Trauma, PTSD and Other Psychiatric Disorders in a Representative Population 145 of Chile." *Salud Mental* 32, no. 2 (2009): 145–53.

Peskin, Victor. "Victor's Justice Revisited: Rwandan Patriotic Front Crimes and the Prosecutorial Endgame at the ICTR." In Straus and Waldorf, *Remaking Rwanda*, 173–83.

Peugny, Camille, and Cécile Van de Velde. "Re-thinking Inter-Generational Inequality." *Revue Française de Sociologie* 54, no. 4 (2013): 641–64.

Pham, Phuong N., Harvey M. Weinstein, and Timothy Longman. "Trauma and PTSD Symptoms in Rwanda: Implications for Attitudes toward Justice and Reconciliation." *Journal of the American Medical Association* 292, no. 5 (2004): 602–12.

Phelps, Teresa. *Shattered Voices: Language, Violence, and the Work of Truth Commissions.* Pennsylvania: University of Pennsylvania Press, 2004.

Pickard, Terry. *Combat Medic: An Eyewitness Account of the Kibeho Massacre.* Sydney: Big Sky, 2010.

Polletta, Francesca. *It Was Like a Fever: Storytelling in Protest and Politics.* Chicago: University of Chicago Press, 2006.

Polletta, Francesca. "Legacies and Liabilities of an Insurgent Past: Remembering Martin Luther King, Jr., on the House and Senate Floor." *Social Science History* 22, no. 4 (1998): 479–512.

Polletta, Francesca, Pang Ching Bobby Chen, Beth Gharrity Gardner, and Alice Motes. "The Sociology of Storytelling." *Annual Review of Sociology* 37 (2011): 109–30.

Porter, Holly. *After Rape: Violence, Justice and Social Harmony in Uganda.* New York: Cambridge University Press, 2017.

Pottier, Johan. *Re-imagining Rwanda: Conflict, Survival and Disinformation in the Late Twentieth Century.* New York: Cambridge University Press, 2002.

Prosecutor v. Jean-Paul Akayesu. Case No. ICTR 96-4-T. Judgment (Sep. 2, 1998).

Prunier, Gérard. *Africa's World War: Congo, the Rwandan Genocide, and the Making of a Continental Catastrophe.* New York: Oxford University Press, 2009.

Prunier, Gérard. *The Rwanda Crisis: History of a Genocide.* New York: Columbia University Press, 1995.

Pugh, Allison. "What Good Are Interviews for Thinking about Culture? Demystifying Interpretive Analysis." *American Journal of Cultural Sociology* 1, no. 1 (2013): 42–68.

Purdeková, Andrea. "Building a Nation in Rwanda? De-ethnicisation and Its Discontents." *Studies in Ethnicity & Nationalism* 8, no. 3 (2008): 502–23.

Purdeková, Andrea. *Making Ubumwe: Power, State and Camps in Rwanda's Unity-Building Project.* New York: Berghahn Books, 2015.

Randazzo, Elisa. "The Paradoxes of the 'Everyday': Scrutinising the Local Turn in Peacebuilding." *Third World Quarterly* 37, no. 8 (2016): 1351–70.

Reconciliation Australia. *2018 Australian Reconciliation Barometer.* https://www.recon ciliation.org.au/wp-content/uploads/2019/02/ra_2019-barometer-brochure_web .single.page_.pdf.

Republic of Rwanda, City of Kigali. "City of Kigalo Master Plan Online." http://www .masterplan2013.kigalicity.gov.rw/.

Republic of Rwanda, National Commission for the Fight Against Genocide. https:// cnlg.gov.rw/index.php?id=10.

Reydams, Luc. "The ICTR Ten Years On: Back to the Nuremberg Paradigm?" *Journal of International Criminal Justice* 3, no. 4 (2005): 977–88.

Reyntjens, Filip. *The Great African War: Congo and Regional Geopolitics, 1996–2006.* Cambridge: Cambridge University Press, 2009.

Reyntjens, Filip. *Political Governance in Post-genocide Rwanda.* New York: Cambridge University Press, 2013.

Reyntjens, Filip. 2016. "(Re-)Imagining a Reluctant Post-genocide Society: The Rwandan Patriotic Front's Ideology and Practice." *Journal of Genocide Research* 18, no. 1 (2016): 61–81.

Reyntjens, Filip. "Rwanda, Ten Years On: From Genocide to Dictatorship." *African Affairs*, no. 103 (2004): 177–210.

Reyntjens, Filip. "Waging (Civil) War Abroad: Rwanda and the DRC." In *Remaking Rwanda: State Building and Human Rights after Mass Violence*, 132–51. Madison: University of Wisconsin Press, 2011.

Rieder, Heide, and Thomas Elbert. "Rwanda—Lasting Imprints of a Genocide: Trauma, Mental Health and Psychosocial Conditions in Survivors, Former Prisoners and Their Children." *Conflict and Health* 7, no. 1 (2013): 1–13.

Rimé, Bernard, Patrick Kanyangara, Vincent Yzerbyt, and Darío Paéz. "The Impact of Gacaca Tribunals in Rwanda: Psychosocial Effects of Participation in a Truth and Reconciliation Process after a Genocide." *European Journal of Social Psychology* 41 (2011): 695–706.

Rittner, Carol, John K. Roth, and Wendy Whitworth. *Genocide in Rwanda: Complicity of the Churches?* St. Paul, MN: Paragon House, 2004.

Rosaldo, Renato. "Grief and Headhunter's Rage." In *Death, Mourning, and Burial: A Cross-Cultural Reader*, edited by Antonius C. G. M. Robben, 166–78. Oxford: Blackwell, 2004.

Rulisa, Stephen, Frederick Kateera, Jean Pierre Bizimana, Steven Agaba, Javier Dukuzumuremyi, Lisette Baas, Jean de Dieu Harelimana, Petra F. Mens, Kimberly R. Boer, and Peter J. de Vries. "Malaria Prevalence, Spatial Clustering and Risk Factors in a Low Endemic Area of Eastern Rwanda: A Cross Sectional Study." *Public Library of Science* 8, no. 7 (2013).

Russell, S. Garnett. *Becoming Rwandan: Education, Reconciliation, and the Making of a Post-genocide Citizen.* New Brunswick, NJ: Rutgers University Press, 2020.

Rwembeho, Stephen. "Over 10,000 Tutsi Perished in Lake Muhazi during the Genocide." *New Times,* April 24, 2014.

Sadat, Leila Nadya. "The Legacy of the International Criminal Tribunal for Rwanda." Paper presented at the Whitney R. Harris World Law Institute, Washington University in St. Louis, MO, 2012.

Sangvic, Major Roger N. *Battle of Mogadishu: Anatomy of a Failure.* Royal Oak, New Zealand: Pickle Partners, 2015.

Sas, Corina, and Alina Coman. "Designing Personal Grief Rituals: An Analysis of Symbolic Objects and Actions." *Death Studies* 40, no. 9 (2016): 558–69.

Saunders, H. H. *A Public Peace Process: Sustained Dialogue to Transform Racial and Ethnic Conflicts.* New York: Palgrave, 2001.

Savelsberg, Joachim, and Ryan King. "Institutionalizing Collective Memories of Hate: Law and Law Enforcement in Germany and the United States." *American Journal of Sociology* 111, no. 2 (2005): 579–616.

Scarry, Elaine. *The Body in Pain: The Making and Unmaking of the World.* New York: Oxford University Press, 1985.

Schaal, Susanne, Jean-Pierre Dusingizemungu, Nadja Jacob, and Thomas Elbert. "Rates of Trauma Spectrum Disorders and Risks of Posttraumatic Stress Disorder in a Sample of Orphaned and Widowed Genocide Survivors." *European Journal of Psychotraumatology* 2 (2011): 6343–53.

Schaal, Susanne, and Thomas Elbert. "Ten Years after the Genocide: Trauma Confrontation and Posttraumatic Stress in Rwandan Adolescents." *Journal of Traumatic Stress* 19, no. 1 (2006): 95–105.

Schaal, Susanne, Nadja Jacob, Jean-Pierre Dusingizemungu, and Thomas Elbert. "Rates and Risks for Prolonged Grief Disorder in a Sample of Orphaned and Widowed Genocide Survivors." *BMC Psychiatry* 10, no. 55 (2010): 55–63.

Schmidt, William E. "Deaths in Rwanda Said to be 20,000 or More." *New York Times,* April 11, 1994.

Schuman, Howard, and Cheryl Rieger. "Historical Analogies, Generational Effects, and Attitudes Toward War." *American Sociological Review,* no. 57 (1992): 315–26.

Schuman, Howard, and Jacqueline Scott. "Generations and Collective Memories." *American Sociological Review* 54, no. 3 (1989): 359.

Schuman, Howard, Vered Vinitzky-Seroussi, and Amiram D. Vinokur. "Keeping the Past Alive: Memories of Israeli Jews at the Turn of the Millennium." *Sociological Forum* 18, no. 1 (2003): 103–36.

Schwartz, Barry. "Social Change and Collective Memory: The Democratization of George Washington." *American Sociological Review* 56, no. 2 (1991): 221–36.

Schwartz, Barry, and Howard Schuman. "History, Commemoration, and Belief: Abraham Lincoln in American Memory: 1945–2001." *American Sociological Review* 70, no. 2 (2005): 183–203.

Sebarenzi, Joseph, and Laura Mullane. *God Sleeps in Rwanda: A Journey of Transformation.* New York: Atria Books, 2009.

Sharlach, Lisa. "Gender and Genocide in Rwanda: Women as Agents and Objects of Genocide." *Journal of Genocide Research* 1, no. 3 (1999): 387–99.

Shearer, Samuel. "The City Is Burning! Street Economies and the Juxtacity of Kigali, Rwanda." *Urban Forum* 31 (2020): 351–71.

Sidelinger, Robert J., Brandi N. Frisby, and Audra L. McMullen. "The Decision to Forgive: Sex, Gender, and the Likelihood to Forgive Partner Transgressions." *Communication Studies* 60, no. 2 (2009): 164–79.

Simic, Olivera. "Feminist Research in Transitional Justice Studies: Navigating Silences and Disruptions in the Field." *Human Rights Review* 17, no. 1 (2016): 95–113.

Simko, Christina. *The Politics of Consolation: Memory and the Meaning of September 11.* New York: Oxford University Press, 2015.

Skilbeck, Rupert. "Funding Justice: The Price of War Crimes Trials." *Human Rights Brief* 15, no. 3 (2008): 1–5.

Smeekes, Anouk, Maykel Verkuyten, and Borja Matinovic. "Longing for the Country's Good Old Days: National Nostalgia, Autochthony Beliefs, and Opposition to Muslim Expressive Rights." *British Journal of Social Psychology* 54, no. 3 (2015): 561–80.

Smith, Dorothy E. *The Everyday as Problematic: Feminist Sociology.* Boston: Northeastern University Press, 1987.

Smith, Steve. "Singing Our World into Existence: International Relations Theory and September 11." *International Studies Quarterly* 48, no. 3 (2004): 499–515.

Sodaro, Amy. *Exhibiting Atrocity: Memorial Museums and the Politics of Past Violence.* New Brunswick, NJ: Rutgers University Press, 2018.

Soler, Angela, and Jared S. Beatrice. "Expanding the Role of Forensic Anthropology in a Humanitarian Crisis: An Example from the USA-Mexico Border." In *Sociopolitics of Migrant Death and Repatriation: Perspectives from Forensic Science*, edited by Krista E. Latham and Alyson J. O'Daniel, 115–28. Cham: Springer International, 2018.

Spasojević, Jasmina, Robert W. Heffer, and Douglas K. Snyder. "Effects of Posttraumatic Stress and Acculturation on Marital Functioning in Bosnian Refugee Couples." *Journal of Traumatic Stress* 13, no. 2 (2000): 205–17.

Stearns, Jason. *Dancing in the Glory of Monsters: The Collapse of the Congo and the Great War of Africa.* New York: Public Affairs, 2012.

Steven Betts, Kim, Gail M. Williams, Jacob M. Najman, and Rosa Alati. "Exploring the Female Specific Risk to Partial and Full PTSD Following Physical Assault." *Journal of Traumatic Stress* 26, no. 1 (2013): 86–93.

Stoler, Linda R. "Researching Childhood Sexual Abuse: Anticipating Effects on the Researcher." *Feminism & Psychology* 12, no. 2 (2002): 69–74.

Stover, Eric, and Harvey M. Weinstein, eds. *My Neighbor, My Enemy: Justice and Community in the Aftermath of Mass Atrocity.* Cambridge: Cambridge University Press, 2004.

Straus, Scott. "How Many Perpetrators Were There in the Rwandan Genocide? An Estimate." *Journal of Genocide Research* 6, no. 1 (2004): 85–98.

Straus, Scott. *The Order of Genocide: Race, Power, and War in Rwanda.* Ithaca, NY: Cornell University Press, 2006.

Straus, Scott, and Lars Waldorf, eds. *Remaking Rwanda: State Building and Human Rights after Mass Violence.* Critical Human Rights. Madison: University of Wisconsin Press, 2011.

Straziuso, Jason. "Rwanda Genocide: Man and Victim Now Friends." *ABC News,* April 6, 2014.

Sturken, Marita. *Tangled Memories: The Vietnam War, the AIDS Epidemic, and the Politics of Remembering.* Berkeley: University of California Press, 1997.

Summerfield, Derek. "A Critique of Seven Assumptions behind Psychological Trauma Programmes in War-Affected Areas." *Social Science & Medicine* 48, no. 10 (1999): 1449–62.

Summerfield, Derek. "The Invention of PTSD and the Social Usefulness of a Psychiatric Category." *BMJ* (Clinical research ed.) 322 (2001): 95–98.

Sundaram, Anjan. *Bad News: Last Journalists in a Dictatorship.* New York: Knopf Doubleday, 2016.

Sundberg, Ralph, and Erik Melander. "Introducing the UCDP Georeferenced Event Dataset." *Journal of Peace Research* 50, no. 4 (2013): 523–32.

Swiss, Liam, Kathleen M. Fallon, and Giovani Burgos. "Does Critical Mass Matter? Women's Political Representation and Child Health in Developing Countries." *Social Forces* 91, no. 2 (2012): 531–57.

Tadjo, Véronique. "Genocide: The Changing Landscape of Memory in Kigali." *African Identities* 8, no. 4 (2010): 379–88.

Tam, S. Y., S. Houlihan, and G. J. Melendez-Torres. "A Systematic Review of Longitudinal Risk and Protective Factors and Correlates for Posttraumatic Stress and Its Natural History in Forcibly Displaced Children." *Trauma, Violence, & Abuse* 18, no. 4 (2015): 377–95.

Tatum, James. "Memorials of the American War in Vietnam." *Critical Inquiry,* no. 22 (1996): 634–80.

Taylor, Christopher C. "The Cultural Face of Terror in the Rwandan Genocide of 1994." In *Annihilating Difference: The Anthropology of Genocide,* edited by Alexander Laban Hinton, 137–78. Berkeley: University of California Press, 2002.

Taylor, Christopher C. *Sacrifice as Terror: The Rwandan Genocide.* Oxford: Berg, 1999.

Taylor, Katriona, and Gerald H. Burgess. "Views of Non-Western Trainee or Recently-Qualified Practitioner Psychologists on the Import of Western Psychology into Their Indigenous Non-Western Cultures." *International Journal of Mental Health* 48, no. 4 (2019): 272–87.

Teeger, Chana. "Collective Memory and Collective Fear: How South Africans Use the Past to Explain Crime." *Qualitative Sociology* 37, no. 1 (2014): 69–92.

Tetreault, Mary Ann, and Sita Ranchod-Nilsson, eds. *Women, States and Nationalism: At Home in the Nation?* New York: Routledge, 2000.

Thakur, Ramesh. "From Peacekeeping to Peace Enforcement: The UN Operation in Somalia." *Journal of Modern African Studies* 32, no. 3 (1994): 387–410.

Thelen, David, ed. *Memory and American History.* Bloomington: University of Indiana Press, 1989.

Thiranagama, Sharika. "Claiming the State: Postwar Reconciliation in Sri Lanka." *Humanity: An International Journal of Human Rights, Humanitarianism, and Development* 4, no. 1 (2013): 93–116.

Thompson, Allan, ed. *The Media and the Rwandan Genocide.* Ann Arbor: Pluto Press, 2007.

Thomson, Susan. "Re-education for Reconciliation: Participant Observations on Ingando." In Straus and Waldorf, *Remaking Rwanda*, 331–39.

Thomson, Susan. *Rwanda: From Genocide to Precarious Peace.* New Haven, CT: Yale University Press, 2018.

Thomson, Susan. *Whispering Truth to Power: Everyday Resistance to Reconciliation in Postgenocide Rwanda.* Madison: University of Wisconsin Press, 2013.

Thurman, Tonya Renee, Leslie A. Snider, Neil W. Boris, Edward Kalisa, Laetitia Nyirazinyoye, and Lisanne Brown. "Barriers to the Community Support of Orphans and Vulnerable Youth in Rwanda." *Social Science & Medicine* 66, no. 7 (2008): 1557–67.

Tiemessen, Alana Erin. "After Arusha: Gacaca Justice in Post-genocide Rwanda." *African Studies Quarterly* 8, no. 1 (2004): 57–76.

Torgovnick, Mariana. "Rereading 'The Iliad' in Times of War." *PMLA* 124, no. 5 (2009): 1838–41.

Toussaint, Loren, and Jon R. Webb. "Gender Differences in the Relationship between Empathy and Forgiveness." *Journal of Social Psychology* 145, no. 6 (2005): 673–85.

Tribea, Rachel. "Culture, Politics and Global Mental Health." *Disability and the Global South* 1, no. 2 (2014): 251–65.

Truth and Reconciliation Commission of Canada. *Honouring the Truth, Reconciling for the Future: Summary of the Final Report of the Truth and Reconciliation Commission of Canada.* University of Manitoba: Truth and Reconciliation Commission of Canada, 2015.

Tutu, Desmond. *No Future without Forgiveness.* New York: Random House, 1999.

Tuzinde, Idi Gaparayi. "Justice and Social Reconstruction in the Aftermath of Genocide in Rwanda: An Evaluation of the Possible Role of the Gacaca Tribunals." In *Law*, 74. Pretoria: University of Pretoria, South Africa, 2000.

Twagiramariya, C., and M. Turshen. "'Favours' to Give and 'Consenting' Victims: The Sexual Politics of Survival in Rwanda." In *What Women Do in Wartime: Gender and Conflict in Africa*, edited by M. Turshen and C. Twagiramariya, 101–17. New York: Zed Books, 1998.

UNICEF. "Ten Years after Genocide, Rwandan Children Suffer Lasting Impact." New York, 2004.

United Nations. "General Assembly Designates 7 April International Day of Reflection on 1994 Genocide against Tutsi in Rwanda, Amending Title of Annual Observance." January 2018. https://www.un.org/press/en/2018/ga12000.doc.htm.

United Nations Development Programme. "Human Development Reports: Human Development Index (HDI)." Accessed April 1, 2020. http://hdr.undp.org/en/content/human-development-index-hdi.

United Nations, Economic and Social Council, Commission on Human Rights. *Report on the Situation of Human Rights in Rwanda.* Mr. René Deqni-Séqui, Special Rapporteur of the Commission on Human Rights, under paragraph 20 of resolution S-3/1 of 25 May 1994.

United Nations, Human Rights Office of the High Commissioner. "Basic Principles and Guidelines on the Right to a Remedy and Reparation for Victims of Gross Violations of International Human Rights Law and Serious Violations of International Humanitarian Law." December 2005. http://www.ohchr.org/EN/Professional Interest/Pages/RemedyAndReparation.aspx.

United Nations, International Criminal Tribunal for the former Yugoslavia. "Timeline." Accessed May 1, 2018. https://www.icty.org/en/features/timeline.

United Nations, International Residual Mechanism for Criminal Tribunals. "The ICTR in Brief." Accessed October 2018. http://unictr.unmict.org/en/tribunal.

United Nations Security Council, Resolution 955 (1994) Adopted by the Security Council at its 3453rd meeting, November 8, 1994. http://unscr.com/en/resolutions/doc/955.

Uvin, Peter. *Aiding Violence: The Development Enterprise in Rwanda.* Hartford: Kumarian Press, 1998.

Valji, Nahla. *Gender Justice and Reconciliation: Dialogue on Globalization.* Berlin: Friedrich-Ebert-Stiftung (FES), 2007.

Van Hoyweghen, Saskia. "The Urgency of Land and Agrarian Reform in Rwanda." *African Affairs* 98, no. 392 (1999): 353–72.

Vansina, Jan. *Antecedents to Modern Rwanda: The Nyiginya Kingdom.* Madison: University of Wisconsin Press, 2004.

Varshney, Ashutosh. *Ethnic Conflict and Civic Life: Hindus and Muslims in India.* New Haven, CT: Yale University Press, 2002.

Veale, Angela, Padraig Quigley, Théoneste Ndibeshye, and Célestin Nyirimihigo. "Struggling to Survive: Orphans and Community Dependent Children in Rwanda." Kigali: UNICEF, 2001.

Verpoorten, Marijke. "The Death Toll of the Rwandan Genocide: A Detailed Analysis for Gikongoro Province." *Population* 60, no. 4 (2005): 331–67.

Verpoorten, Marijke. "How Many Died in Rwanda?" *Journal of Genocide Research* 22, no. 1 (2020): 94–103.

Verwimp, Phillip. "Machetes and Firearms: The Organization of Massacres in Rwanda." *Journal of Peace Research* 43, no. 1 (2006): 5–22.

Verwimp, Philip. *Peasants in Power: The Political Economy of Development and Genocide in Rwanda.* New York: Springer, 2013.

Vinitzky-Seroussi, Vered. "Commemorating a Difficult Past: Yitzhak Rabin's Memorial." *American Sociological Review* 67, no. 1 (2002): 30–51.

Von Joeden-Forgey, Elisa. "The Devil in the Details: 'Life Force Atrocities' and the Assault on the Family in Times of Conflict." *Genocide Studies and Prevention* 5, no. 1 (2010): 1–19.

Wagner-Pacifici, Robin. "Memories in the Making: The Shapes of Things That Went." *Qualitative Sociology* 19, no. 3 (1996): 301–21.

Wagner-Pacifici, Robin, and Barry Swartz. "The Vietnam Veterans Memorial: Commemorating a Difficult Past." *American Journal of Sociology* 97, no. 2 (1991): 376–420.

Waldorf, Lars. "Instrumentalizing Genocide: The RPF's Campaign against 'Genocide Ideology.'" In Straus and Waldorf, *Remaking Rwanda*, 48–66.

Waldorf, Lars. "'Like Jews Waiting for Jesus': Posthumous Justice in Post-Genocide Rwanda." In *Localizing Transitional Justice: Interventions and Priorities after Mass Violence,* edited by Rosalind Shaw, Lars Waldorf, and Pierre Hazan, 183–202. Stanford: Stanford University Press, 2010.

Waldorf, Lars. "Revisiting Hotel Rwanda: Genocide Ideology, Reconciliation, and Rescuers." *Journal of Genocide Research* 11, no. 1 (2009): 101–25.

Waldorf, Lars. "Rwanda's Failing Experiment in Restorative Justice." In *Handbook of Restorative Justice: A Global Perspective,* edited by Dennis Sullivan and Larry Tifft, 422–32. London: Routledge, 2006.

Warshauer-Freedman, Sarah, Harvey M. Weinstein, K. L. Murphy, and Timothy Longman. "Teaching History in Post-Genocide Rwanda." In Straus and Waldorf, *Remaking Rwanda*, 297–316.

Weil, Frederick D. "Cohorts, Regimes, and the Legitimation of Democracy: West Germany since 1945." *American Sociological Review* 52, no. 3 (1987): 308–24.

Weiner, Phillip. "The Evolving Jurisprudence of the Crime of Rape in International Criminal Law." *Boston College Law Review* 54, no. 3 (2013): 1207–37.

Wenzel, Michael, Tyler G. Okimoto, Norman T. Feather, and Michael J. Platow. "Retributive and Restorative Justice." *Law and Human Behavior* 32, no. 5 (2008): 375–89.

Werner, Jayne S. "Between Memory and Desire: Gender and the Remembrance of War in Doi Moi Vietnam." *Gender, Place and Culture* 13, no. 3 (2006): 303–15.

West, Brad. "Collective Memory and Crisis: The 2002 Bali Bombing, National Heroic Archetypes and the Counter-narrative of Cosmopolitan Nationalism." *Journal of Sociology* 44, no. 4 (2008): 337–53.

Whitlinger, Claire. *Between Remembrance and Repair: Commemorating Racial Violence in Philadelphia, Mississippi.* Chapel Hill: University of North Carolina Press, 2020.

Whitlinger, Claire. "From Countermemory to Collective Memory: Acknowledging the 'Mississippi Burning' Murders." *Sociological Forum* 30 (2015): 648–70.

Wicke, T. and R. C. Silver. "A Community Responds to Collective Trauma: An Eco-logical Analysis of the James Byrd Murder in Jasper, Texas." *American Journal Community Psychology* 44, nos. 3–4 (2009): 233–48.

Williams, Paul. *Memorial Museums: The Global Rush to Commemorate Atrocities.* New York: Oxford International, 2007.

Wilson, Richard Ashby. *The Politics of Truth and Reconciliation in South Africa: Legitimizing the Post-Apartheid State.* Cambridge: Cambridge University Press, 2001.

Winter, Jay. *Sites of Memory, Sites of Mourning: The Great War in European Cultural History.* Cambridge: Cambridge University Press, 1995.

Women's Commission for Refugee Women and Children. *Rwanda's Women and Children: The Long Road to Reconciliation: A Field Report Assessing the Protection and Assistance Needs of Rwandan Women and Children.* New York: Women's Commission for Refugee Women and Children, 1997.

World Health Organization. *World Report on Violence and Health.* Geneva, 2002.

Young, James E. *The Texture of Memory: Holocaust Memorials and Meaning.* New Haven, CT: Yale University Press, 1993.

Yuval-Davis, Nira. *Gender & Nation.* London: SAGE, 1997.

Yuval-Davis, Nira. *The Politics of Belonging: Intersectional Contestations.* London: SAGE, 2011.

Zehr, Howard. *The Little Book of Restorative Justice: Revised and Updated.* New York: Good Books, 2014.

Zelizer, Barbara. "Reading the Past against the Grain: The Shape of Memory Studies." *Critical Studies in Mass Communication* 12, no. 2 (1999).

Zelizer, Barbara, ed. *Visual Culture and the Holocaust.* New Brunswick, NJ: Rutgers University Press, 2001.

Zerubavel, Eviatar. "Social Memories: Steps to a Sociology of the Past." *Qualitative Sociology* 19, no. 3 (1996): 283–99.

Zerubavel, Eviatar. *Time Maps: Collective Memory and the Social Shape of the Past.* Chicago: University of Chicago Press, 2003.

Zorbas, Eugenia. "What Does Reconciliation after Genocide Mean? Public Transcripts and Hidden Transcripts in Post-genocide Rwanda." *Journal of Genocide Research* 11, no. 1 (2009): 127–47.

Zraly, Maggie, and Laetitia Nyirazinyoye. "Don't Let the Suffering Make You Fade Away: An Ethnographic Study of Resilience among Survivors of Genocide-Rape in Southern Rwanda." *Social Science & Medicine* 70, no. 10 (2010): 1656–64.

Zraly, Maggie, Sarah E. Rubin, and Donatilla Mukamana. "Motherhood and Resilience among Rwandan Genocide-Rape Survivors." *Ethos* 41, no. 4 (2013): 411–39.

Zraly, Maggie, Julia Rubin-Smith, and Theresa Betancourt. "Primary Mental Health Care for Survivors of Collective Sexual Violence in Rwanda." *Global Public Health* 6, no. 3 (2011): 257–70.

Zussman, Robert. "Autobiographical Occasions." *Contemporary Sociology* 25, no. 2 (1996): 143–48.

Index

Page numbers in italics refer to illustrations.

Burnet, Jennie, 45, 103, 188n4, 200n36
Burundi, 24, 31–32, 149, 187n1, 191n32

Cambodia, 43, 146
Campbell, Rebecca, 158–59
Canada, 169n26
cannibalism, 159
Catholics: culpability and, 62–63; nuns, 5, 158; priests, 155, 161, 164, 174n22; research methodologies and, 163–64; schools of, 27, 163, 175n24
cattle, 25–26
Center for Commemoration (CFC): gendered violence and, 51–52, 65–66, 97, 98, 104–6, 108, 110, 126, 132, 134, 196, 199n26; human rights and, 49–52; memory of atrocities and, 49–52, 65–68, 196n17; preparing displays at, 49–51; reconciliation and, 119–20, 122, 126; resources of, 53–54; sexual and gender-based violence (SGBV) and, 98, 105–6, 108, 110, 134; survivors and, 49–51, 65–68, 98, 105, 110, 119–20, 122, 126
Center for Genocide Prevention and Education (CGPE): gendered violence and, 97, 98, 108–10, 134; mass graves and, 50; methodologies and, 151; reconciliation and, 119, 122; remembering human rights violations and, 50–52, 54; sexual and gender-based violence (SGBV) and, 98, 108–10, 134
Center for Memory, Survivors, and Reconciliation (CMSR): forgiveness and, 119; gendered violence and, 97, 98, 106–10, 134–35; remembering human rights violations and, 49–53; violence prevention and, 65
Chakravarty, Anuradha, 186n152
Chhang, Youk, 43
child-headed household (CHH): context of violence and, 37; human rights

and, 54; reconciliation and, 113; research methodologies and, 148, 153, 156, 163; trauma and, 71, 77, 81, 88–90
children, 18; adopted, 37, 66, 140; babies, 19, 34, 51–52, 65, 84, 103–5, 122, 140, 159–60, 208n5; born out of rape, 95, 99, 101–2, 104, 106, 201n56; Canadian indigenous, 169n26; context of violence and, 27, 32, 34–38, 163; gendered violence and, 95, 99, 106, 108–9, 135, 199n26; hiding of, 32, 37, 70, 177n73, 196n17; Holocaust survivors and, 159; host family's, 161; human rights and, 44, 52; killing of in front of parents, 34, 80, 159; number killed, 79; orphans, 13 (*see also* orphans); parents' sacrificing selves for, 32, 177n73; reconciliation and, 122; soccer and, 13, 156; trauma and, 71–72, 75–76, 79–84, 92; UNICEF and, 37–38, 75; violence prevention and, 63–66, 70
China, 30, 39, 193n27
churches: bone displays and, 49; Catholic, 27, 163, 175n24; context of violence and, 27, 29, 33–34, 36; demolition of, 36; education and, 27; ethnic tensions in, 27; as false safety zones, 105; gendered violence and, 104–5; genocide involvement of, 13, 33–34, 179n86; Habyarimana and, 29; human remains in, 36, 196n17; human rights and, 45, 49, 52, 54–55; inequality and, 27; memorials and, 3, 45, 49, 54–55, 62–63, 65, 104, 132, 190n27; nuns and, 5, 158; priests and, 155, 161, 164, 174n22; rituals and, 132; sheltering in, 3, 34; trauma and, 71, 79; violence prevention and, 62–63, 65
closure, 51, 119, 121, 128, 132–33, 139, 194n30
clothes, 3, 49–52, 67, 104, 189n22

Coalition pour la Défense de la République (CDR, Coalition for the Defense of the Republic), 30, 176n52

Codere, Helen, 25–26

coffee, 23, 29, 100

Cold War, 11

collective memory: banality of everyday memory and, 138–40; commemorations and, 6, 14–21, 45, 71–93, 98, 110, 112, 134, 137, 139, 207n18; concretizing memories by, 132; construction of, 14–19; culpability and, 20, 60–64, 108; different forms of, 44–45; ethnicity and, 6, 8; gendered violence and, 98, 110–12; guilt and, 17; Halbwachs and, 15–16; individuals and, 207n18; institutional power and, 137; legal effects of, 172n64; marginalization and, 15, 21, 45, 73–74, 84, 90, 93, 98, 112, 121, 134; memorials and, 4 (*see also* memorials); mourning months and, 3, 5, 19–20, 43–44, 73, 76–78, 86–88, 127–28, 149, 151; national, 4, 17–18, 138; reconciliation and, 118, 121; rituals and, 131–34 (*see also* rituals); stratification of, 6, 8, 20–21, 71–93, 121, 131, 134, 138–40, 146; survivors and, 4, 6–8, 14–15, 18, 20–21, 45, 73–74, 76, 78, 92–93, 98, 110, 112, 118, 121, 130, 134, 137–38; transitional justice and, 18, 136–38; trauma and, 71–93, 194n2, 194n6, 195n15

colonialism: context of violence and, 25–28, 40; culpability and, 20, 60–64, 108, 133; inequality and, 25, 27–28, 59, 174n13, 193nn15–16; schools and, 27; violence prevention and, 59–63, 68–69, 193n16

commemorations: bones and, 49–50, 89, 189nn21–22; CFC and, 49 (*see also* Center for Commemoration (CFC)); collective memory and, 6, 14–21, 45, 71–93, 98, 110, 112, 134, 137, 139, 207n18; environment of, 46–47; gendered violence and, 94–99, 104, 106, 108, 110–12; graves and, 44–45, 53, 73, 108, 188n15; memorials, 3 (*see also* memorials); mourning months, 3, 5, 19–20, 43–44, 73, 76–78, 86–88, 127–28, 149, 151; narratives and, 6, 15, 17–18, 22, 45, 73–74, 81, 84–87, 90, 92–93, 97, 104, 110, 112, 132, 134–35, 139, 145; observing silences and, 151–53; plaques, 45; reconciliation and, 122; rituals and, 6, 14–15, 17, 44, 46, 73, 84, 90, 132, 165; stadiums and, 44, 91, 93; trauma and, 5–6, 14, 17, 20–22, 53, 72–93, 98, 134, 140, 160, 194n2; violence prevention and, 56, 66; week of, 45, 50, 80

Commission Nationale de Lutte contre le Génocide (CNLG, National Commission for the Fight Against Genocide), 188n15

communism, 27, 29

Connerton, Paul, 46

constituencies, 9–10, 144–48

context of violence: AIDS and, 29, 37, 41; children and, 27, 32, 34–38, 163; churches and, 27, 29, 33–34, 36; ethnicity and, 19–20, 23, 25–30, 33, 35; grenades and, 3–4, 31, 34–36, 52, 71, 105–6, 154, 176n58; human immunodeficiency virus (HIV) and, 37–38, 41; Hutus and, 25–35, 175n31, 176nn52–53, 177n64, 177nn69–70; identity and, 19–20, 26–27, 33; internally displaced persons (IDP) and, 35–36; International Criminal Tribunal for Rwanda and, 39–42; machetes and, 3–4, 30–36, 68, 71, 106, 176n58; marginalization and, 28; militia and, 30–31, 34; mutilation and, 34, 37, 69, 95, 102, 105; narratives and, 39; nongovernmental organizations

trauma (*continued*)

72–93, 98, 134, 140, 160, 194n2; in context, 36, 40–41, 50–55, 74–79, 182n110, 185n146, 186n148; definition of, 167n2, 194n2; disruption of order by, 130; ethics and, 194n1; flashbacks and, 3, 72, 76, 80–81, 154, 161, 163, 194n2; gendered violence and, 95, 98, 102, 104, 106, 110, 134; graves and, 73; guilt and, 17, 158–60; hospitals and, 54, 77–80, 84, 87–89, 91, 93; lasting effects of, 75–93, 130–31, 133, 136, 140, 144–45, 147, 152, 154, 158–61, 163, 182n108, 205n1; memorials and, 133 (*see also* memorials); militia and, 71–72, 79; mourning months and, 73, 76–78, 86–88; narratives and, 6, 18, 20, 22, 58, 73–74, 81, 84–93, 117, 130–34, 152, 205n1; nongovernmental organizations (NGOs) and, 75, 77, 88; observing silences and, 151–53; orphans and, 71–72, 79–83, 92; post-traumatic stress disorder (PTSD), 36, 74–75, 182n108, 194n6, 196n18; psychological issues from, 5, 36, 53–54, 58, 74–75, 78–79, 82–84, 87, 92, 136, 194n2, 194n6, 195n15, 196n18; rape and, 21, 72, 79–86, 90–93; reconciliation and, 117, 121, 203n18; research methodologies and, 144–45, 147, 152, 154, 158–61, 163; rituals and, 73, 81, 84, 90; schools and, 78, 83–84; secondary, 22, 81, 144, 160–61, 173n66; stratification and, 79–84; suicide and, 37, 200n41; testimony and, 71–74, 78, 81, 85, 87–92; torture and, 80; United Nations (UN) and, 75, 145; victimhood and, 45, 95, 97, 102, 111, 187n1, 196n1, 196n18, 198n20; vulnerables and, 79–82, 84, 93; women and, 8, 12, 18, 36, 41, 51, 54, 72–74, 79–82, 85–86, 90–95, 98, 104, 110, 134, 136, 140, 154, 163, 196n18

Trauma Recovery Programme (TRP), 75

tribute, 4, 105, 130, 133, 137

Truth and Reconciliation Commission (TRC), 12–13, 119, 201n2

truth commissions, 11–14, 98, 136, 169n26, 198n21

tsetse flies, 25, 62

Tutsis: cattle and, 25–26; colonialism and, 25–28, 59, 61–63, 133, 193nn15–16; context of violence and, 25–35, 130, 174n22, 176n52, 176n56, 177nn69–70; gendered violence and, 94, 96, 98–104, 107–8, 111; Hamitic hypothesis and, 26, 174n16; human rights and, 43, 45, 187n1, 193n16; identification of, 199n31; inequality and, 25–28; as *inyenzi* (cockroaches), 30, 100, 199n27; naming and, 9–10, 25, 144; protecting, 32, 63, 100, 187n1; reconciliation and, 5–6, 13, 118, 121–26, 204nn25–26; research methodologies and, 143–48, 159, 163, 208n5; rescuing, 3–5, 9, 144, 147, 208n5; school quotas and, 28; Statement of Views of, 27–28; transitional justice and, 136; violence prevention and, 59–63, 133

Tutu, Desmond, 10, 201n2

Twas: colonialism and, 25, 27–28, 59, 61–62, 193nn15–16; context of violence and, 25, 27; inequality and, 25–28; methodologies and, 144–45, 148; naming and, 9, 25, 144; as potters, 25; violence prevention and, 59, 61–62

Twagiramungu, Faustin, 34

Uganda, 4, 24, 28–29, 39, 164, 191n32

umuganda (obligatory community service), 39, 175n40

Union Nationale Rwandaise (UNAR, Rwandese National Union), 28

United Nations Assistance Mission for Rwanda (UNAMIR), 31, 35, 177n73

Critical Human Rights